PART 1

Paper 1.2

Financial Information for Management

REVISION SERIES

Official Publisher

FOULKS LYNCH
PUBLICATIONS

British Library Cataloguing-in-Publication Data

A catalogue record for this book is available from the British Library.

Published by AT Foulks Lynch Ltd
4, The Griffin Centre
Staines Road
Feltham
Middlesex
TW14 0HS

ISBN 0 7483 5997 4

© AT Foulks Lynch Ltd, 2003

Printed and bound in Great Britain, by Ashford Colour Press Ltd.

Acknowledgements

The past ACCA examination questions are the copyright of the Association of Chartered Certified Accountants. The original answers to the questions from June 1994 onwards were produced by the examiners themselves and have been adapted by AT Foulks Lynch Ltd.

We are grateful to the Chartered Institute of Management Accountants and the Institute of Chartered Accountants in England and Wales for permission to reproduce past examination questions. The answers have been prepared by AT Foulks Lynch Ltd.

CONTENTS

This book includes a wide selection of questions from past ACCA exams, both objective test questions and longer questions, and including the latest papers. In addition, there are full answers, many prepared by the examiner. This is the ONLY publication to include actual questions and official answers from the previous four sittings of the 'paper-based' examination (at the date of publication).

INDEX TO QUESTIONS AND ANSWERS

OBJECTIVE TEST QUESTIONS

PRACTICE QUESTIONS

SYLLABUS AND EXAMINATION FORMAT

Format of the paper-based examination

	Number of marks
Section A: 25 compulsory choice questions (2 marks each)	50
Section B: 5 compulsory short form questions (8–12 marks each)	50
	100

Total time allowed: 3 hours

Format of the computer-based examination

	Number of marks
Objective test questions	100

Total time allowed: 3 hours

Aim

To develop knowledge and understanding of the application of management accounting techniques to support the management processes of planning, control and decision making.

Objectives

On completion of this paper candidates should be able to:

- explain the role of management accounting within an organisation and the requirement for management information

- describe costs by classification and purpose

- identify appropriate material, labour and expense costs

- understand the principles of costing and apply them in straightforward scenarios

- understand and demonstrate the cost factors affecting production and pricing decisions

- understand the basic principles of performance management

- demonstrate the skills expected in Part 1.

Position of the paper in the overall syllabus

No prior knowledge is required before commencing study for Paper 1.2. Some understanding of the accounting principles and practices from Paper 1.1 Preparing Financial Statements and a basic competence in numeracy are assumed.

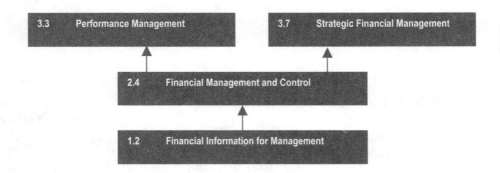

This paper provides the basic techniques required to enable the candidate to develop the various methods into more complex problems at later parts. Candidates will, therefore, need a sound understanding of the methods and techniques encountered in this paper to ensure that they can take them further in subsequent papers. The methods introduced in this paper are revisited and extended in Paper 2.4 Financial Management and Control and taken yet further in Papers 3.3 Performance Management and 3.7 Strategic Financial Management.

Syllabus content

1 Accounting for management

(a) The nature, purpose, scope and interrelations of functions carried out by management in relation to resources, costs, operations, performance

    (i) setting objectives (long and short-term, strategic and operational, corporate and personal)

    (ii) planning to meet objectives

    (iii) implementing objectives

    (iv) monitoring and controlling against objectives and plans

(b) Nature of internal reporting

    (i) financial and non-financial information for managers

    (ii) cost centres, revenue centres, profit centres and investment centres and the impact of these on management information.

(c) Management information requirements

    (i) importance and definition of good information

    (ii) presentation of information

    (iii) role of accountants and accounting information

    (iv) role of IT.

(d) Maintaining and improving an appropriate system

    (i) cost units

    (ii) cost/profit/responsibility centres

    (iii) methods for recording relevant information

    (iv) sources of information and recording/processing information

    (v) computer based information, storage and processing

    (vi) analysis of output information and its dissemination to relevant individuals/ departments.

2 Cost accounting

(a) Cost accounting versus management accounting

(i) purposes of cost and management accounting and financial accounting

(ii) role of cost accounting in a management information system

(iii) non-financial information.

(b) Nature and purpose of cost classification and definitions.

3 Elements of cost

(a) Materials

(i) standard and actual costs for materials including the use of FIFO, LIFO and weighted average for material valuation and the pricing of material issues

(ii) optimal purchase quantities to include discounts

(iii) optimal batch quantities

(iv) reorder levels

(v) material losses.

(b) Labour

(i) direct and indirect labour

(ii) different remuneration methods

(iii) labour efficiency

(iv) labour turnover.

(c) Overheads

(i) direct and indirect expenses

(ii) principles and processes of overhead cost analysis

(iii) allocation and apportionment of overhead costs including reciprocal service centre situations

(iv) absorption rates

(v) under- and over-absorption

(vi) fixed overhead expenditure and volume variances

(vii) fixed overhead efficiency and capacity variances where appropriate

(viii) changes in the cost structure of a business over time.

4 Costing systems

(a) Job, batch and process costing

(i) characteristics

(ii) direct and indirect costs (including waste, scrap and rectification costs)

(iii) valuation of process transfers and work-in-progress using equivalent

units of production and based on FIFO and weighted average pricing methods

(iv) process costing normal losses, abnormal losses and gains

(v) joint and by-products in process costing

(b) Operation/service costing

(i) scope of operation/service costing

(ii) appropriate cost units

(iii) collection, classification and ascertainment of costs.

5 Costing methods and techniques

(a) Standard costing

(i) establishment of standard costs

(ii) variance analysis

(iii) explanations of variances and control

(iv) implications for management

(v) operating statements.

(b) Marginal and absorption costing

(i) marginal and absorption costing profit and loss accounts

(ii) reconciliation of the profits under the two methods

(iii) contrast of absorption and marginal costing.

6 Short-term decision making

(a) Cost behaviour

(i) fixed, variable and semi-variable costs

(ii) cost behaviour using an appropriate graph

(iii) high-low method

(iv) regression analysis.

(b) CVP analysis

(i) break-even point and revenue

(ii) margin of safety

(iii) target profit

(iv) contribution to sales ratio

(v) break-even chart and profit/volume graph.

(c) Limiting factors

(i) optimal production plan given a scarce resource

(ii) linear programming techniques

(iii) other methods for more than two variable problems.

(d) Preparation of cost estimates for decision making

(i) relevant costing techniques to include opportunity/sunk, avoidable/unavoidable, fixed/variable applied to such situations as make or buy, shut down and one-off contracts.

(e) Pricing of goods and services

(i) price/demand relationships

(ii) full cost plus pricing

(iii) marginal costing.

(f) Price skimming, penetration pricing, premium pricing and price discrimination.

Excluded topics

The syllabus content outlines the areas for assessment. No areas of knowledge are specifically excluded from the syllabus.

Key areas of the syllabus

The key topic areas are as follows:

- cost classification and behaviour

- material, labour and overhead costs

- absorption and marginal costing

- process costing

- standard costing

- CVP analysis

- pricing methods.

ANALYSIS OF PAST PAPERS (PAPER-BASED EXAMINATIONS)

Section A questions

Section A consists of 25 objective test questions that have so far all been multiple choice questions. The question topics cover the entire syllabus.

An analysis of the Section B questions is given below. Note, however, that the syllabus for Paper 1.2 has been reduced in scope, and some of the topics examined in the past are no longer examinable from 2004 onwards. Check the new syllabus for details.

Section B questions

Pilot paper 2001

1   NPV and IRR (no longer in the syllabus)
2   Overhead allocation, apportionment (reciprocal method) and absorption
3   Limiting factors and linear programming
4   Regression analysis to estimate variable and fixed costs
5   Materials: EOQ and bulk purchase discounts

December 2001

1   Cost plus pricing and other pricing strategies
2   Variance analysis
3   CVP analysis, breakeven chart
4   Budget preparation (no longer in the syllabus)
5   Absorption costing and marginal costing

June 2002

1   Labour costs (earnings with indices)
2   Relevant costs (minimum contract price)
3   Operational planning and strategic planning. Stages in the planning and control process
4   Investment mathematics: terminal value and annuities (no longer in the syllabus)
5   Process costing

December 2002

1   Linear regression analysis
2   Decision tree analysis (no longer in the syllabus)
3   Absorption costing and marginal costing
4   Advantages of a computer system; management information system; stock-take procedures
5   ROI and residual income. Performance measures for a service sector company (no longer in the syllabus)

June 2003

1   Fixed overhead variances
2   Process costing: joint products
3   Service centre and production centre overheads. Activity-based costing
4   Linear programming
5   Discounted cash flow.

December 2003

1   Apportionment of service centre overheads (reciprocal method)
2   Breakeven chart. Profit-volume chart
3   Flexible budget variances
4   Economic order quantity
5   Marginal revenue, marginal cost and profit maximisation

REVISION GUIDANCE

Planning your revision

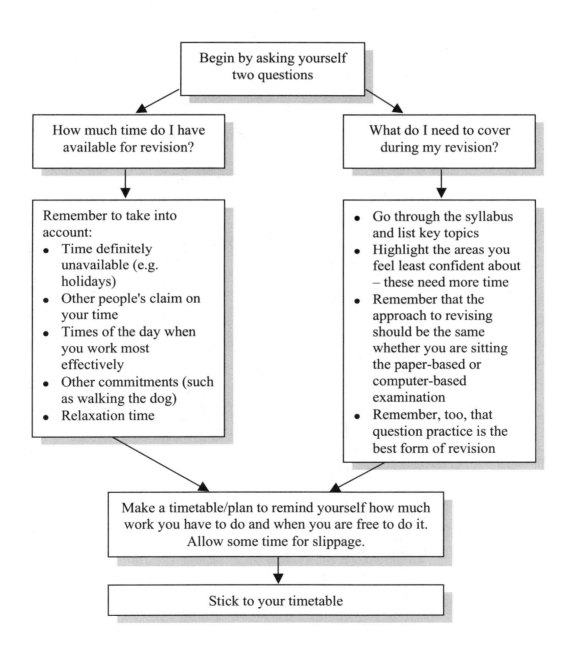

Begin by asking yourself
two questions

How much time do I have
available for revision?

What do I need to cover
during my revision?

Remember to take into
account:
- Time definitely
  unavailable (e.g.
  holidays)
- Other people's claim on
  your time
- Times of the day when
  you work most
  effectively
- Other commitments (such
  as walking the dog)
- Relaxation time

- Go through the syllabus
  and list key topics
- Highlight the areas you
  feel least confident about
  – these need more time
- Remember that the
  approach to revising
  should be the same
  whether you are sitting
  the paper-based or
  computer-based
  examination
- Remember, too, that
  question practice is the
  best form of revision

Make a timetable/plan to remind yourself how much
work you have to do and when you are free to do it.
Allow some time for slippage.

Stick to your timetable

Revision techniques

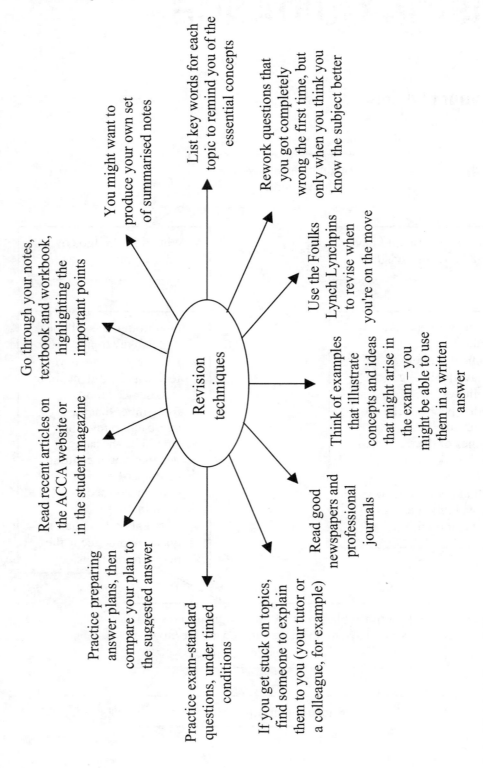

EXAMINATION TECHNIQUES

Paper-based examinations – tips

- You might want to spend the first few minutes of the examination **reading the paper**.

- Where you have a **choice of question**, decide which questions you will do.

- Unless you know exactly how to answer the question, spend some time **planning** your answer.

- **Divide the time** you spend on questions in proportion to the marks on offer. One suggestion is to allocate 1½ minutes to each mark available, so a 10 mark question should be completed in 15 minutes.

- Spend the last **five minutes** reading through your answers and **making any additions or corrections**.

- If you **get completely stuck** with a question, leave space in your answer book and **return to it later.**

- Stick to the question and **tailor your answer** to what you are asked. Pay particular attention to the verbs in the question.

- If you do not understand what a question is asking, **state your assumptions**. Even if you do not answer in precisely the way the examiner hoped, you should be given some credit, if your assumptions are reasonable.

- You should do everything you can to make things easy for the marker. The marker will find it easier to identify the points you have made if your **answers are legible**.

- **Essay questions**: Your essay should have a clear structure. It should contain a brief introduction, a main section and a conclusion. Be concise. It is better to write a little about a lot of different points than a great deal about one or two points.

- **Multiple-choice questions**: don't treat these as an easy option – you could lose marks by rushing into your answer. Read the questions carefully and work through any calculations required. If you don't know the answer, eliminate those options you know are incorrect and see if the answer becomes more obvious.

- **Objective test questions** might ask for numerical answers, but could also involve paragraphs of text which require you to fill in a number of missing blanks, or for you to write a definition of a word or phrase. Others may give a definition followed by a list of possible key words relating to that description. Whatever the format, these questions require that you have *learnt* definitions, *know* key words and their meanings and importance, and *understand* the names and meanings of rules, concepts and theories.

- **Computations**: It is essential to include all your workings in your answers. Many computational questions require the use of a standard format: company profit and loss account, balance sheet and cash flow statement for example. Be sure you know these formats thoroughly before the examination and use the layouts that you see in the answers given in this book and in model answers.

- **Case studies**: to write a good case study, first identify the area in which there is a problem, outline the main principles/theories you are going to use to answer the question, and then apply the principles/theories to the case.

- **Reports, memos and other documents**: some questions ask you to present your answer in the form of a report or a memo or other document. So use the correct format - there could be easy marks to gain here.

Computer-based examinations – tips

- Be sure you understand how to use the **software** before you start the exam. If in doubt, ask the assessment centre staff to explain it to you.

- Questions are **displayed on the screen** and answers are entered using keyboard and mouse. At the end of the examination, you are given a certificate showing the result you have achieved.

- In addition to the traditional multiple-choice question type, CBEs might also contain **other types of questions**, such as number entry questions, formula entry questions, and stem questions with multiple parts. There are also questions that carry several marks.

- You need to be sure you **know how to answer questions** of this type before you sit the exam, through practice.

- Do not attempt a CBE until you have **completed all study material** relating to it.

- **Do not skip any of the material** in the syllabus.

- **Read each question** *very* carefully.

- **Double-check your answer** before committing yourself to it.

- Answer *every* question – if you do not know an answer, you don't lose anything by guessing. Think carefully before you **guess**.

- If you are answering a multiple-choice question, eliminate first those answers that you know are wrong. Then choose the most appropriate answer from those that are left.

- Remember that **only one answer to a multiple-choice question can be right**. After you have eliminated the ones that you know to be wrong, if you are still unsure, guess. But only do so after you have double-checked that you have only eliminated answers that are *definitely* wrong.

- **Don't panic** if you realise you've answered a question incorrectly. Getting one question wrong will not mean the difference between passing and failing.

MATHEMATICAL TABLES AND FORMULAE

Formulae

Regression analysis

$$a = \frac{\sum y}{n} - \frac{b\sum x}{n}$$

$$b = \frac{n\sum xy - \sum x \sum y}{n\sum x^2 - \left(\sum x\right)^2}$$

$$r = \frac{n\sum xy - \sum x \sum y}{\sqrt{\left(n\sum x^2 - \left(\sum x\right)^2\right)\left(n\sum y^2 - \left(\sum y\right)^2\right)}}$$

Economic order quantity $\quad = \sqrt{\dfrac{2C_0 D}{C_h}}$

Economic batch quantity $\quad = \sqrt{\dfrac{2C_0 D}{C_h\left(1 - \dfrac{D}{R}\right)}}$

Section 1

OBJECTIVE TEST QUESTIONS

ACCOUNTING FOR MANAGEMENT AND COST ACCOUNTING

1   **Which of the following could be true with regard to a management information system (MIS)?**

An MIS is

(i)   a database system.

(ii)   used for planning, directing and controlling activities.

(iii)   a hierarchy of information within an organisation.

A   (i) and (ii) only

B   (i) and (iii) only

C   (ii) and (iii) only

D   (i), (ii) and (iii)

2   **Which of the following is correct?**

A   Qualitative data is numerical information only.

B   Information can only be extracted from external sources.

C   Operational information gives details of long-term plans only.

D   Data can be either discrete or continuous.

3   **Which of the following are purposes of a budget?**

(i)   establishing strategic options

(ii)   motivating management

(iii)   establishing long term objectives

(iv)   planning operations

A   (i) and (iii) only

B   (i) and (iv) only

C   (ii) and (iv) only

D   (ii), (iii) and (iv) only

4   **The following statements relate to business objectives:**

(i)   The short-term objectives of an organisation are described in very general terms.

(ii)   Corporate objectives relate to the organisation as a whole.

(iii)   It is possible for a division of an organisation to have its own specific objectives.

Which of the above are correct?

A   (i) and (ii) only

B   (i) and (iii) only

C   (ii) and (iii) only

D   (i), (ii) and (iii)

5 **What level of planning is the Board of Directors generally responsible for?**

A   Strategic planning

B   Operational planning

C   Tactical planning

D   Directional planning

6 **An MIS helps managers in which of the following areas?**

(i)   Planning

(ii)   Control

(iii) Co-ordination

(iv)   Decision-making

A   (i) (ii) and (iii) only

B   All of them

C   (i) and (ii) only

D   (iii) and (iv) only

7 **Cost centres are:**

A   units of product or service for which costs are ascertained

B   amounts of expenditure attributable to various activities

C   functions or locations for which costs are ascertained and related to cost units

D   a section of an organisation for which budgets are prepared and control exercised.

8 **Which of the following is NOT CORRECT?**

A   Cost accounting can be used for stock valuation to meet the requirements of internal reporting only.

B   Management accounting provides appropriate information for decision-making, planning, control and performance evaluation.

C   Routine information can be used for both short-term and long run decisions.

D   Financial accounting information can be used for internal reporting purposes.

9 **Which of the following could be carried out by higher level management?**

(i)   Making short term decisions

(ii)   Defining the objectives of the business

(iii) Making long run decisions

A   (i), (ii) and (iii)

B   (i) and (ii) only

C   (i) and (iii) only

D   (ii) and (iii) only

10 **Which of the following techniques would be useful for controlling costs?**

(i)   Actual versus flexed budget

(ii)   Variance analysis

(iii) Trend of costs analysis

A   (i) and (ii) only

B   (i) and (iii) only

C   (ii) and (iii) only

D   (i), (ii) and (iii)

ELEMENTS OF COST

11   Direct costs are:

A   costs which can be identified with a cost centre but not identified to a single cost unit

B   costs which can be economically identified with a single cost unit

C   costs which can be identified with a single cost unit, but it is not economic to do so

D   costs incurred as a direct result of a particular decision.

12   The following relate to procedures for materials:

1   Check the goods received note

2   Raise a stores requisition note

3   Update the stores ledger account for the purchase

4   Raise a purchase order

What would be the correct order of the above when in the process of purchasing and using materials?

A   4, 2, 1, 3

B   2, 1, 3, 4

C   4, 1, 3, 2

D   1, 4, 3, 2

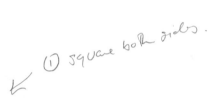

13   In the formula $Q = \sqrt{2CoD/Ch}$, if C = £20, D = 24,000 and Q = 400, then H is closest in value to:

A   £2.45

B   £6.00

C   £12.00

D   £36.00

The following information applies to questions 14 to 17

Marlows manufactures one product – jeans. As management accountant at Marlows you have determined the following information:

		£
Direct materials		10
Direct labour		29
Direct expenses		3
Factory expenses	– variable	7
	– fixed	5
Non-manufacturing costs	– variable	2
	– fixed	4
		60

Profit is 33.33% of total cost.

14   What is the final selling price?

A   £75

B   £60

C   £80

D   £20

15   **What is the unit stock valuation figure, if an absorption costing system is used?**

A   £54 per unit

B   £60 per unit

C   £42 per unit

D   £49 per unit

16   **What is the variable cost/unit?**

A   £54 per unit

B   £42 per unit

C   £51 per unit

D   £49 per unit

17   **What is the prime cost/unit?**

A   £54 per unit

B   £60 per unit

C   £42 per unit

D   £49 per unit

The following information applies to questions 18 and 19

An enterprise uses a raw material T. Movements in T for the month of August are set out below.

	Goods received			Issued to production	
Date	Kilos	Price per kilo		Date	Kilos
12 August	4,000	£5.00		15 August	3,900
19 August	1,200	£6.00		21 August	1,100
24 August	2,800	£7.50			

There were no stocks of T held at 1 August.

18   **What would be the stock valuation at 31 August on a FIFO basis, to the nearest £?**

A   £22,200

B   £22,500

C   £15,000

D   £18,000

19   **What would be the closing stock valuation at 31 August on a weighted average cost basis to the nearest £?**

A   £18,075

B   £18,500

C   £22,185

D   £22,046

20   **WL has closing stock at 31 July of 400 units valued, using LIFO, at £10,000. Stock movements in July were:**

5 July   300 units bought for £25 per unit

10 July   500 units issued

15 July   400 units bought for £22 per unit

20 July   200 units issued

What was the value of the opening stock?

A   £11,200

B   £10,000

C   £9,400

D   Cannot be found from the information available

Data for questions 21 and 22

Aberdeen Ltd holds stocks of ratchets that it uses in production. Over the last month receipts and issues were as follows:

	Receipts	Issues	
Opening balance	200 at £5	7th May	400
5 May	300 at £4.50	23rd May	400
12 May	100 at £6	30th May	200
22 May	400 at £5.50		
29 May	200 at £7		

21   If a FIFO stock valuation method were used, the value of stocks at the month end would be:

A   £1,000

B   £1,100

C   £1,200

D   £1,400

22   If a LIFO stock valuation method were used, the cost of ratchets issued to production in the month would be:

A   £5,150

B   £5,350

C   £5,450

D   £5,550

23   A firm has a high level of stock turnover and uses the FIFO (first in first out) issue pricing system. In a period of rising purchase prices, the closing stock valuation is:

A   close to current purchase prices

B   based on the prices of the first items received

C   much lower than current purchase prices

D   the average of all goods purchased in the period.

24   What is the economic batch quantity used to establish?

Optimal

A   reorder quantity

B   reorder level

C   cumulative production quantity

D   stock level for production

25 **A company uses the Economic Order Quantity (EOQ) model to establish reorder quantities. The following information relates to the forthcoming period:**

Order costs = £25 per order

Holding costs = 10% of purchase price = £4/unit

Annual demand = 20,000 units

Purchase price = £40 per unit

EOQ = 500 units

No safety stocks are held.

What are the total annual costs of stock (i.e. the total purchase cost plus total order cost plus total holding cost)?

A   £22,000

B   £33,500

C   £802,000

D   £803,000

Handwritten annotations: AOC + ASHC + PD = TAC; $\frac{D}{EOQ} \times Co$; CH $\times \frac{EOQ}{2}$; P×D

The following information is to be used for questions 26 and 27

A national chain of tyre fitters stocks a popular tyre for which the following information is available:

Average usage:	140 tyres per day
Minimum usage:	90 tyres per day
Maximum usage:	175 tyres per day
Lead time:	10 to 16 days
Re-order quantity:	3,000 tyres

26 **Based on the data above, at what level of stocks should a replenishment order be issued?**

A   2,240

B   2,800

C   3,000

D   5,740

Handwritten annotation: ROL — MAX USAGE × MAX LEAD TIME

27 **Based on the data above, what should be the maximum level of stocks possible?**

A   2,800

B   3,000

C   4,900

D   5,800

Handwritten annotation: ROL + ROQ − (MIN USAGE × MIN LEAD); 2800 + 3000 − (90 × 10); 5800 − 900

28 **Moura uses the economic order quantity formula (EOQ) to establish its optimal reorder quantity for its single raw material. The following data relates to the stock costs:**

Purchase price:	£15 per item
Carriage costs:	£50 per order
Ordering costs:	£5 per order
Storage costs:	10% of purchase price plus £0.20 per unit per annum

Annual demand is 4,000 units.

Handwritten annotation: Co = cost to place order.

What is the EOQ to the nearest whole unit?

A   153 units

B   170 units

C   485 units

D   509 units

29   **When considering the economic batch quantity model what does (1–D/R) represent?**

A   The rate at which production decreases.

B   The rate at which production increases.

C   The rate at which stock decreases.

D   The rate at which stock increases.

30   **Which of the following statements is correct?**

A   A stores ledger account will be updated from a goods received note only.

B   A stores requisition will only detail the type of product required by a customer.

C   The term 'lead time' is best used to describe the time between receiving an order and paying for it.

D   To make an issue from stores authorisation should be required.

31   **What would be the most appropriate cost unit for a cake manufacturer?**

Cost per:

A   Cake

B   Batch produced

C   Kilogram produced

D   Production run

The following information relates to questions 32 and 33

Turner Limited has the following stock record:

Date	Number of units		Cost	
1 March	Opening stock	100 units	at £3.00/unit	
3 March	Receipt	200 units	at £3.50/unit	
8 March	Issue	250 units		
15 March	Receipt	300 units	at £3.20/unit	
17 March	Receipt	200 units	at £3.30/unit	
21 March	Issue	500 units		
23 March	Receipt	450 units	at £3.10/unit	
27 March	Issue	350 units		

---

32   **What is the valuation of closing stock using LIFO at each issue?**

A   £460

B   £465

C   £467

D   £469

33   **What is the valuation of issues using the weighted average method of stock valuation at each issue?**

  A   £3,248

  B   £3,548

  C   £3,715

  D   £4,015

34   **Hill Limited wishes to minimise its stock costs. At the moment its reorder quantity is 1,000 units. Order costs are £10 per order and holding costs are £0.10 per unit per month. Hill Limited estimates annual demand to be 15,000 units.**

  What is the optimal reorder quantity (to the nearest 100 units)?

  A   500 units

  B   1,000 units

  C   1,200 units

  D   1,700 units

35   **Which of the following is correct with regard to stocks?**

  (i)   Stock-outs arise when too little stock is held.

  (ii)   Safety stocks are the level of units maintained in case there is unexpected demand.

  (iii)   A reorder level can be established by looking at the maximum usage and the maximum lead-time.

  A   (i) and (ii) only

  B   (i) and (iii) only

  C   (ii) and (iii) only

  D   (i), (ii) and (iii)

36   **The following data relates to a wage index for a company:**

Year	Wages per week	Index
20X1	£275	117
20X6	£315	157

  What were the 20X6 weekly wages at 20X1 prices (to the nearest £)?

  A   £201

  B   £235

  C   £275

  D   £369

37   **A company has a budget for two products A and B as follows:**

	Product A	Product B
Sales (units)	2,000	4,500
Production (units)	1,750	5,000
Labour:		
Skilled at £10/hour	2 hours/unit	2 hours/unit
Unskilled at £7/hour	3 hours/unit	4 hours/unit

What is the budgeted cost for unskilled labour for the period?

A   £105,000

B   £135,000

C   £176,750

D   £252,500

A

$£7 \times 3 \times 1750$

36750

B

$£7 \times 4 \times 5000$

$140,000$

38   The following statements relate to labour costs:

There would be an increase in the total cost for labour as a result of

(i)   additional labour being employed on a temporary basis.

(ii)   a department with spare capacity being made to work more hours.

(iii)   a department which is at full capacity switching from the production of one product to another.

Which of the above is/are correct?

A   (i) only

B   (ii) only

C   (iii) only

D   (i) and (iii) only

39   A manufacturing firm is very busy and overtime is being worked.

The amount of overtime premium contained in direct wages would normally be classed as:

A   part of prime cost

B   factory overheads

C   direct labour costs

D   administrative overheads.

INDIRECT PROD'N COST

40   Gross wages incurred in Department 1 in June were £135,000. The wages analysis shows the following summary breakdown of the gross pay.

	Paid to direct labour £	Paid to indirect labour £
Ordinary time	62,965	29,750
Overtime:		
Basic pay	13,600	8,750
Premium	3,400	2,190
Shift allowance	6,750	3,495
Sick pay	3,450	650
	90,165	44,835

What is the direct wages cost for Department 1 in June?

A   £62,965

B   £76,565

C   £86,715

D   £90,165

41 **Scaynes employs two types of labour: skilled workers, considered to be direct workers, and semi-skilled workers, considered to be indirect workers. Skilled workers are paid £10 per hour and semi-skilled £6 per hour.**

The skilled workers have worked 30 hours overtime this week, 10 hours on a specific order and 20 hours on general overtime. Overtime is paid at a rate of time and a half.

The semi-skilled workers have worked 45 hours overtime, 15 hours for a specific order at a customer's request and the rest for general purposes. Overtime again is paid at time-and-a-half.

What would be the total overtime pay considered to be a direct cost for this week?

A £195

B £285

C £350

D £485

42 **Which of the following relates to the cost of replacing (rather than retaining) labour due to high employee turnover?**

A Improving working conditions

B Suffering the learning curve effect

C Provision of a pension

D Provision of welfare services.

43 **A job requires 2,400 actual labour hours for completion but it is anticipated that idle time will be 20% of the total time required. If the wage rate is £10 per hour, what is the budgeted labour cost for the job, including the cost of the idle time?**

A £19,200

B £24,000

C £28,800

D £30,000

44 **The following information relates to a small production unit during a period:**

Budgeted hours   9,500 hours

Actual hours worked   9,200 hours

Standard hours of work produced   9,300 hours

What is the efficiency ratio for the period to the nearest 1%?

A 97%

B 98%

C 99%

D 101%

45 **A manufacturing firm is very busy and overtime is being worked.**

The amount of overtime premium contained in direct wages would normally be classed as:

A part of prime cost

B factory overheads

C direct labour costs

D administrative overheads

46   A job is budgeted to require 3,300 productive hours after incurring 25% idle time. If the total labour cost budgeted for the job is £36,300, what is the labour cost per hour?

A   £8.25

B   £8.80

C   £11.00

D   £13.75

47   At the beginning of the year, a company employed 4,600 individuals. During the year, 1,800 individuals were recruited and at the end of the year, the company employed a total of 5,500 individuals.

What was labour turnover during the year, as a percentage of the average employment level? Give your answer to the nearest 1%.

	%

48   A contract cleaning firm estimates that it will take 2,520 actual cleaning hours to clean an office block. Unavoidable interruptions and lost time are estimated to take 10% of the operatives' time. If the wage rate is £4 per hour, what is the budgeted labour cost?

A   £10,080

B   £11,088

C   £11,200

D   £12,197

49   Which of the following would be classed as indirect labour?

A   Assembly workers in a company manufacturing televisions.

B   A stores assistant in a factory store.

C   Plasterers in a construction company.

D   An audit clerk in a firm of auditors.

50   Which ONE of the following would be classified as direct labour?

A   Personnel manager in a company servicing cars.

B   Bricklayer in a construction company.

C   General manager in a DIY shop.

D   Maintenance manager in a company producing cameras.

51   The earnings index for employees in an industry for the past five years has been as follows:

Year	Average earnings index
20X1	247
20X2	255
20X3	265
20X4	271
20X5	278

Using the index, what (to the nearest £100) would be the expected labour cost of a job in 20X5 if an identical job in 20X2 cost £24,600 and no improvement in efficiency is anticipated?

A   £22,600

B   £26,800

C   £26,900

D   £27,700

COSTING METHODS – OVERHEADS, ABSORPTION COSTING AND MARGINAL COSTING

52   A manufacturing company absorbs overheads based on units produced. In one period 110,000 units were produced and the actual overheads were £500,000. Overheads were £50,000 over-absorbed in the period.

The overhead absorption rate was:

A   £4.00 per unit.

B   £4.50 per unit.

C   £5.00 per unit.

D   £5.50 per unit.

53   **Over-absorbed overheads occur when:**

A   Absorbed overheads exceed actual overheads.

B   Absorbed overheads exceed budgeted overheads.

C   Actual overheads exceed budgeted overheads.

D   Budgeted overheads exceed absorbed overheads.

54   **A company has four production departments. Fixed costs have been apportioned between them as follows:**

Department	K	L	M	N
Fixed costs	£10,000	£5,000	£4,000	£6,000

The time taken in each department to manufacture the company's only product, X, is 5 hours, 5 hours, 4 hours and 3 hours respectively.

If the company recovers overheads on the basis of labour hours and plans to produce 2,000 units, then the fixed cost per unit is:

A   £3.00

B   £12.00

C   £12.50

D   £17.00

55   **Which of the following is correct when considering the allocation, apportionment and reapportionment of overheads in an absorption costing situation?**

A   Only production related costs should be considered.

B   Allocation is the situation where part of an overhead is assigned to a cost centre.

C   Costs may only be reapportioned from production centres to service centres.

D   Any overheads assigned to a single department should be ignored.

The following information relates to questions 56 and 57:

A company has established the following budgeted fixed overheads for the forthcoming period:

	£'000	*Bases of apportionment*
Heating and lighting	12	Cubic capacity
Welfare costs	7	Number of employees
Power	42	Kwh usage
Total	61	

Other information:

	Department 1	Department 2	Maintenance	Total
Cubic capacity (m³)	6,000	7,500	2,500	16,000
Employees (number)	20	30	6	56
Power				
(kwh usage)	35,000	25,000		60,000
Labour hours	28,000	48,500		76,500
Machine hours	40,000	39,000		79,000

The maintenance department splits its time between Department 1 and Department 2 on a ratio of 2:3.

The management accountant has partially completed an allocation and apportionment statement:

	Department 1 £	Department 2 £	Maintenance £
Heat and light	4,500	5,625	1,875
Welfare	2,500		
Power	24,500		
	———		
Total	31,500		
	———		

56 **What would be the total cost allocated and apportioned to Department 2 excluding the reapportionment of the maintenance costs?**

    A   £21,250

    B   £26,875

    C   £27,625

    D   £29,500

57 **What would be the overhead absorption rate in Department 1 (to 3 decimal places)?**

    A   £0.788/machine hour

    B   £0.814/machine hour

    C   £1.125/labour hour

    D   £1.163/labour hour

58 **The process of cost apportionment is carried out so that:**

    A   costs may be controlled

    B   cost units gather overheads as they pass through cost centres

    C   whole items of cost can be charged to cost centres

    D   common costs are shared among cost centres.

59 **Floaters manufactures a product called the IC. It has the following production and fixed overhead budgets for the coming year.**

Production department	1	2
Fixed overhead	£2,400,000	£4,000,000
Total production hours	240,000	200,000
Total materials cost	£200,000	£400,000

Department 1 labour is paid £5 per hour and department 2 labour £4 per hour. The variable production cost of an IC is as follows:

		£
Labour		
Department 1 : 3 hours		15
Department 2 : 2 hours		8
Materials		
Department 1 : 1kg	@ £4 per kg	4
Department 2 : 2 kgs	@ £5 per kg	10
Variable overheads		7
		___
		44
		___

If fixed overheads are absorbed on the basis of labour hours, the fixed overhead cost per unit of IC is:

A   £70.00

B   £72.72

C   £102.67

D   £148.00

60   **Carrell produces two types of jacket, Blouson and Bomber, in its factory that is divided into two departments, cutting and stitching. The firm wishes to calculate a fixed overhead cost per unit figure from the following budgeted data.**

	Cutting dept	*Stitching dept*
Direct and allocated fixed overheads	£120,000	£72,000
Labour hours per unit		
Blouson	0.05 hours	0.20 hours
Bomber	0.10 hours	0.25 hours
Budgeted production		
Blouson	6,000 units	6,000 units
Bomber	6,000 units	6,000 units

If fixed overheads are absorbed by reference to labour hours, the fixed overhead cost of a Bomber would be:

A   £5.33

B   £6.67

C   £12.00

D   £20.00

61   **What is cost apportionment?**

A   The charging of discrete identifiable items of cost to cost centres or cost units.

B   The collection of costs attributable to cost centres and cost units using the costing methods, principles and techniques prescribed for a particular business entity.

C   The process of establishing the costs of cost centres or cost units.

D   The division of costs amongst two or more cost centres in proportion to the estimated benefit received, using a proxy e.g. square feet.

62   **An overhead absorption rate is used to:**

A   share out common costs over benefiting cost centres

B   find the total overheads for a cost centre

C   charge overheads to products

D   control overheads.

63 In a factory, there are 15 machines which are given a routine servicing every two weeks, and each machine takes the same amount of time to service. The factory uses a system of absorption costing, and some of the machines are in Production Centre 1 and some are in Production Centre 2.

Which of the following bases of apportionment would be most appropriate for machine maintenance expenses?

A Number of machines

B Value of machines

C Machine hours operated

D Floor space occupied

64 A company absorbs overheads on machine hours which were budgeted at 11,250 with overheads of £258,750. Actual results were 10,980 hours with overheads of £254,692.

Overheads were:

A under-absorbed by £2,152

B over-absorbed by £4,058

C under-absorbed by £4,058

D over-absorbed by £2,152.

65 A firm absorbs overheads on labour hours. In one period 11,500 hours were worked, actual overheads were £138,000 and there was £23,000 over-absorption. The overhead absorption rate per hour was:

A £10

B £12

C £13

D £14

66 When opening stocks were 8,500 litres and closing stocks 6,750 litres, a firm had a profit of £62,100 using marginal costing.

Assuming that the fixed overhead absorption rate was £3 per litre, what would be the profit using absorption costing?

A £41,850

B £56,850

C £67,350

D £82,350

67 A company budgeted to produce 3,000 units of a single product in a period at a budgeted cost per unit, built up as follows:

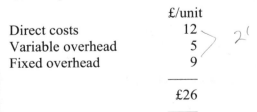

	£/unit
Direct costs	12
Variable overhead	5
Fixed overhead	9
	£26

In the period covered by the budget:

(a) Actual sales were 3,500 units and finished stocks decreased by 300 units.

(b) Actual fixed overhead expenditure was 5% above that budgeted – all other costs were as budgeted.

Determine which of the following statements is correct.

A   Overheads in the period were £450 over-absorbed.

B   Overheads in the period were £450 under-absorbed.

C   Overheads in the period were £1,450 over-absorbed.

D   Overheads in the period were £1,450 under-absorbed.

68   **QRL uses a standard absorption costing system. The following details have been extracted from its budget for April 20X7:**

Fixed production overhead cost	£48,000
Production (units)	4,800

In April 20X7 the fixed production overhead cost was under-absorbed by £8,000 and the fixed production overhead expenditure variance was £2,000 adverse.

The actual number of units produced was:

A   3,800

B   4,000

C   4,200

D   5,400

69   **A company uses a standard absorption costing system. The following details are taken from its budget for March 20X8:**

Fixed production overhead cost	£72,000
Production (units)	7,200

The accounts for March 20X8 show that the fixed production overhead cost was over-absorbed by £12,000, and the fixed production overhead expenditure variance was £3,000 adverse.

The actual number of units produced was:

A   5,700

B   6,300

C   8,100

D   8,700

70   **A management consultancy recovers overheads on chargeable consulting hours. Budgeted overheads were £615,000 and actual consulting hours were 32,150. Overheads were under-recovered by £35,000.**

If actual overheads were £694,075 what was the budgeted overhead absorption rate per hour?

A   £19.13

B   £20.50

C   £21.59

D   £22.68

71   **Canberra has established the following information regarding fixed overheads for the coming month:**

Budged information

Fixed overheads	£180,000
Labour hours	3,000 hours
Machine hours	10,000 hours
Units of production	5,000 units

Actual fixed costs for the last month were £160,000.

Canberra produces many different products using highly automated manufacturing processes and absorbs overheads on the most appropriate basis.

What will be the pre-determined overhead absorption rate?

A   £16

B   £18

C   £36

D   £60

72   **The management accountant of Gympie Limited has already allocated and apportioned the fixed overheads for the period although she has yet to reapportion the service centre costs. Information for the period is as follows:**

	Production departments		Service departments		Total
	1	*2*	*Stores*	*Maintenance*	
Allocated and apportioned	£17,500	£32,750	£6,300	£8,450	£65,000
Work done by:					
Stores	60%	30%	-	10%	
Maintenance	75%	20%	5%	-	

What are the total overheads including in production department 1 if the reciprocal method is used to reapportion service centre costs?

A   £27,618

B   £28,171

C   £28,398

D   £28,453

73   **A company produces and sells a single product whose variable cost is £6 per unit.**

Fixed costs have been absorbed over the normal level of activity of 200,000 units and have been calculated as £2 per unit.

The current selling price is £10 per unit.

How much profit is made under marginal costing if the company sells 250,000 units?

A   £500,000

B   £600,000

C   £900,000

D   £1,000,000

74   **A company has established a marginal costing profit of £72,300. Opening stock was 300 units and closing stock is 750 units. The fixed production overhead absorption rate has been calculated as £5/unit.**

What was the profit under absorption costing?

A   £67,050

B   £70,050

C   £74,550

D   £77,550

The following information relates to questions 75 and 76

Haywards Limited reported an annual profit of £47,500 for the year ended 31 March 20X4. The company uses absorption costing. One product is manufactured, the Heath, which has the following standard cost per unit:

	£
Direct material (2kg at £5/kg)	10
Direct labour (4 hours at £6.50/hour)	26
Variable overheads (4 hours at £1/hour)	4
Fixed overheads (4 hours at £3/hour)	12
	52

The normal level of activity is 10,000 units although actual production was 11,500 units. Fixed costs were as budgeted.

Stock levels at 1 April 20X3 were 400 units and at the end of the year were 600 units.

75   **What would be the profit under marginal costing?**

   A   £44,300
   B   £45,100
   C   £49,900
   D   £50,700

76   **What were the budgeted fixed overheads for the year ended 31 March 20X4 and the actual under- or over-absorption?**

	Budgeted overheads	Under-/over-absorbed
A	£120,000	£18,000 over-absorbed
B	£120,000	£18,000 under-absorbed
C	£138,000	£18,000 over-absorbed
D	£138,000	£18,000 under-absorbed

The following data are for questions 77 and 78

The budget for Bright's first month of trading, producing and selling boats was as follows:

	£'000
Variable production cost of boats	45
Fixed production costs	30
Production costs of 750 boats	75
Closing stock of 250 boats	(25)
Production cost of 500 sold	50
Variable selling costs	5
Fixed selling costs	25
	80
Profit	10
Sales revenue	90

The budget has been produced using an absorption costing system.

77   If a marginal costing system were used, the budgeted profit would be:

A   £22,500 lower

B   £10,000 lower

C   £10,000 higher

D   £22,500 higher

78   **Assume that at the end of the first month unit variable costs and fixed costs and selling price for the month were in line with the budget and any stock was valued at the same unit cost as in the above budget.**

However, if production was actually 700 and sales 600, what would be the reported profit using absorption costing?

A   £9,000

B   £12,000

C   £14,000

D   £15,000

The following data are for questions 79 and 80

Dundee makes cakes, for which the standard cost card is as follows:

	£
Materials	2
Labour	3
Variable production overhead	3
Fixed production overhead	4
Variable selling cost	1
Fixed selling overhead	2
Profit	5
Sales price	20

Both types of fixed overheads were based on a budget of 10,000 cakes a year.

In the first year of production, the only difference from the budget was that Dundee produced 11,000 cakes and sold 9,000.

---

79   **What was the profit made under an absorption costing system?**

A   £39,000

B   £43,000

C   £47,000

D   £51,000

80   **What would the profit have been using a marginal costing system?**

A   £35,000

B   £39,000

C   £42,000

D   £47,000

81   In a period, a company had opening stocks of 31,000 units of Product G and closing stocks of 34,000 units. Profits based on marginal costing were £850,500 and profits based on absorption costing were £955,500.

If the budgeted fixed costs for the company for the period were £1,837,500, what was the budgeted level of activity?

A   24,300 units

B   27,300 units

C   52,500 units

D   65,000 units

82   The absorption cost budget of a company shows a profit per unit of £5. This is based on production of 10,000 units and sales of 8,000 units.

If all fixed costs are related to production and a change to a marginal cost profit produces a budgeted decrease in profit of £2,000, the standard contribution per unit must be:

A   £6

B   £5

C   £4.80

D   £4

83   A new company has set up a marginal costing system and has a budgeted contribution for the period of £26,000 based on sales of 13,000 units and production of 15,000 units. This level of production represents the firm's expected long-term level of production. The company's budgeted fixed production costs are £3,000 for the period.

If the company were to change to an absorption costing system the budgeted profit would be:

A   £22,600

B   £23,400

C   £25,600

D   £26,400

COSTING SYSTEMS

84   Jill is trying to establish a budgeted quantity of material purchases for the coming month.

Opening stock of material was 300kg and closing stock is expected to be 400kg.

Jill produces two products, the Pye and the Combe, to which the following information applies:

	Pye	*Combe*
Raw material input per unit	10kg	4kg
Material lost in production	10%	–
Demand per month	450 units	375 units

How many kilograms of raw material should be purchased?

A   5,900

B   6,100

C   6,400

D   6,600

85 **A company is preparing a production budget for the next year. The following information is relevant:**

Budgeted sales 10,000 units
Opening stock 600 units
Closing stock 5% of budgeted sales

The production process is such that 10% of the units produced are rejected.

What is the number of units required to be produced to meet demand?

A 8,900 units

B 9,900 units

C 10,900 units

D 11,000 units

86 **Burgess operates a continuous process into which 3,000 units of material costing £9,000 was input in a period.**

Conversion costs for this period were £11,970 and losses, which have a scrap value of £1.50, are expected at a rate of 10% of input. There were no opening or closing stocks and output for the period was 2,900 units.

What was the output valuation?

A £20,271

B £20,520

C £20,970

D £22,040

87 **Which of the following best describes the term 'equivalent units' when using the FIFO method?**

A The number of units worked on during a period including the opening and closing stock units.

B The number of whole units worked on during a period ignoring the levels on completion of opening and closing stock units.

C The number of effective whole units worked on during a period allowing for the levels of completion of opening and closing stock units.

D The total number of whole units started during a period ignoring the opening stock units as these were started in the previous period.

88 **The costs of process 1 in month 6 were as follows:**

	Degree of completion	Units	Cost
			£
Opening stock	40%	3,000	6,750
Direct materials cost in the month		5,000	10,000
Conversion costs in the month			19,925
Closing stock	75%	2,000	

Materials are added gradually throughout the production process. There is no loss in process.

What is the cost of the finished output in the month if the FIFO method of stock valuation is used?

A £22,800

B £28,800

C £29,340

D £29,550

89   Charleville operates a continuous process producing three products and one by-product. Output from the process for a month was as follows:

Product	Selling price per unit	Units of output from process
1	£18	10,000
2	£25	20,000
3	£20	20,000
4 (by-product)	£2	3,500

Total output costs were £277,000.

What was the unit valuation for product 3 using the sales revenue basis for allocating joint costs?

A   £4.70

B   £4.80

C   £5.00

D   £5.10

90   Perth operates a process costing system. The process is expected to lose 25% of input and this can be sold for £8 per kg.

Inputs for the month were:

Direct materials   3,500 kg at a total cost of £52,500

Direct labour   £9,625 for the period

There is no opening or closing work in progress in the period. Actual output was 2,800 kg. What is the valuation of the output?

A   £44,100

B   £49,700

C   £58,800

D   £56,525

91   A company uses process costing to value its output and all materials are input at the start of the process.

The following information relates to the process for one month:

Input	3,000 units
Opening stock	400 units
Losses	10% of input is expected to be lost
Closing stock	200 units

How many good units were output from the process if actual losses were 400 units?

A   2,800 units

B   2,900 units

C   3,000 units

D   3,200 units

92   A company uses process costing to value output. During the last month the following information was recorded:

Output:	2,800 kg valued at £7·50/kg
Normal loss:	300 kg which has a scrap value of £3/kg
Actual loss:	200 kg

What was the value of the input?

A   £22,650

B   £21,900

C   £21,600

D   £21,150

93   **A chemical process has a normal wastage of 10% of input. In a period, 2,500 kgs of material were input and there was an abnormal loss of 75 kgs.**

What quantity of good production was achieved?

A   2,175 kgs

B   2,250 kgs

C   2,325 kgs

D   2,475 kgs

94   **A company produces Inverness in a continuous process.**

At the beginning of November work in progress of 400 litres was 30% complete as regards labour and overheads. At the end of the month, work in progress was 200 litres and was 60% complete. During the month 2,000 litres were introduced to the process.

If the labour and overheads in November cost £3,300, and FIFO is used for stock valuation, the cost per equivalent unit in the month was:

A   £1.42

B   £1.50

C   £1.62

D   £1.65

95   **Vare Ltd produces various inks at its Normanton factory. Production details for Process 1 are as follows:**

Opening work in progress, 1 April	400 units	60% complete
Closing work in progress, 30 April	600 units	20% complete
Units started	1,000	
Units finished	800	

The degree of completion quoted relates to labour and overhead costs. Three-quarters of the materials are added at the start of the process and the remaining quarter added when the process is 50% complete.

The equivalent units of production for materials in the period are:

A   1,250

B   1,000

C   850

D   680

96   **ABC manufactures product X in a single process. Normal loss (scrap) in the process is 10% of output and scrapped units can be sold off for £4/unit.**

In period 8 there was no opening stock and no closing stock. Process costs of direct materials, direct labour and production overheads totalled £184,800. Input to the process in the month was 13,200 units.

What was the cost/unit produced?

A   £12.50

B   £15.00

C   £15.15

D   £15.40

97   **The costs of Process 2 during period 3 were:**

	Degree of completion	Total units	Materials cost £	Conversion costs £
Opening stock	75%	2,000	9,400	4,800
Transferred from Process 1		8,000	41,600	
Conversion costs				16,450
Closing stock	50%	3,000		

Units transferred from Process 1 are all added at the start of processing in Process 2. There is no loss in process.

What is the value of closing stock at the end of the period if the weighted average method of stock valuation is used?

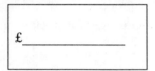

£_____

98   **The following process account has been drawn up for the last month:**

Process account

	Units	£		Units	£
Opening WIP	250	3,000	Normal loss	225	450
Input:			Output	4,100	
Materials	4,500	22,500	Abnormal loss	275	
Labour		37,500	Closing WIP	150	
	4,750			4,750	

Work in progress has the following level of completion:

	Material	Labour
Opening WIP	100%	40%
Closing WIP	100%	30%

The company uses the FIFO method for valuing the output from the process and all losses occurred at the end of the process.

What were the equivalent units for labour?

A   4,380 units

B   4,270 units

C   4,320 units

D   4,420 units

The following data are to be used for questions 99 and 100

A firm uses job costing and recovers overheads on a direct labour cost basis.

Three jobs were worked on during a period, the details of which were:

	Job 1	Job 2	Job 3
	£	£	£
Opening work-in-progress	8,500	0	46,000
Material in period	17,150	29,025	0
Labour for period	12,500	23,000	4,500

The overheads for the period were exactly as budgeted, £140,000. Actual labour costs were also the same as budgeted.

99 **Jobs 1 and 2 were the only incomplete jobs at the end of the period.**

What was the value of closing work-in-progress?

A   £81,900

B   £90,175

C   £140,675

D   £214,425

100 **Job 3 was completed during the period and consisted of 2,400 identical circuit boards. The firm adds 50% to total production costs to arrive at a selling price.**

What is the selling price of a circuit board?

A   It cannot be calculated without more information

B   £31.56

C   £41.41

D   £58.33

101 **A jobbing enterprise calculates the prices of its jobs by adding overheads to the prime cost and adding 30% to total costs as a profit margin. Job number 256 was sold for £1,690 and incurred overheads of £694. What was the prime cost of the job?**

A   £489

B   £507

C   £606

D   £996

102 **For operational purposes, for a company operating a fleet of delivery vehicles, which of the following cost units would be most useful?**

A   Cost per mile run

B   Cost per driver hour

C   Cost per tonne mile

D   Cost per kilogram carried

103 A cleaning fluid is produced by a series of processes. The following information relates to the final process:

	Litres
Opening work in progress	2,000
Closing work in progress	1,500
Input of new materials	42,300
Transfer to finished goods stock	40,100
Normal loss	400

The abnormal loss is:

A   800 litres

B   1,300 litres

C   1,800 litres

D   2,300 litres

104 A factory manufactures model cars. During October work commenced on 110,000 new cars. This was in addition to 20,000 which were 50% complete at the start of the month. At the end of October there were 40,000 cars which were 50% complete.

Costs for October were:

	£'000
Brought forward	11,000
Incurred this period	121,000
	£132,000

If this factory chooses the weighted average method of spreading costs, what is the cost per car for October production?

A   £1,100

B   £1,200

C   £1,210

D   £1,320

The following data are to be used for questions 105 to 107

A firm makes special assemblies to customers' orders and uses job costing. The data for a period are:

	Job number AA10 £	Job number BB15 £	Job number CC20 £
Opening WIP	26,800	42,790	0
Material added in period	17,275	0	18,500
Labour for period	14,500	3,500	24,600

The budgeted overheads for the period were £126,000. Overheads are absorbed on the basis of labour costs. Actual labour costs in the period were the same as budgeted labour costs.

---

105 What overhead should be added to job number CC20 for the period?

A   £24,600

B   £65,157

C   £72,761

D   £126,000

106 **Job number BB15 was completed and delivered during the period and the firm wishes to earn 33% profit on sales.**

What is the selling price of job number BB15?

A   £69,435

B   £70,804

C   £75,521

D   £84,963

107 **What was the approximate value of closing work-in-progress at the end of the period?**

A   £58,575

B   £101,675

C   £147,965

D   £217,323

108 **An error was made in a firm's computation of the percentage of completion of closing work-in-progress. The error resulted in assigning a lower percentage of completion than actually was the case.**

What was the effect of this error upon the cost per equivalent unit and the cost of goods completed for the period?

	Cost per equivalent unit	*Cost of goods completed*
A	Understated	Understated
B	Understated	Overstated
C	Overstated	Understated
D	Overstated	Overstated

109 **Which one of the following statements is incorrect?**

A   Job costs are collected separately, whereas process costs are averages.

B   In job costing the progress of a job can be ascertained from the materials requisition notes and job tickets or time sheet.

C   In process costing information is needed about work passing through a process and work remaining in each process.

D   In process costing, but not job costing, the cost of normal loss will be incorporated into normal product costs.

110 **The following details relate to the main process a chemical manufacturer:**

Opening work-in-progress	2,000 litres, fully complete as to materials and 40% complete as to conversion
Material input	24,000 litres
Normal loss is 10% of input.	
Output to process 2	19,500 litres
Closing work-in-progress	3,000 litres, fully complete as to materials and 45% complete as to conversion

The numbers of equivalent units to be included in the calculation of the cost per equivalent unit, using a weighted average basis of valuation, are:

	Materials	Conversion
A	21,400	20,850
B	22,500	21,950
C	22,500	20,850
D	23,600	21,950

111 Two joint products X and Y and a by-product B are produced from a process. Data relating to the period just ended are:

Opening and closing stocks	Nil
Direct materials cost	£40,000
Direct labour and overhead costs	£44,000
Output:	
Product X	8,000 units
Product Y	6,000 units
Product B	3,000 units

Joint processing costs are shared between the joint products on the basis of net realisable value at the split-off point. The unit sales price of Product X is £12, the unit price of product Y is £6 and the price of by-product B is £0.50/unit. Product Y is sold immediately as output from the common process, but product X needs further processing before it is ready for sale, costing £3/unit.

What was the cost/unit of Product Y in the period?

A £3.80

B £4.58

C £4.67

D £4.75

112 Which of the following would be considered a service industry?

(i) an airline company

(ii) a railway company

(iii) a firm of accountants

A (i) and (ii) only

B (i) and (iii) only

C (ii) and (iii) only

D (i), (ii) and (iii)

COSTING METHODS AND TECHNIQUES – STANDARD COSTING AND VARIANCE ANALYSIS

The following data are common to questions 113 - 117

A company manufactures special electrical equipment. The company employs a standard costing system with separate standards established for each product.

A special transformer is manufactured in the transformer department. Production volume is measured by direct labour hours in this department, and a flexible budget system is used to plan and control departmental overheads.

Standard costs for the special transformer are determined annually. The standard cost of a transformer is shown below.

		£
Direct materials		
Iron	5 sheets at £2 per sheet	10
Copper	3 spools at £3 per spool	9
Direct labour	4 hours at £7 per hour	28
Variable overhead	4 hours at £3 per hour	12
Fixed overhead	4 hours at £2 per hour	8
		____
		67
		____

Overhead rates were based upon normal and expected monthly capacity, both of which were 4,000 direct labour hours. Practical capacity for this department is 5,000 direct labour hours per month. The variable overhead costs are expected to vary with the number of direct labour hours actually used.

During the month 800 transformers were produced.

The following costs were incurred in the month:

Direct materials

Type	Quantity purchased	Quantity used
Iron	5,000 sheets at £2.00 per sheet	3,900 sheets
Copper	2,200 spools at £3.10 per spool	2,600 spools

Direct labour

2,000 hours at £7.00
1,400 hours at £7.20

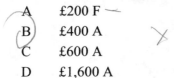

Overheads expenditure

Variable overheads: £10,000
Fixed overheads: £8,800

---

113 **The total material usage variance is:**

    A   £200 A

    B   £400 A

    C   £600 A

    D   £800 A

114 **The labour rate variance is:**

    A   £280 A

    B   £340 A

    C   £1,680 A

    D   £2,440 A

115 **The variable overhead expenditure variance is:**

    A   £200 F

    B   £400 A

    C   £600 A

    D   £1,600 A

116 The expenditure variance for fixed overhead is:

A £2,400 A

B Nil

C £800 A

D £1,000 F

117 The fixed overhead volume variance is:

A £400 A

B £2,200 A

C £2,400 A

D £1,600 A

The following information relates to questions 118 and 119:

A company has a budgeted material cost of £125,000 for the production of 25,000 units per month. Each unit is budgeted to use 2 kg of material. The standard cost of material is £2.50 per kg.

Actual materials in the month cost £136,000 for 27,000 units and 53,000 kg were purchased and used.

118 What was the adverse material price variance?

A £1,000

B £3,500

C £7,500

D £11,000

119 What was the favourable material usage variance?

A £2,500

B £4,000

C £7,500

D £10,000

120 FGH has the following budget and actual data:

Budget fixed overhead cost	£120,000
Budget production (units)	20,000
Actual fixed overhead cost	£115,000
Actual production (units)	21,000

The fixed overhead volume variance:

A is £4,500 adverse

B is £5,500 favourable

C is £6,000 favourable

D is £10,500 favourable

121 In the month just ended, a factory made 12,500 units of a product, and there was a favourable labour efficiency variance of £11,250.

If 41,000 hours were worked and the standard labour rate is £6 per hour, how many standard hours are allowed per unit of production (to two decimal places)?

A   3.13
B   3.28
C   3.43
D   4.18

122 During a period, 25,600 labour hours were worked at a standard cost of £7.50 per hour. The direct labour efficiency variance was £8,250 adverse. How many standard hours were produced?

A   1,100
B   24,500
C   25,600
D   26,700

123 The following information relates to April production of product CK:

	Actual	Budget
Units produced	580	600
Input of material (kg)	1,566	1,500
Cost of material purchased and input	£77,517	£76,500

What is the materials usage variance?

A   £2,349 F
B   £3,366 A
C   £5,742 A
D   £5,916 A

124 For product DR, the material price variance for the month of August was £1,000 (F) and the material usage variance was £300 (A).

The standard material usage per unit is 3 kg, and the standard material price is £2 per kg. 500 units were produced in the period. Opening stocks of raw materials were 100 kg and closing stocks 400 kg.

Material purchases in the period were:

A   1,050 kg
B   1,350 kg
C   1,650 kg
D   1,950 kg

125 The following information relates to a month's production of product CN:

	Budget	Actual
Units produced	600	580
Input of material P (kg)	1,500	1,566
Cost of material P purchased and input	£25,500	£25,839

What is the price variance for material P?

A   £783 F

B   £339 A

C   £1,189 A

D   £1,972 A

126 **Direct labour cost data relating to last month is as follows:**

Actual hours worked	28,000
Total direct labour cost	£117,600
Direct labour rate variance	£8,400 Adverse
Direct labour efficiency variance	£3,900 Favourable

To the nearest thousand hours, what were the standard labour hours produced last month?

A   31,000 hrs

B   29,000 hrs

C   27,000 hrs

D   25,000 hrs

127 **In a period, 11,280 kilograms of material were used at a total standard cost of £46,248. The material usage variance was £492 adverse.**

What was the standard allowed weight of material for the period?

A   11,520 kgs

B   11,280 kgs

C   11,400 kgs

D   11,160 kgs

128 **During a period 17,500 labour hours were worked at a standard cost of £6.50 per hour. The labour efficiency variance was £7,800 favourable.**

How many standard hours were produced?

A   1,200

B   16,300

C   17,500

D   18,700.

129 **ABC Ltd uses standard costing. It purchases a small component for which the following data are available:**

Actual purchase quantity	6,800 units
Standard allowance for actual production	5,440 units
Standard price	85p/unit
Purchase price variance	£544 Adverse

What was the actual purchase price/unit?

A   £0.75

B   £0.77

C   £0.93

D   £0.95

130 Trim Ltd's materials price variance for the month of January was £1,000 F and the usage variance was £200 F.

The standard material usage per unit is 3 kg, and the standard material price is £2 per kg. 500 units were produced in the period. Opening stocks of raw materials were 100 kg and closing stocks 300 kg.

Material purchases in the period were:

A   1,200 kg

B   1,400 kg

C   1,600 kg

D   1,800 kg

131 The following information relates to R plc for October 20X7:

Bought 7,800 kg of material R at a total cost of £16,380.

Stocks of material R increased by 440 kg.

Stocks of material R are valued using standard purchase price.

Material price variance was £1,170 Adverse.

The standard price per kg for material R is:

A   £1.95

B   £2.10

C   £2.23

D   £2.25

132 XY Ltd purchased 6,850 kilograms of material at a total cost of £21,920. The material price variance was £1,370 favourable. The standard price per kilogram was:

A   £0.20

B   £3.00

C   £3.20

D   £3.40

133 XYZ uses standard costing. It makes an assembly for which the following standard data are available:

Standard labour hours per assembly   24

Standard labour cost per hour   £8

During a period 850 assemblies were made, there was a Nil rate variance and an adverse efficiency variance of £4,400.

How many actual labour hours were worked?

A   19,850

B   20,400

C   20,950

D   35,200

134 AB purchased a quantity of materials costing £43,250. The standard cost was £2.00 per kg and there was an adverse price variance of £3,250.

How many kilograms were purchased?

A   20,000

B   21,625

C   23,250

D   24,875

135 **F Ltd has the following budget and actual data:**

Budget fixed overhead cost	£100,000
Budget production (units)	20,000
Actual fixed overhead cost	£110,000
Actual production (units)	19,500

The fixed overhead volume variance is:

A   £500 adverse

B   £2,500 adverse

C   £10,000 adverse

D   £17,500 adverse.

136 **JDC operates a standard cost accounting system. The following information has been extracted from its standard cost card and budgets:**

Budgeted sales volume	5,000 units
Budgeted selling price	£10.00 per unit
Standard variable cost	£5.60 per unit
Standard total cost	£7.50 per unit

If it used a standard marginal cost accounting system and its actual sales were 4,500 units at a selling price of £12.00, its sales volume variance would be:

A   £1,250 adverse

B   £2,200 adverse

C   £2,250 adverse

D   £3,200 adverse.

137 **PQ operates a standard costing system for its only product. The standard cost card is as follows:**

Direct materials	(4 kg at £2 per kg)	£8.00
Direct labour	(4 hours at £4 per hour)	£16.00
Variable overhead	(4 hours at £3 per hour)	£12.00
Fixed overhead	(4 hours at £5 per hour)	£20.00

Fixed overheads are absorbed on the basis of labour hours. Fixed overhead costs are budgeted at £120,000 per annum arising at a constant rate during the year.

Activity in month 3 of 20X5 is budgeted to be 10% of total activity for the year. Actual production during period 3 was 500 units, with actual fixed overhead costs incurred being £9,800 and actual hours worked being 1,970.

The fixed overhead expenditure variance for month 3 of 20X5 was:

A   £2,200 (F)

B   £200 (F)

C   £50 (F)

D   £200 (A)

138 Sheffield operates a standard costing system for production and uses variance analysis to identify deviations from budget.

Information with regard to variable overhead costs for the period was as follows:

Budgeted cost	£180,000
Actual costs	£173,800

Labour hours:

Budgeted	90,000 hours
Actual	82,650 hours

Variable overheads are absorbed on a direct labour hour basis.

What was the variable overhead expenditure variance?

A   £6,200 favourable

B   £8,500 adverse

C   £14,700 favourable

D   £15,455 adverse

139 When considering setting standards for costing which of the following would NOT be appropriate?

A   The normal level of activity should always be used for absorbing overheads.

B   Average prices for materials should be used, encompassing any discounts that are regularly available.

C   The labour rate used will be the rate at which labour is paid.

D   Average material usage should be established based on generally-accepted working practices.

140 Which of the following statements is correct with regard to the material price variance calculation?

The material price variance is calculated by comparing the:

A   actual quantity purchased at standard cost with the actual quantity used at standard cost

B   actual quantity purchased at actual cost with the actual quantity used at standard cost

C   actual quantity purchased at actual cost with the actual quantity purchased at standard cost

D   actual quantity purchased at actual cost with the actual quantity used at actual cost.

141 Bowen has established the following with regard to fixed overheads for the past month:

Actual costs incurred	£132,400
Actual units produced	5,000 units
Actual labour hours worked	9,750 hours
Budgeted costs	£135,000
Budgeted units of production	4,500 units
Budgeted labour hours	9,000 hours

Overheads are absorbed on a labour hour basis.

What was the fixed overhead capacity variance?

A   £750 favourable

B   £11,250 favourable

C   £22,500 favourable

D   £11,250 adverse.

142 The following details relate to product T, which has a selling price of £44.00:

	£/unit
Direct materials	15.00
Direct labour (3 hours)	12.00
Variable overhead	6.00
Fixed overhead	4.00
	37.00

During April 20X6, the actual production of T was 800 units, which was 100 units fewer than budgeted. The budget shows an annual production target of 10,800, with fixed costs accruing at a constant rate throughout the year. Actual overhead expenditure totalled £8,500 for April 20X6.

The overhead variances for April 20X6 were:

	Expenditure	Volume
	£	£
A	367 A	1,000 A
B	500 A	400 A
C	100 A	1,000 A
D	100 A	400 A

143 QR Limited uses a standard absorption costing system. The following details have been extracted from its budget for April 20X7:

Fixed production overhead cost   £48,000

Production (units)   4,800

In April 20X7 the fixed production overhead cost was under-absorbed by £8,000 and the fixed production overhead expenditure variance was £2,000 adverse.

The actual number of units produced was:

A   3,800

B   4,000

C   4,200

D   5,400

144 A company is reviewing actual performance to budget to see where there are differences. The following standard information is relevant:

	£ per unit
Selling price	50
Direct materials	4
Direct labour	16
Fixed production overheads	5
Variable production overheads	10
Fixed selling costs	1
Variable selling cost	1
Total costs	37
Budgeted sales units	3,000
Actual sales units	3,500

What was the favourable sales volume variance using marginal costing?

A   £9,500

B   £7,500

C   £7,000

D   £6,500

SHORT-TERM DECISION MAKING

145   **A company achieves bulk buying discounts on quantities above a certain level. These discounts are only available for the units above the specified level and not on all the units purchased.**

Which of the following graphs of total purchase cost against units best illustrates the above situation?

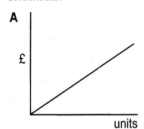 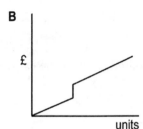

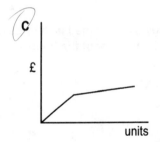 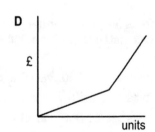

146

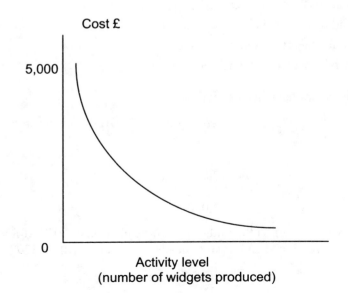

Which of the following descriptions best suits the graph?

A   Total fixed costs

B   Total variable costs

C   Variable costs/unit

D   Fixed costs/unit

147   **Which of the following costs are fixed over a large range of activity levels?**

A   Telephone costs

B   Office rental cost

C   Direct material

D   Supervisory costs

148   **The following data relate to the overhead expenditure of contract cleaners at two activity levels:**

Square metres cleaned	12,750	15,100
Overheads	£73,950	£83,585

Using the high-low method, what is the estimate of the overhead cost if 16,200 square metres are to be cleaned?

A   £88,095

B   £89,674

C   £93,960

D   £98,095

149   **A company's weekly costs (£C) were plotted against production level (P) for the last 50 weeks and a regression line calculated to be C = 1,000 +250P. Which statement about the breakdown of weekly costs is true?**

A   Weekly fixed costs are £1,000, variable costs per unit are £5.

B   Weekly fixed costs are £250, variable costs per unit are £1000.

C   Weekly fixed costs are £1,000, variable costs per unit are £250.

D   Weekly fixed costs are £20, variable costs per unit are £5.

150   **The 'high low' method of cost estimation can be used to:**

A   calculate the budget cost for the actual activity

B   calculate the highest and lowest costs in the budget period

C   measure the actual cost for the budget activity

D   predict the range of costs expected in the budget period.

151   **Overhead costs in the past four years have been as follows:**

Year	Output units	Overhead cost £	Overheads price index
20X3	7,000	91,350	315
20X4	7,500	97,000	331
20X5	6,400	93,500	340
20X6	8,000	112,000	352

Using the high-low method, what should be the budgeted overhead costs in 20X7 if it is expected that 7,500 units will be produced and the overheads price index will be 370?

A   £103,200

B   £107,250

C   £112,500

D   £112,700

152   The following information for advertising and sales has been established over the past six months:

Month	Sales revenue £'000	Advertising expenditure £'000
1	155	3
2	125	2.5
3	200	6
4	175	5.5
5	150	4.5
6	225	6.5

Using the high-low method which of the following is the correct equation for linking advertising and sales from the above data?

A   sales revenue = 62,500 + (25 × advertising expenditure)

B   advertising expenditure = –2,500 + (0.04 × sales revenue)

C   sales revenue = 95,000 + (20 × advertising expenditure)

D   advertising expenditure = –4,750 + (0.05 × sales revenue)

153   The following data relate to two output levels of a department:

Machine hours	17,000	18,500
Overheads	£246,500	£251,750

The amount of fixed overheads is:

A   £5,250

B   £59,500

C   £187,000

D   £246,500.

154   Tindall Ltd sells a single product for £40 per unit. Fixed costs are £48,000 and variable costs are 80% of revenue. If fixed costs increase by £8,000 the break-even number of units will increase by:

A   10,000 units

B   5,000 units

C   1,000 units

D   200 units

155   HH manufactures and sells two products, J and K. Annual sales are expected to be in the ratio of J : 1 K : 3. Total annual sales are planned to be £420,000. Product J has a contribution to sales ratio of 40% whereas that of product K is 50%. Annual fixed costs are estimated to be £120,000.

The budgeted break-even sales value (to the nearest £1,000) is:

A   £196,000

B   £200,000

C   £253,000

D   £255,000

156 A company wishes to make a profit of £150,000. It has fixed costs of £75,000 with a C/S ratio of 0.75 and a selling price of £10 per unit.

How many units would the company need to sell in order to achieve the required level of profit?

A   10,000 units

B   15,000 units

C   22,500 units

D   30,000 units

[handwritten: = FC + PROFIT / CONT/UNIT   75,000 + 150,000 / 7.50]

157 A company has established the following information for the costs and revenues at an activity level of 500 units:

	£
Direct materials	2,500
Direct labour	5,000
Production overheads	1,000
Selling costs	1,250
Total cost	9,750
Sales revenue	17,500
Profit	7,750

[handwritten next to Production overheads: ×50% 500]
[handwritten next to Selling costs: ×20% 250]

20% of the selling costs and 50% of the production overheads are fixed over all levels of activity.

What would be the profit at an activity level of 1,000 units?

A   £15,500

B   £16,250

C   £16,500

D   £17,750

[handwritten: 1000 = 750 + x]

158 A company has been reviewing its total costs over the last few periods and has established the following:

Period	Sales (units)	Total cost £
1	225	2,300
2	150	1,500
3	350	2,800

The company is aware that fixed costs increase by £500 when sales exceed 200 units.

What would be the total cost at a sales level of 180 units?

A   £2,120

B   £1,800

C   £1,695

D   £1,620

159   **The following data relates to output levels and overhead costs of a department in two time periods.**

	Period 1	Period 2
Labour hours	14,000	18,000
Overhead costs	£277,500	£321,880

If there was 4% inflation in costs between period 1 and period 2, what (to the nearest £0.01) was the variable overhead rate per labour hour in period 1?

A   £8.00

B   £11.09

C   £17.88

D   £19.82

160   **A company uses regression analysis to establish a total cost equation for budgeting purposes.**

Data for the past four months is as follows: x y

$y = a + bx$

Month	Total cost £'000	Quantity produced 000s
1	57.5	1.25
2	37.5	1.00
3	45.0	1.50
4	60.0	2.00
	200.0	5.75

The gradient of the regression line is 17.14.

What is the value of a?

A   25.36

B   48.56

C   74.64

D   101.45

Data for questions 161 and 162

The following data is available for output volumes and total costs during a period of five months.

Month	Output 000 units	Total cost £'000
1	5	132
2	4	127
3	6	139
4	4	119
5	7	153

---

161   **On the basis of this data, and using regression analysis, what is the best estimate, to the nearest £1, of the variable cost per unit?**

£ [   ]   B

162   **On the basis of this data, and using regression analysis, what is the best estimate, to the nearest £1,000, of the fixed costs per month?**

£ [   ]   A

Data for questions 163 to 165

The costs of carrying out maintenance checks is semi-fixed and semi-variable. The cost varies to some extent with the time taken for each check. The following data is available for a sample of four checks carried out recently.

Check	Time taken hours	Cost £
1	1.0	16.0
2	1.5	21.0
3	0.5	14.0
4	1.0	17.0

163   On the basis of this data, and using regression analysis, what is the best estimate, to the nearest £1, of the variable cost per hour of maintenance checking?

£ _____

164   On the basis of this data, and using regression analysis, what is the best estimate, to the nearest £1, of the fixed costs per maintenance check?

£ _____

165   What is the correlation coefficient (r) for your estimates of the fixed and variable cost elements in maintenance checking? Give your answer to 2 decimal places.

_____

166   E plc operates a marginal costing system. For the forthcoming year, variable costs are budgeted to be 60% of sales value and fixed costs are budgeted to be 10% of sales value.

If E plc increases its selling prices by 10%, and if fixed costs, variable costs per unit and sales volume remain unchanged, the effect on E plc's contribution would be:

A   a decrease of 2%

B   an increase of 10%

C   an increase of 25%

D   an increase of 66.67%

167   A company manufactures and sells a single product. The following data have been extracted from the current year's budget

Sales and production (units)	5,000
Variable production and distribution cost per unit	£50
Fixed cost per unit	£70
Contribution/sales ratio	75%

The selling price per unit for next year is budgeted to increase by 8%, whereas both the variable production and distribution cost per unit and the total fixed costs are expected to increase by 12%.

The objective for next year is that the total budgeted profit should remain the same as that budgeted for the current year.

What is the minimum number of units which should be produced and sold next year in order to achieve the objective?

A   4,688
B   4,950
C   5,209
D   5,280

168   **A company which makes a single product has a contribution to sales ratio of 30%. Each unit is sold at £8. In a period when fixed costs were £30,000 the net profit was £56,400. What was the total of direct wages for the period if direct wages were 20% of variable costs?**

A   £17,280
B   £26,400
C   £40,320
D   £57,600

169

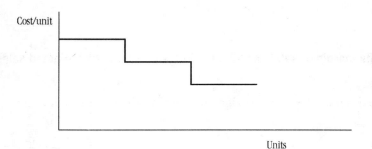

Which of the following descriptions best suits the above graph?

Cost/unit falls due to:

A   A learning curve effect
B   Overtime being worked
C   The availability of discounts for materials
D   Actual overheads being more than expected

170   **Hill Ltd sells a single product. In the coming month, it is budgeted that this product will generate a total revenue of £300,000 with a contribution of £125,000. Fixed costs are budgeted at £100,000 for the month.**

What is the margin of safety?

A   0%
B   10%
C   20%
D   25%

171   **Consider the following graph for total costs and total revenue:**

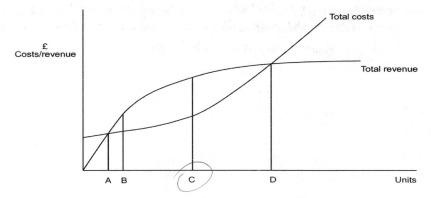

At which point on the above graph is it most likely that profits will be maximised?

A

B

C

D

172   **A company has established a budgeted sales revenue for the forthcoming period of £500,000 with an associated contribution of £275,000. Fixed production costs are £137,500 and fixed selling costs are £27,500.**

What is the breakeven sales revenue?

A   £76,625

B   £90,750

C   £250,000

D   £300,000

173   **A company has calculated its margin of safety as 20% on budgeted sales and budgeted sales are 5,000 units per month.**

What would be the budgeted fixed costs if the budgeted contribution was £25 per unit?

A   £100,000

B   £125,000

C   £150,000

D   £160,000

TOTAL CONT'N = TOTAL F.C.

174   **Balcombe has recorded the following costs over the last six months:**

Month	Total cost	Units produced
	£'000	000
1	74	3
2	72.75	1.75
3	73.25	2
4	75	2.5
5	69.5	1.5
6	72.75	2

Using the high – low method what would be the total cost equation?

A   Total cost = 61,250 + 5.5 Quantity

B   Total cost = 65,000 + 3 Quantity

C   Total cost = 70,250 + 1.25 Quantity

D   Total cost = 71,000 + 1 × Quantity

175   **Dane makes and sells a single product which has a selling price of £26, prime costs are £10 and overheads (all fixed) are absorbed at 50% of prime cost. Fixed overheads are £50,000.**

What is the break-even point (to the nearest whole unit)?

A   1,923

B   3,125

C   4,545

D   5,000

176 **A company produces three products which have the following details:**

		I Per unit	II Per unit	III Per unit
		Product		
Direct materials	(at £5/kg)	8 kg	5 kg	6 kg
Contribution per unit		£35	£25	£48
Contribution per kg of material		£4.375	£5	£8
Demand (excluding special contract)	(units)	3,000	5,000	2,000

The company must produce 1,000 units of Product I for a special contract before meeting normal demand.

Unfortunately there are only 35,000 kg of material available.

What is the optimal production plan?

	I	II	III
		Product	
A	1,000	4,600	2,000
B	1,000	3,000	2,000
C	2,875	–	2,000
D	3,000	2,200	–

177 **A company originally budgeted production and sales of 48 units of X and 100 units of Y. These figures represent maximum demand for each product.**

Details of each product are:

	X	Y
Contribution per unit	£10	£22.50
Labour time per unit (at £10 per hour)	0.5 hours	1.5 hours

If the total labour time available is cut to 150 hours, what is the *minimum* drop in contribution that can be expected?

A £360

B £480

C £2,370

D £2,730

178 **Worth produces four products L, E, W and S which have the following costs per unit:**

	L £	E £	W £	S £
Direct materials (at £10/kg)	15	10	12.50	20
Direct labour (at £12/hour)	12	12	18.00	18
Overheads (at £6 /labour hour)	12	6	9.00	9
Total cost	39	28	39.50	47
Contribution/unit	10	15	12.00	20
Maximum demand per month	3,000	2,000	1,500	2,500

Only 15,000 kg of materials and 10,250 labour hours are available.

What is the optimal production plan given that the company wish to maximise contribution?

	L	*E*	*W*	*S*
	units	units	units	units
A	3,000	2,000	1,500	2,500
B	2,250	2,000	1,500	2,500
C	3,000	2,000	1,500	1,500
D	3,000	2,000	1,000	2,500

179   Brisbane Limited has recorded the following sales information for the past six months:

Month	Advertising expenditure	Sales revenue
	£'000	£'000
1	1.5	30
2	2	27
3	1.75	25
4	3	40
5	2.5	32
6	2.75	38

The following has also been calculated:

- (Advertising expenditure) = £13,500
- (Sales revenue) = £192,000
- (Advertising expenditure × Sales revenue) = £447,250,000
- (Sales revenue^2) = £6,322,000,000
- (Advertising expenditure^2) = £32,125,000

What is the value of b, i.e. the gradient of the regression line?

A   0.070

B   0.086

C   8.714

D   14.286.

180   The standard cost of the only type of product made in the factory of SD, based on an expected monthly level of production and sales of 1,000 is as follows:

	£
Variable production costs	5.60
Fixed production costs	5.80
Variable selling costs	3.40
Fixed selling costs	4.60
Profit	5.50
Selling price	£24.90

The break-even point is:

A   365 units

B   513 units

C   654 units

D   920 units

181   The unit price of a product is higher than its variable cost of manufacture and sale. If both the selling price per unit and variable cost per unit rise by 10%, the break-even point will:

A   remain constant

B   increase

C   fall

D   be impossible to determine without further information.

182   AL makes a single product which it sells for £10 per unit. Fixed costs are £48,000 per month and the product has a contribution to sales ratio of 40%.

In a period when actual sales were £140,000, AL's margin of safety, in units, was:

A   2,000

B   6,000

C   8,000

D   14,000

183   A company uses limiting factor analysis to calculate an optimal production plan given a scarce resource.

The following applies to the three products of the company:

Product	I	II	III
Direct materials (at £6/kg)	£	£	£
Direct labour (at £10/hour)	36	24	15
Variable overheads (£2/hour)	40	25	10
	8	5	2
	84	54	27
Maximum demand (units)	2,000	4,000	4,000
Optimal production plan	2,000	1,500	4,000

How many kg of material were available for use in production?

A   15,750 kg

B   28,000 kg

C   30,000 kg

D   38,000 kg

184   The sales price of a product is higher than its variable cost of sale. If both the selling price per unit and variable cost per unit of a company fall by 5%, the break-even point:

A   will remain constant

B   will increase

C   will fall

D   could be unchanged, higher or lower.

185   E plc operates a marginal costing system. For the forthcoming year, variable costs are budgeted to be 60% of sales value and fixed costs are budgeted to be 10% of sales value.

If E plc increases its selling prices by 10%, but if fixed costs, variable costs per unit and sales volume remain unchanged, the effect on E plc's contribution would be:

A   a decrease of 2%

B   an increase of 5%

C   an increase of 10%

D   an increase of 25%.

186   Taree Limited uses linear programming to establish the optimal production plan for the production of its two products, A and U, given that it has the objective of minimising costs.

The following graph has been established bearing in mind the various constraints of the business. The clear area indicates the feasible region.

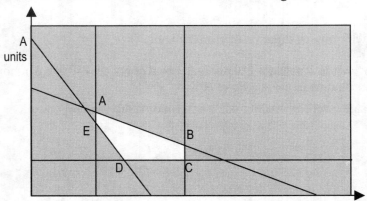

Which points are most likely to give the optimal solution?

A   A or B only

B   A, B or C only

C   D or E only

D   B, D or E only

187   A company manufactures three products (X, Y, Z) all of which pass through the same finishing process. For the coming month the number of hours available in the finishing process is 6,000.

Data relating to each product are as follows:

Product	X	Y	Z
Selling price per unit (£)	30	36	41
Variable cost per unit (£)	20	27	35
Minutes in the finishing process per unit	45	36	25
Maximum monthly demand (units)	4,500	4,500	4,500

Determine the production plan that will maximise profits for the coming month.

	X Units	Y Units	Z Units
A	4,500	4,375	Nil
B	4,500	1,250	4,500
C	4,400	4,500	Nil
D	1,900	4,500	4,500

188   A company's existing production plan is as follows:

	Product A	Product B
Units	750	1,000
	£	£
Unit selling price	13.00	21.00
Unit variable costs		
Direct material	1.00	1.00
Direct labour at £2 per hour	5.00	12.00
Overhead	0.50	1.20
	6.50	14.20

This represents the maximum demand for each product. The company is limited to 7,000 labour hours availability. A contract to produce 200 units of product C is under review. These are required by a customer who will provide his own materials. Net proceeds from the contract after deducting labour and overhead costs amount to £3,000 and will utilise 1,500 labour hours.

Assuming that the company wishes to maximise profit, which is the optimum production plan?

	A	B	C
A	400	750	200
B	1,000	750	0
C	1,000	500	200
D	0	750	200

189 **A company makes three products as follows:**

	Kilts	Skirts	Dresses
	£	£	£
Material at £5 per square metre	5.0	2.50	10.0
Labour at £2 per hour	6.0	2.00	2.0
Fixed costs absorbed	6.0	2.00	2.0
Profit	6.0	3.50	5.0
Sales price	23.0	10.00	19.0

Maximum demand is 1,000 for each product, but supplies of material are limited to 4,000 square metres while the labour force will only work 1,000 hours.

To maximise its profits the company should produce:

A   1,000 kilts

B   1,000 skirts

C   1,000 dresses

D   333 kilts

190 **The costs most relevant to be used in decision-making are:**

A   Sunk costs

B   Current costs

C   Estimated future costs

D   Notional and full costs

191 **A firm has some material which originally cost £45,000. It has a scrap value of £12,500 but if reworked at a cost of £7,500, it could be sold for £17,500.**

What would be the incremental effect of reworking and selling the material?

A   A loss of £27,500

B   A loss of £2,500

C   A profit of £5,000

D   A profit of £10,000

192 **In order to utilise some spare capacity, Zola is preparing a quotation for a special order which requires 1,000 kilograms of material R.**

Zola has 600 kilograms of material R in stock (original cost £5.00 per kg). Material R is used in the company's main product Q.

The resale value of material R is £4.00 per kg. The present replacement price of material R is £6.00. Material R is readily available on the market.

The relevant cost of the 1,000 kilograms of material R to be included in the quotation is:

A   £4,000

B   £5,000

C   £5,400

D   £6,000

193 **BB makes three components – S, T and W. The following costs have been recorded:**

	Component S Unit cost £	Component T Unit cost £	Component W Unit cost £
Variable cost	2.50	8.00	5.00
Fixed cost	2.00	8.30	3.75
Total cost	4.50	16.30	8.75

Another company has offered to supply the components to BB at the following prices:

	Component S	Component T	Component W
Price each	£4	£7	£5.50

Which component(s), if any, should BB consider buying in?

A   Buy in all three components

B   Do not buy any

C   Buy in S and W

D   Buy in T only

194 **A sunk cost is:**

A   a cost committed to be spent in the current period

B   a cost that is irrelevant for decision-making

C   a cost connected with oil exploration in the North Sea

D   a cost unaffected by fluctuations in the level of activity

195 **A company is considering accepting a one-year contract that will require four skilled employees.**

The four skilled employees could be recruited on a one-year contract at a cost of £40,000 per employee. The employees would be supervised by an existing manager who earns £60,000 per annum. It is expected that supervision of the contract would take 10% of the manager's time.

Instead of recruiting new employees, the company could retrain some existing employees who currently earn £30,000 per year. The training would cost £15,000 in total. If these employees were used they would need to be replaced at a total cost of £100,000.

The relevant labour cost of the contract is:

A   £100,000

B   £115,000

C   £135,000

D   £166,000

196   A company is considering its options with regard to a machine which cost £60,000 four years ago.

If sold the machine would generate scrap proceeds of £75,000. If kept, this machine would generate net income of £90,000.

The current replacement cost for this machine is £105,000.

What is the deprival value of the machine?

A   £105,000

B   £90,000

C   £75,000

D   £60,000

197   A company has just purchased a new machine, costing £150,000, for a contract. It has an installation cost of £25,000 and is expected to have a scrap value of £10,000 in five years' time. The machine will be depreciated on a straight line basis over five years.

What is the relevant cost of the machine for the contract?

A   £140,000

B   £150,000

C   £165,000

D   £175,000

198   An engineering company has been offered the opportunity to bid for a contract which requires a special component.

Currently, the company has a component in stock, which has a net book value of £250. This component could be used in the contract, but would require modification at a cost of £50. There is no other foreseeable use for the component held in stock. Alternatively, the company could purchase a new specialist component for £280.

What is the relevant cost of using the component currently held in stock for this contract?

A   £50

B   £250

C   £280

D   £300

199   P Ltd is considering accepting a contract. The materials required for the contract are currently held in stock at a book value of £3,000. The materials are not regularly used by the organisation and currently have a scrap value of £500. Current replacement cost for the materials is £4,500.

What is the relevant cost to P Ltd of using the materials on this contract?

A   £500

B   £3,500

C   £4,500

D   £5,000

200 In order to manufacture a new product, a firm needs two materials, S and T. There are ample quantities of both in stock. S is commonly used within the business whereas T is now no longer used for other products. Relevant information for the two types of material is:

	Quantity required per unit	Original cost	Replacement cost	Scrap value
	kg	£/kg	£/kg	£/kg
Material S	2	2.40	4.20	1.80
Material T	3	1.00	1.40	0.40

The opportunity cost of materials to be used in making one unit of the new product is:

A £4.80

B £7.80

C £9.60

D £12.60

201 The labour requirements for a special contract are 250 skilled labour hours paid £10 per hour and 750 semi-skilled labour hours paid £8 per hour.

At present skilled labour is in short supply, and all such labour used on this contract will be at the expense of other work which generates £12 contribution per hour (after charging labour costs). There is currently a surfeit of 1,200 semi-skilled labour hours, but the firm temporarily has a policy of no redundancies.

The relevant cost of labour for the special contract is:

A £3,000

B £5,500

C £8,500

D £11,500

202 A company has a fixed asset that originally cost £58,000, but would now cost just £37,000 to replace. The asset could be sold for scrap to earn £11,000. Alternatively, it could be used in a small project that would earn net income of £17,500. The asset has no other use.

What is the deprival value of the asset?

A £11,000

B £17,500

C £37,000

D £58,000

203 GR is currently experiencing a shortage of skilled labour. In the coming quarter only 3,600 hours will be available for the production of the firm's three products for which details are shown below:

Product	X	Y	Z
Selling price per unit	£66	£100	£120
Variable cost per unit	£42	£75	£90
Fixed cost per unit	£30	£34	£40
Skilled labour per unit	0.40 hours	0.50 hours	0.75 hours
Maximum quarterly demand	5,000	5,000	2,000

The optimum production plan that will maximise profit for the quarter is:

A   0 Xs, 2,200 Ys and 2,000 Zs

B   5,000 Xs, 200 Ys and 2,000 Zs

C   5,000 Xs, 3,200 Ys and 0 Zs

D   9,000 Xs, 0 Ys and 0 Zs

204   For decision-making purposes, which of the following are relevant costs?

(i)   Avoidable cost

(ii)   Future cost

(iii)   Opportunity cost

(iv)   Differential cost

A   (i), (ii), (iii) and (iv)

B   (i) and (ii) only

C   (ii) and (iii) only

D   (i) and (iv) only

205   WW makes three components – X, Y and Z. The following costs have been recorded:

	Component X Unit cost	Component Y Unit cost	Component Z Unit cost
	£	£	£
Variable cost	5.00	16.00	10.00
Fixed cost	4.00	16.60	7.50
Total cost	9.00	32.60	17.50

Another company has offered to supply the components to WW at the following prices:

Component	Price per unit
	£
X	8.00
Y	14.00
Z	11.00

Which components, if any, should WW consider buying in from the other company?

A   All three components

B   Component Y only

C   Components X and Y only

D   None

206   You are currently working as an accountant in an insurance company, but you are thinking of starting up your own business. In considering whether or not to start your own business, your current salary would be:

A   a sunk cost

B   an incremental cost

C   an irrelevant cost

D   an opportunity cost.

The following information relates to questions 207 and 208

Wakehurst is about to tender for a one-off contract. Requirements for this contract have been established as follows:

		£
Labour:	Skilled workers (100 hours at £9/hour)	900
	Semi-skilled workers (200 hours at £5/hour)	1,000
	Management (20 hours at £20/hour)	400
	Materials: N (100 litres at £4.50/litre)	450
	T (300kg at £7/kg)	2,100
		4,850

The skilled workers will be diverted from production of product P with resulting loss of sales. Each unit of P generates a contribution of £7 and takes two skilled labour hours to make. Semi-skilled workers will be hired as required. The management cost represents an allocated amount for hours expected to be spent. At the moment the management team has spare capacity.

Current stocks of material N are 200 litres and it is in continuous use by the business. It cost £4.50/litre originally but new supplies now cost £4.00/litre due to improved negotiating by the purchasing department. It could be sold as scrap for £2/litre.

The current stocks of material T are 200kg, which cost £7/kg some years ago but has not been used by the business for some time. If not used for the contract it would be scrapped for £4/kg. The current purchase price is £8/kg.

207 **What is the relevant cost of labour?**

A £1,350

B £2,250

C £2,600

D £2,650

208 **What is the relevant cost of materials?**

A £1,200

B £1,600

C £2,000

D £2,400

209 **Which of the following statements are correct with regard to marginal costing?**

(i) Period costs are costs treated as expenses in the period incurred.

(ii) Product costs can be identified with goods produced.

(iii) Unavoidable costs are relevant for decision-making.

A (i), (ii) and (iii)

B (i) and (ii) only

C (i) and (iii) only

D (ii) and (iii) only

210 Camden has three divisions. Information for the year ended 30 September is as follows:

	Division A £'000	Division B £'000	Division C £'000	Total £'000
Sales	350	420	150	920
Variable costs	280	210	120	610
Contribution	70	210	30	310
Fixed costs				262.5
Net profit				47.5

General fixed overheads are allocated to each division on the basis of sales revenue. 60% of the total fixed costs incurred by the company are specific to each division, and are exactly the same for each division. Specific fixed costs would be avoided if the division were closed.

Using relevant costing techniques, which divisions should remain open if Camden wishes to maximise profits?

A   A, B and C

B   A and B only

C   B only

D   B and C only

211 Lindfield has established that for one of its products the following cost and revenue functions apply:

Price = $30 - 0.25 \times$ Quantity

Marginal revenue = $30 - 0.5 \times$ Quantity

Total cost = £100,000 + £5 × Quantity

At what price would profits be maximised?

A   £12.50

B   £17.50

C   £50

D   £70

212 TV has established that for one of its products, the following cost and revenue functions apply:

$P = 60 - 0.04Q$

$MR = 60 - 0.08Q$

$TC = 15,000 + 2Q$

where

P is the sales price/unit

Q is the quantity of units produced and sold

MR is the marginal revenue for each additional unit sold

TC is total cost.

At what level of total sales revenue will profit be maximized?

A   £120

B   £1,450

C   £22,475

D   £43,500

213   **Which of the following would be considered to be a pricing strategy?**

(i)   target costing

(ii)   price skimming

(iii)   discrimination pricing

A   (i) and (ii) only

B   (i) and (iii) only

C   (ii) and (iii) only

D   (i), (ii) and (iii)

214   **R Ltd has been asked to quote for a job. The company aims to make a profit margin of 20% on sales. The estimate total variable production cost for the job is £125.**

Fixed production overheads for the company are budgeted to be £250,000 and are recovered on the basis of labour hours. There are 12,500 budgeted labour hours and this job is expected to take 3 labour hours.

Other costs in relation to selling and distribution, and administration are recovered at the rate of £15 per job.

The company quote for the job should be:

A   £200

B   £220

C   £240

D   £250

215   **Which of the following would NOT be considered when pricing a product?**

A   Price charged by competitors

B   Cost of making the product

C   Elasticity of demand

D   Cost of making other products within the business

216   **A firm has decided to enter a new overseas market with a strategy of pricing its product very low in order to win a large share of the market. This type of pricing strategy is known as:**

A   price skimming

B   price penetration

C   premium pricing

D   price discrimination.

217   **A railway company has two sets of rail fares, standard and off-peak. Off-peak fares are available in the middle of the day on weekdays and at weekends.**

The purpose of having two sets of prices is to encourage more customers to use trains during off-peak times, when trains would otherwise be largely unused.

The pricing policy of the railway company is an example of:

A price skimming

B price penetration

C premium pricing

D price discrimination.

218 **A company makes a single product whose variable cost is £16/unit. Annual fixed costs are £240,000. The company expects to sell 32,500 units of the product, provided that the sales price is kept below £30/unit. The company would like to make an annual profit of £150,000.**

What selling price would it have to set for the product to make a profit of exactly £150,000?

A £30.00

B £29.00

C £28.00

D £27.50

214.

125

+ 60

+ 15

_____

200 × .1.

$\frac{250,500}{12,500}$ = £20

×3 = 60

COST 80   200
PROFIT 20   50
    ___   ___
    100   250.

Section 2

PRACTICE QUESTIONS

ACCOUNTING FOR MANAGEMENT AND COST ACCOUNTING

1   SWAINSTHORPE LTD

Swainsthorpe Limited is a small old-fashioned company. They have a very simple manual accounting system to record all of the information of the business.

A bookkeeper comes in once a week to make all the relevant entries to the various manual ledgers. Complete stock-takes take place once a month, during which the business shuts down for the day, and the information from the stock-take is used to check that the store bin cards are correct. The stock-take information is also used to prepare a profit and loss account and balance sheet for the owners of the business.

The business has just been taken over by Ms Swainsthorpe who wishes to change the manual accounting system to a computerised management information system.

Required:

Prepare a report for Ms Swainsthorpe that:

(a)   gives three advantages and three disadvantages of introducing a computer system

(b)   explains what a management information system is and what Ms Swainsthorpe should hope to be able to use it for in general terms

(c)   comments critically on the current stock-take procedures and explains how the system could be improved.   **(10 marks)**

2   PLANNING

(a)   Define the terms 'operational planning' and 'strategic planning' and explain how one impacts upon the other.   **(3 marks)**

(b)   List the stages in a planning and control process and briefly explain what is involved at each stage.   **(7 marks)**

                                                                  (Total: 10 marks)

3   CHOICE OF COST CENTRES

Define the term 'cost centre' and detail the factors influencing the choice of cost centres within a business.   **(10 marks)**

4   COMPUTER PACKAGES

'Computerised financial planning packages have revolutionised the process of budget preparation.'

Describe the main features of such packages and give your views on the quotation.

(10 marks)

5   COST INFORMATION

Discuss the main purposes served by cost information, illustrating your answer with appropriate examples in relation to the operation of a manufacturing business, and state two differences between cost accounting and financial accounting.   **(10 marks)**

6   CHARACTERISTICS

(a)   Briefly describe three characteristics of useful information, giving one example of how each would apply to cost accounting information.   **(5 marks)**

(b)   Discuss the importance of non-financial information within a management information system.   **(5 marks)**

(Total: 10 marks)

7   COST CLASSIFICATIONS

Distinguish between, and provide an illustration of:

(a)   'Avoidable' and 'unavoidable' costs.

(b)   'Cost centres' and 'cost units'.   **(10 marks)**

ELEMENTS OF COST

MATERIALS

8   WIVELSFIELD

Wivelsfield currently uses the economic order quantity (EOQ) to establish the optimal reorder levels for their main raw material. The company has been approached by an alternative supplier who would be willing to offer the following discounts:

Order level	Discount
0 – 199 units	1%
200 – 499 units	3%
500 – 699 units	5%
700 units or more	7%

Information regarding current stock costs are as follows:

Holding cost per unit per annum = 10% of purchase price

Order costs = £2 per order

Annual demand = 15,000 units

Purchase price = £15

Current EOQ = 200 units

Required:

(a) Calculate the new optimal reorder level. **(6 marks)**

(b) Explain your approach with regard to each discount band. **(4 marks)**

(Total: 10 marks)

9 MATERIAL Z

A company uses Material Z (cost £3.50 per kg) in the manufacture of Products A and B. The following forecast information is provided for the year ahead:

	Product A	Product B
Sales (units)	24,600	9,720
Finished goods stock increase by year end (units)	447	178
Post-production rejection rate (%)	1	2
Material Z usage (kg per completed unit, net of wastage)	1.8	3.0
Material Z wastage (%)	5	11

Additional information:

- Average purchasing lead time for Material Z is two weeks.
- Usage of Material Z is expected to be even over the year.
- Annual stock holding costs are 18% of the material cost.
- The cost of placing orders is £30 per order.
- The re-order level for Material Z is set at the average usage in average lead time, plus 1,000kg of safety (buffer) stock.

Required:

(a) State two items that would be regarded as 'stock holding costs' and explain how they may be controlled effectively. **(5 marks)**

(b) Calculate for the year ahead:

　(i) the required production of Products A and B (in units), **(3 marks)**

　(ii) the total requirement for Material Z (in kgs), **(3 marks)**

　(iii) the Economic Order Quantity for Material Z (in kgs). **(5 marks)**

(c) Calculate the average stock investment (£) and the annual stock holding costs (£) for Material Z. **(4 marks)**

(Total: 20 marks)

10 EOQ

A company is planning to purchase 90,800 units of a particular item in the year ahead. The item is purchased in boxes, each containing 10 units of the item, at a price of £200 per box. A safety stock of 250 boxes is kept.

The cost of holding an item in stock for a year (including insurance, interest and space costs) is 15% of the purchase price. The cost of placing and receiving orders is to be estimated from cost data collected relating to similar orders, where costs of £5,910 were incurred on 30 orders. It should be assumed that ordering costs change in proportion to the number of orders placed. 2% should be added to the above ordering costs to allow for inflation.

Required:

Calculate the order quantity that would minimise the cost of the above item, and determine the required frequency of placing orders, assuming that usage of the item will be even over the year. **(10 marks)**

11 MATERIALS ISSUED

(a)   Explain the meaning of:

(i)   continuous stocktaking, and

(ii)   perpetual inventory

in the context of a material control system. **(5 marks)**

(b)   A company operates an historical batch costing system, which is not integrated with the financial accounts, and uses the weighted average method of pricing raw material issues. A weighted average price (to 3 decimal places of a pound £) is calculated after each purchase of material.

Receipts and issues of Material X for a week were as follows:

	Receipts into stock		Issues from stock	
Day	Kgs	Cost (£)	Day	Kgs
1	1,400	£1,092.00	2	1,700
4	1,630	£1,268.14	5	1,250

At the beginning of the week, stock of Material X was 3,040 kgs at a cost of £0.765 per kg. Of the issues of material on Day 2, 60 kgs were returned to stock on Day 3. Of the receipts of material on Day 1, 220 kgs were returned to the supplier on Day 4. Invoices for the material receipts during the week remained unpaid at the end of the week.

Required:

Prepare a tabulation of the movement of stock during the week, showing the changes in the level of stock, its valuation per kilogram and the total value of stock held.

(5 marks)

(Total: 10 marks)

12 RETAIL STOCK CONTROL

A retail company has been reviewing the adequacy of its stock control systems and has identified three products for investigation. Relevant details for the three products are set out below:

Item code	EOQ	Stock (warehouse and stores)		Weekly sales (£'000)			Gross* margin
	(000 units)	(000 units)	(£/unit at cost)	minimum	normal	maximum	(% of sales)
14/363	25	32.5	2.25	26	28	30	42
11/175	500	422.7	0.36	130	143	160	46
14/243	250	190	0.87	60	96	128	37

* Gross margin = sales − purchase cost of product.

Outstanding order: Item code 14/243 - order for 250,000 units placed 2 trading days previously.

There are 6 trading days in each week.

All orders are delivered by suppliers into the retailer's central warehouse. The lead time is one week from placement of order. A further week is required by the retailer in order to transfer stock from central warehouse to stores. Both of these lead times can be relied upon.

Required:

Calculate for each product:

(i)   The minimum and maximum weekly sales units.

(ii)   The stock re-order level.

(iii)   The maximum stock control level.   **(10 marks)**

13   EOQ OF COMPONENT

(a)   A company uses 2,600 units of a component per annum in the manufacture of one of its products. The bought-in cost of the component is £4.00 per unit. Each purchase order costs £65. The cost of carrying stock is 20% of the bought-in cost per annum.

Required:

Calculate the Economic Order Quantity of the component.   **(4 marks)**

(b)   In the previous month, stock movements of another component used by the company were:

Purchase:	320 units at £1.778/unit	Working Day 4
Purchase:	275 units at £1.785/unit	Working Day 15
Usage:	494 units	Throughout month

Opening stock was 228 units (£401.81)

Required:

Calculate:

(i)   The amount charged to production in the month for component usage, using a weighted average price calculated to three decimal places of £.

(ii)   The value of the closing stock of the component, using FIFO.   **(6 marks)**

(Total: 10 marks)

LABOUR

14   LABOUR COSTS

(a)   Explain how the following cost items, relating to direct personnel, would be processed in the cost accounting system of a manufacturing business:

(i)   idle time   **(3 marks)**

(ii)   overtime.   **(3 marks)**

(b) The following information is available regarding the labour costs in a factory department for a week:

	Direct personnel	Indirect personnel
Payroll hours:		
Production	432	117
Training	24	–
Idle time	32	4
Total	488	121
Rate per hour:		
Basic	£7.50	£6.00
Overtime premium	£2.50	£2.00

The following additional information is provided:

(i) There are 12 direct personnel and 3 indirect personnel in the department.

(ii) Group bonuses for the week, shared by all workers in the department, total £520.

(iii) The basic wage rates apply to a normal working week of 37 hours.

(iv) Overtime is worked in order to meet the general requirements of production.

(v) The idle time and the time spent training during the week are regarded as normal.

(vi) The expected number of payroll hours of direct personnel in the week (excluding time spent training), required to produce the output achieved, is 470.

Required:

(i) Calculate the total amounts paid in the week (before share of group bonus) to direct personnel and indirect personnel respectively. **(4 marks)**

(ii) Determine the total amounts to be charged as direct wages and indirect wages respectively. **(5 marks)**

(iii) Calculate the efficiency ratio to the direct personnel (expressed as a percentage to one decimal place). **(2 marks)**

(Total: 17 marks)

15 EARNINGS

Jim is reviewing his pay rises over the last four years compared with the Retail Price Index (RPI) and the Average Earnings Index (AEI). He has obtained the following:

Year	Jim's wage increase	Retail Price Index	Average Earnings Index
	%		
2000	–	157.5	108.0
2001	5.0	169.2	113.5
2002	3.0	165.4	119.0
2003	4.0	170.3	124.4

Jim earned £150 per week in 2000 and is carrying out the review in the year 2003 after receiving the 4% increase.

Required:

(a)   Calculate Jim's actual weekly earnings in each year from 2000 to 2003 using the percentage wage increase (to one decimal place). **(2 marks)**

(b)   Using your answer from part (a) calculate Jim's weekly earnings in each year in year 2003 terms using:

    (i)   the Retail Price Index (RPI); and

    (ii)   the Average Earnings Index (AEI).

    Your calculations should be to one decimal place.

(4 marks)

(c)   Comment on the results obtained from parts (a) and (b). **(2 marks)**

(d)   The Average Earnings Index for 1998 is 100. What does this mean? **(2 marks)**

(Total: 10 marks)

16   KL LTD

KL Ltd currently pays its direct production workers on a time basis at a rate of £6.50 per hour. In an effort to improve productivity, the company will introduce a bonus based on (time taken/time allowed) × time saved × rate per hour; this will be effective as from Week 24. The standard time allowed for a worker in the Assembly Department to perform his particular operation once has been agreed at 37.5 minutes.

In Week 23, Employee No 0035/A, an assembly worker, worked for a total of 41 hours and performed 87 operations. In Week 24, the same employee worked for a total of 44 hours and performed 94 operations.

Required:

(a)   Calculate the gross wages for Employee No 0035/A for Week 24 based on a time rate of £6.50 per hour plus the productivity bonus based on (time taken/time allowed) × time saved × rate per hour. **(4 marks)**

(b)   Determine the efficiency ratio for employee 0035/A for *each* of weeks 23 and 24. Provide a brief comment on your answer. **(4 marks)**

(c)   As an alternative to the productivity bonus above, the Production Supervisor has suggested that a piece rate coupled with a lower basic rate per hour of £2 would be more effective as an incentive. State and explain *one* advantage and *one* disadvantage which may be associated with this approach. **(2 marks)**

(Total: 10 marks)

OVERHEADS

17   SERVICE AND PRODUCTION CENTRES

Explain the following terms giving an example of each:

(a)   service centre; and

(b)   production centre.

Explain how the treatment of overheads differs between the two different types of centre.

(6 marks)

18 WARNINGLID

Warninglid has two production centres and two service centres to which the following applies:

| | Production departments | | Service centres | | |
	1	2	Stores	Maintenance	Total
Floor area (m²)	5,900	1,400	400	300	8,000
Cubic capacity (m³)	18,000	5,000	1,000	1,000	25,000
Number of employees	14	6	3	2	25
Direct labour hours	2,400	1,040			
Machine hours	1,500	4,570			

The following overheads were recorded for the month just ended:

	£'000
Rent	12
Heat and light	6
Welfare costs	2
Supervisors	
Department 1	1.5
Department 2	1

The service centres work for the other centres as follows:

	1	2	Stores	Maintenance
Work done by:				
Stores	50%	40%	–	10%
Maintenance	45%	50%	5%	–

Required:

(a) What would be the overheads allocated and apportioned to each department?

(3 marks)

(b) Calculate the total overheads included in the production departments after reapportionment using the reciprocal method. **(4 marks)**

(c) Calculate the overhead absorption rate for each production department. Justify the basis that you have used. **(3 marks)**

(Total: 10 marks)

19 TWO PRODUCTION COST CENTRES

A manufacturing company has two production costs centres (Departments A and B) and one service cost centre (Department C) in its factory.

A predetermined overhead absorption rate (to two decimal places of £) is established for each of the production cost centres on the basis of budgeted overheads and budgeted machine hours.

The overheads of each production cost centre comprise directly allocated costs and a share of the costs of the service cost centre.

Budgeted production overhead data for a period is as follows:

	Department A	Department B	Department C
Allocated costs	£217,860	£374,450	£103,970
Apportioned costs	£45,150	£58,820	(£103,970)
Machine hours	13,730	16,110	
Direct labour costs	16,360	27,390	

Actual production overhead costs and activity for the same period are:

	Department A	Department B	Department C
Allocated costs	£219,917	£387,181	£103,254
Machine hours	13,672	16,953	
Direct labour hours	16,402	27,568	

70% of the actual costs of Department C are to be apportioned to production cost centres on the basis of actual machine hours worked and the remainder on the basis of actual direct labour hours.

Required:

(a)   Establish the production overhead absorption rates for the period.   **(3 marks)**

(b)   Determine the under or over absorption of production overhead for the period in each production cost centre. (Show workings clearly).   **(12 marks)**

(c)   Explain when, and how, the repeated distribution method may be applied in the overhead apportionment process.   **(5 marks)**

(Total: 20 marks)

20   COST CENTRES

One of the cost centres in a factory is involved in the final stage of production. Budgeted fixed overhead costs for the cost centre for a period were:

Apportioned costs	£74,610
Directly incurred costs	£98,328

A predetermined machine hour rate is established for the absorption of fixed production overhead into product cost. Budgeted machine hours for the cost centre in the period were 1,900.

Actual overheads (apportioned and directly incurred) in the period were £173,732. The volume variance was £4,551 favourable.

Required:

Calculate for the period:

(a)   The predetermined fixed overhead absorption rate.   **(2 marks)**

(b)   The actual machine hours.   **(4 marks)**

(c)   The over/under absorption of fixed overhead.   **(4 marks)**

(Total: 10 marks)

21   A, B AND C

A company makes a range of products with total budgeted manufacturing overheads of £973,560 incurred in three production departments (A, B and C) and one service department.

Department A has 10 direct employees who each work 37 hours per week. Department B has five machines each of which is operated for 24 hours per week. Department C is expected to produce 148,000 units of final product in the budget period.

The company will operate for 48 weeks in the budget period.

Budgeted overheads incurred directly by each department are:

Production Department A	£261,745
Production Department B	£226,120
Production Department C	£93,890
Service Department	£53,305

The balance of budgeted overheads are apportioned to departments as follows:

Production Department A	40%
Production Department B	35%
Production Department C	20%
Service Department	5%

Service department overheads are apportioned equally to each production department.

Required:

(a)   Calculate an appropriate predetermined overhead absorption rate in each production department.   **(8 marks)**

(b)   Calculate the manufacturing overhead cost per unit of finished product in a batch of 100 units which take nine direct labour hours in Department A and three machine hours in Department B to produce.   **(2 marks)**

(Total: 10 marks)

22   SOLICITORS' COSTING

A large firm of solicitors use a job costing system to identify costs with individual clients. Hours worked by professional staff are used as the basis for charging overhead costs to client services. A predetermined rate is used derived from budgets drawn up at the beginning of each year commencing on 1 April.

In the year to 31 March 20X6, the overheads of the solicitors' practice, which were absorbed at a rate of £7.50 per hour of professional staff, were over-absorbed by £4,760. Actual overheads incurred were £742,600. Professional hours worked were 1,360 over budget.

The solicitors' practice has decided to refine its overhead charging system by differentiating between hours of senior and junior professional staff respectively. A premium of 40% is to be applied to the hourly overhead rate for senior staff compared with junior staff.

Budgets for the year to 31 March 20X7 are as follows:

Senior professional staff hours	21,600
Junior professional staff hours	79,300
Practice overheads	£784,000

Required:

(a)   Calculate for the year ended 31 March 20X6:

   (i)   Budgeted professional staff hours.

   (ii)   Budgeted overhead expenditure.   **(5 marks)**

(b)   Calculate, for the year ended 31 March 20X7, the overhead absorption
         rates (to three decimal places of a £) to be applied to

   (i)   Senior professional staff hours.

   (ii)   Junior professional staff hours.   **(5 marks)**

                                                                        (Total: 10 marks)

23   DIVISIONS A AND B

A company has two divisions (A and B). In Division A, small mechanical assemblies are
manufactured to customer order in two production departments. The following information
is available for the two production departments for a period:

	Machining Dept	Welding Dept
Budgeted production overhead	£256,200	£168,100
Budgeted machine hours	4,200	820
Budgeted direct labour hours	8,100	15,500
Actual machine hours	4,384	734
Actual direct labour hours	8,296	15,109
Job No 1763 (order for 800 assemblies):		
Materials issued	£16,740	£264
Machine hours	293	40
Direct labour hours	440	726

Labour hourly rates are £8 in the Machining Department and £10 in the Welding
Department.

Division A operates an absorption costing system, with predetermined overhead absorption
rates calculated to two decimal places of £.

Actual production overhead in Division A in the period consisted of:

Indirect materials	£47,440
Indirect labour	£203,740
General expenses (on credit)	£172,838

Payments to general expense creditors in the period totalled £169,763.

Required:

(a)   Calculate the total production cost of Job No 1763:

   (i)   If production overheads are absorbed on the basis of machine hours in the
           Machining Department and direct labour hours in the Welding Department.

                                                                        (5 marks)

   (ii)   If production overheads are absorbed on a plant-wide direct labour hour basis.

                                                                        (3 marks)

(b)   Calculate the amount of under-absorbed production overhead for Division A. (Assume that overheads are absorbed on a plant-wide direct labour hour basis.)   **(2 marks)**

(Total: 10 marks)

24   HOTEL

A company operates a hotel and analyses trading performance into three separate trading areas, Bedrooms, Catering and Meetings. Direct costs of the three areas for a period were:

	Bedrooms £	Catering £	Meetings £
Food and beverages	–	239,702	–
Staff	96,217	191,123	47,891
Other direct costs	24,762	17,654	15,337

There are 79 bedrooms in the hotel at an average bed/night rate of £64. Bedroom occupancy in the 365 day period was 61%.

38,760 meals were served at an average price of £10.80. Bar sales were £182,572. The Catering area is expected to achieve a profit margin (net of direct costs) of 30%.

Revenue from meetings in the period was £293,100.

There are two service (support) departments in the hotel:

General Administration

Domestic Services

Costs allocated to the two departments in the period were:

General Administration   £167,255

Domestic Services   £155,108

In addition, hotel occupancy costs (e.g. rent & rates, heating & lighting, insurance, general depreciation) totalled £876,230 in the period. Occupancy costs are apportioned according to floor space, an analysis of which is as follows:

Bedrooms	75%
Catering	9%
Meetings	13%
General Administration	2%
Domestic Services	1%

The costs of the two service (support) departments are apportioned as follows:

	Bedrooms	Catering	Meetings	Gen Admin	Domestic Serv
General Admin	30%	30%	30%	–	10%
Domestic Services	60%	14%	23%	3%	–

Required:

(a)   Apportion the hotel overhead costs, for the 365 day period, to the three trading areas within the hotel.   **(6 marks)**

(b)   Tabulate the trading performance of each area.   **(7 marks)**

(c)   Comment upon the trading performance.   **(7 marks)**

(Total: 20 marks)

25 PTS LTD

PTS Ltd is a manufacturing company which uses three production departments to make its product. It has the following factory costs which are expected to be incurred in the year to 31 December 20X2:

		£
Direct wages	Machining	234,980
	Assembly	345,900
	Finishing	134,525
Indirect wages and salaries	Machining	120,354
	Assembly	238,970
	Finishing	89,700
Factory rent		12,685,500
Business rates		3,450,900
Heat and lighting		985,350
Machinery power		2,890,600
Depreciation		600,000
Canteen subsidy		256,000

Other information is available as follows:

	Machining	Assembly	Finishing
Number of employees	50	60	18
Floor space occupied (m²)	1,800	1,400	800
Horse power of machinery	13,000	500	6,500
Value of machinery (£'000)	250	30	120
Number of labour hours	100,000	140,000	35,000
Number of machine hours	200,000	36,000	90,000

Required:

(a) Prepare the company's overhead analysis sheet for 20X2. **(9 marks)**

(b) Calculate appropriate overhead absorption rates (to two decimal places) for each department. **(6 marks)**

(Total: 15 marks)

26 UTOPIAN HOTEL

The Utopian Hotel is developing a cost accounting system. Initially it has been decided to create four cost centres: Residential and Catering deal directly with customers whilst Housekeeping and Maintenance are internal service cost centres.

The following overhead details have been estimated for the next period:

	Residential	Catering	House-keeping	Maintenance	Total
	£	£	£	£	£
Consumable materials	14,000	23,000	27,000	9,000	73,000
Staff costs	16,500	13,000	11,500	5,500	46,500
Rent and rates					37,500
Contents insurance					14,000

Heating and lighting	18,500
Depreciation of equipment	37,500
	227,000

The following information is also available:

	Residential	Catering	House-keeping	Maintenance	Total
Floor area (m²)	2,750	1,350	600	300	5,000
Value of equipment	£350,000	£250,000	£75,000	£75,000	£750,000
Number of employees	20	20	15	5	60

In the period it is estimated that there will be 2,800 guest-nights and 16,000 meals will be served. Housekeeping works 70% for Residential and 30% for Catering, and Maintenance works 20% for Housekeeping, 30% for Catering and 50% for Residential.

Required:

(a)   Prepare an overhead statement showing clearly allocations and apportionments to each cost centre.   **(7 marks)**

(b)   Calculate appropriate overhead absorption rates for Residential and Catering.
    (2 marks)

(c)   Calculate the under/over absorption of overheads if actual results were as follows:

Residential: 3,050 guest-nights with overheads of £144,600.

Catering: 15,250 meals with overheads of £89,250.   **(3 marks)**

(d)   Comment briefly on possible future developments in the Utopian Hotel's cost accounting system.   **(3 marks)**

(Total: 15 marks)

27   QRS LTD

QRS Ltd has three main departments - casting, dressing and assembly - and for period 3 has prepared the following production overhead budgets for an output level of 110,000 units:

Department	Casting	Dressing	Assembly
Production overheads	£225,000	£175,000	£93,000
Expected production hours	7,500	7,000	6,200

During period 3, actual results were as follows for an output level of 117,500 units:

Department	Casting	Dressing	Assembly
Production overheads	£229,317	£182,875	£94,395
Expected production hours	7,950	7,280	6,696

Required:

(a)   Calculate predetermined departmental overhead absorption rates for period 3.

(3 marks)

(b)   Calculate the under/over absorption of overheads for *each* department for period 3 and suggest possible reasons for the value of under/over absorbed overheads you have calculated for the *casting* department.

(7 marks)

(c)   Analyse the values of under/over absorbed overheads you have calculated for *dressing* and *assembly* and briefly discuss whether the calculated values assist departmental management with the operations of their departments or in the control of their overheads.

(5 marks)

(Total: 15 marks)

COSTING SYSTEMS

28   PRINTING

A printing and publishing company has been asked to provide an estimate for the production of 100,000 catalogues, of 64 pages (32 sheets of paper) each, for a potential customer.

Four operations are involved in the production process: photography, set-up, printing and binding.

Each page of the catalogue requires a separate photographic session. Each session costs £150.

Set-up would require a plate to be made for each page of the catalogue. Each plate requires four hours of labour at £7 per hour and £35 of materials. Overheads are absorbed on the basis of labour hours at an hourly rate of £9.50.

In printing, paper costs £12 per thousand sheets. Material losses are expected to be 2% of input. Other printing materials will cost £7 per 500 catalogues. 1,000 catalogues are printed per hour of machine time. Labour and overhead costs incurred in printing are absorbed at a rate of £62 per machine hour.

Binding costs are recovered at a rate per machine hour. The rate is £43 per hour and 2,500 catalogues are bound per hour of machine time.

A profit margin of 10% of selling price is required.

Determine the total amount that should be quoted for the catalogue job by the printing and publishing company.

(10 marks)

29   JOB COST

(a)   Explain how the following documents are used in a job costing system:

(i)   materials requisition

(3 marks)

(ii)   job cost card.

(3 marks)

(b)   A company uses a job costing system in order to identify the production costs incurred in carrying out a range of work to customer specification in its factory. The system allocates costs to each job wherever these can be identified directly, as long as they are considered as being 'normal'. 'Abnormal' costs are analysed by cost centre and are charged indirectly to jobs.

In the completion of Job XYZ, £17,560 of raw materials were initially allocated to the job. This included £620 of raw materials that were wasted, and a further £756 that were used for rectification work on the job. 'Normal' wastage and rectification costs (raw materials only) are allowed at 2% and 3% respectively of the direct raw material costs of each job.

During the period, raw materials totalling £234,720 were initially allocated to jobs, including £5,164 and £6,105 for wastage and rectification respectively.

Required:

(i)   Identify the 'normal' raw material costs that are to be allocated to Job XYZ.

(3 marks)

(ii)   Evaluate the efficiency of the company in respect to wastage and rectification both on Job XYZ and for the period as a whole.   **(4 marks)**

(Total: 13 marks)

30   JOB Y COSTS

A company carries out production jobs in its factory to customer requirements.

Production overheads are absorbed using a factory wide direct labour hour rate based upon the actual overhead expenditure and hours worked in the most recent calendar quarter. Relevant information for the most recent quarter is:

Direct labour:

Grade 1	80,000 hours:	£480,000
Grade 2	130,000 hours:	£650,000

Indirect labour:

Grade M	30,000 hours at	£4.50 per hour
Grade N	45,000 hours at	£4.00 per hour

Indirect materials	£85,000
General factory expenses	£325,000
Depreciation of plant and machinery	£370,000
Rent and rates	£249,000

Issues of raw materials to production jobs are charged at a weighted average cost (to four decimal places of £) calculated at the end of each week. Each stock issue is rounded in total to the nearest £.

During the week just ended, stock movements of Material X were as follows:

Opening stock	962 kilos: £2,532.16
Day 1	273 kilos issued
Day 2	660 kilos received: £1,745.70
Day 3	328 kilos issued
Day 5	114 kilos issued

Stores requisitions for Material X included:

Day 1	177 kilos to Job Y
Day 3	185 kilos to Job Y

Direct labour hours worked in the week just ended included:

Grade 1	105 hours on Job Y at £6/hr
Grade 2	192 hours on Job Y at £5/hr

Required:

Calculate the production costs, charged to Job Y for the week just ended, from the above information.

31 ADAM

Adam, the management accountant of Mark Limited, has on file the costs per equivalent unit for the company's process for the last month but the input costs and quantities appear to have been mislaid.

Information that is available to Adam for last month is as follows:

> Opening work in progress 100 units, 30% complete.
>
> Closing work in progress 200 units, 40% complete.
>
> Normal loss 10% of input valued at £2 per unit.
>
> Output 1,250 units.

The losses were as expected and Adam has a record of there being 150 units scrapped during the month. All materials are input at the start of the process. The cost per equivalent unit for materials was £2.60 and for conversion costs was £1.50.

Mark Limited uses the FIFO method of stock valuation in its process account.

Required:

(a)	Calculate the units input into the process.	**(2 marks)**
(b)	Calculate the equivalent units for materials and conversion costs.	**(4 marks)**
(c)	Using your answer from (b) calculate the input costs.	**(4 marks)**

(Total: 10 marks)

32 TWO PROCESSES

A company manufactures a product that requires two separate processes for its completion. Output from Process 1 is immediately input to Process 2.

The following information is available for Process 2 for a period:

(i)   Opening work-in-progress units:
12,000 units: 90% complete as to materials, 50% complete as to conversion costs.

(ii) Opening work-in-progress value:

Process 1 output:	£13,440
Process 2 materials added:	£4,970
Conversion costs:	£3,120

(iii) Costs incurred during the period:

Process 1 output:	£107,790 (95,000 units)
Process 2 materials added:	£44,000
Conversion costs:	£51,480

(iv) Closing work-in-progress units
10,000 units: 90% complete as to materials, 70% complete as to conversion costs.

(v)   The product is inspected when it is complete. 200 units of finished product were rejected during the period, in line with the normal allowance. Units rejected have no disposal value.

Required:

(a)   Calculate the unit cost of production for the period in Process 2 (to three decimal places of £), using the periodic weighted average method.   **(7 marks)**

(b)   Prepare the Process 2 Account for the period using the unit cost of production calculated in (a) above.   **(5 marks)**

(c)   Explain why, and how, the Process 2 Account would be different if there was no normal allowance for rejects. NB the process account should not be reworked.

          (5 marks)

(d)   Explain how the process account workings, required in (a) above to calculate the unit cost, would differ if the FIFO valuation method was used instead.   **(3 marks)**

          (Total: 20 marks)

33   FINAL PROCESS

(a)   The following information relates to the final process in a factory for the month just ended:

Units:

Opening work-in-progress: 500 units
Transfers in from previous process: 6,500 units
Closing work-in-progress: 600 units

Costs (£):

Opening work-in-progress: £1,527

Transfers in:

  Previous process costs: £14,625
  Materials added: £5,760
  Conversion costs: £3,608

The degree of completion of work-in-progress (WIP) rates was:

	Opening WIP	Closing WIP
Previous process costs	100%	100%
Materials added	80%	80%
Conversion costs	40%	60%

There is no loss of units in the process. The company uses the FIFO method for charging out the costs of production.

Required:

Prepare the process account for the period.   **(11 marks)**

(b)   Another process in the factory produces joint products (M and N). Each joint product is further processed to produce saleable output. The following data is available for a period:

	Total	Product M	Product N
Joint processing costs (£)	44,730		
Production (kg)		2,760	6,640
Selling price (£ per kg)		11.00	4.80
Further processing costs (£ per kg)		1.20	0.90

Required:

(i)   Apportion the joint costs for the period using the net realisable value method
                                                                                    (4 marks)

(ii)   Contrast the accounting treatment of joint products with that applied to by-
        products.   **(5 marks)**

                                                                    (Total: 20 marks)

34   MANUFACTURING PROCESS

The following information relates to a manufacturing process for a period:

Materials costs	£16,445
Labour and overhead costs	£28,596

10,000 units of output were produced by the process in the period, of which 420 failed testing and were scrapped. Scrapped units normally represent 5% of total production output. Testing takes place when production units are 60% complete in terms of labour and overheads. Materials are input at the beginning of the process. All scrapped units were sold in the period for £0.40 per unit.

Required:

Prepare the process accounts for the period including those for process scrap and abnormal losses/gains.   **(10 marks)**

35   EQUIVALENT UNITS

A firm operates a process, the details of which for the period were as follows.

There was no opening work-in-progress.

During the period 8,250 units were received from the previous process at a value of £453,750, labour and overheads were £350,060 and material introduced was £24,750.

At the end of the period the closing work-in-progress was 1,600 units, which were 100% complete in respect of materials, and 60% complete in respect of labour and overheads.

The balance of units were transferred to finished goods.

Required:

(a)   Calculate the number of equivalent units produced.   **(3 marks)**

(b)   Calculate the cost per equivalent unit.   **(2 marks)**

(c)   Prepare the process account.   **(7 marks)**

(d)   Distinguish between joint products and by-products, and briefly explain the difference
        in accounting treatment between them.   **(3 marks)**

                                                                    (Total: 15 marks)

36   PROCESS MANUFACTURING LTD

Process Manufacturing Ltd makes product X using two processes - 1 and 2.

The following details are available for the last period:

Process 1

No opening work-in-progress

Input materials 24,000 kgs costing	£168,000
Labour	£52,800
Overheads	£13,200

There were no process losses and 19,000 kgs were transferred to process 2. The unfinished production was complete as to materials and 60% complete as to labour and overheads.

Process 2

No opening work-in-progress

Completed good production   15,200 kgs

Labour	£45,752
Overheads	£27,353

The normal process loss is 5% of input which was exactly achieved in the period. The unfinished production was estimated to be 40% complete as to labour and overheads.

Requirements:

(a)   Prepare a process account for process 1.   **(5 marks)**

(b)   Prepare a process account for process 2.   **(7 marks)**

(c)   Briefly explain what is meant by a process gain.   **(3 marks)**

                                                                                                  (Total: 15 marks)

37   CHEMICAL COMPOUND

A chemical compound is made by raw material being processed through two processes. The output of Process A is passed to Process B where further material is added to the mix. The details of the process costs for the financial period number 10 were as shown below:

Process A

Direct material	2,000 kilograms at £5 per kg
Direct labour	£7,200
Process plant time	140 hours at £60 per hour

Process B

Direct material	1,400 kilograms at £12 per kg
Direct labour	£4,200
Process plant time	80 hours at £72.50 per hour

The departmental overhead for Period 10 was £6,840 and is absorbed into the costs of each process on direct labour cost.

	Process A	*Process B*
Expected output was	80% of input	90% of input
Actual output was	1,400 kgs	2,620 kgs

Assume no finished stock at the beginning of the period and no work-in-progress at either the beginning or the end of the period.

Normal loss is contaminated material which is sold as scrap for £0.50 per kg from Process A and £1.825 per kg from Process B, for both of which immediate payment is received.

You are required to prepare the accounts for Period 10, for:

(i)   Process A

(ii)   Process B

(iii)   Normal loss/gain

(iv)   Abnormal loss/gain

(v)   Finished goods

(vi)   Profit and loss (extract).   **(15 marks)**

38   NET REALISABLE VALUE

A business uses process costing to establish stock valuations and profitability of its products. Output from the process consists of three separate products: two joint products and a by-product. Details of the process is as follows:

Input costs:
Materials   £45,625 for 12,500 kg
Labour   £29,500
Overheads   £26,875

The process is expected to lose 20% of the input. This is sold for scrap for £4 per unit.

The following details relate to the output from the process:

Product	Type	% of output	Final sales value per unit	Further costs to complete
A	Joint	50%	£20	£10
B	Joint	40%	£25	
C	By-product	10%	£2	

Joint costs are allocated on the basis of net realisable value at split-off.

Required:

(a)   Establish the total cost of the output from the process.   **(4 marks)**

(b)   Calculate the profit per unit for each of the joint products, A and B.   **(6 marks)**

(Total: 10 marks)

39   JOINT PRODUCTS PROCESS

(a)   A company operates a manufacturing process which produces joint products A and B, and by-product C.

Manufacturing costs for a period total £272,926, incurred in the manufacture of:

Product   A – 16,000 kgs (selling price £6.10/kg)
               B – 53,200 kgs (selling price £7.50/kg)
               C –   2,770 kgs (selling price £0.80/kg)

Required:

Calculate the cost per kg (to 3 decimal places of a pound £) of Products A and B in the period, using market values to apportion joint costs.   **(5 marks)**

(b) In another of the company's processes, Product X is manufactured using raw materials P and T which are mixed in the proportions 1:2.

Material purchase prices are:

  P £5.00 per kilo

  T £1.60 per kilo

Normal weight loss of 5% is expected during the process.

In the period just ended 9,130 kilos of Product X were manufactured from 9,660 kilos of raw materials. Conversion costs in the period were £23,796. There was no work in process at the beginning or end of the period.

Required:

Prepare the Product X process account for the period.   **(5 marks)**

(Total: 10 marks)

40 PROCESS ACCOUNT

A company operates a manufacturing process where six people work as a team and are paid a weekly group bonus based upon the actual output of the team compared with output expected.

A basic 37 hour week is worked during which the expected output from the process is 4,000 equivalent units of product.

Basic pay is £5.00 per hour and the bonus for the group, shared equally, is £0.80 per unit in excess of expected output.

In the week just ended, basic hours were worked on the process. The following additional information is provided for the week:

    Opening work in process (1,000 units):
      Materials £540 (100% complete)
      Labour and overheads £355 (50% complete).
    During the week:
      Materials used £2,255
      Overheads incurred £1,748
      Completed production 3,800 units
    Closing work in process (1,300 units):
      Materials (100% complete)
      Labour and overheads (75% complete).

There are no process losses.

The FIFO method is used to apportion costs.

Required:

Prepare the process account for the week just ended.   **(10 marks)**

41 TRANSPORT BUSINESS

(a) Describe the characteristics of service costing.   **(3 marks)**

(b) A transport business with a fleet of four similar vehicles is working at 80% of practical capacity for three-quarters of the time. For the remainder of the time operations are at

60% of practical capacity. Measured in operating hours, practical capacity of the business is 8,000 per annum; this is equivalent to 160,000 kilometres.

Operating costs of the business are as follows:

Vehicle depreciation: £4,000 per vehicle per annum.

Basic maintenance: £110 per vehicle per 6 monthly service.

Spares/replacement parts: £100 per 1,000 kilometres.

Vehicle licence: £140 per vehicle per annum.

Vehicle insurance: £450 per vehicle per annum.

Tyre replacements: after 40,000 kilometres, six at £90 each.

Fuel: £0.40 per litre.

Average kilometres per litre: 4.0.

Drivers: £8,000 per annum each.
(Four drivers are employed at all times, on a time rate basis)

General administration costs: £19,700 per annum.
(These are absorbed into the costs of jobs at 25% of total costs before general administration).

Required:

(i) Define the term 'cost unit' and discuss appropriate cost unit(s) for the transport business. **(4 marks)**

(ii) Calculate the variable and total costs that would be charged to a job if it requires one vehicle driving 64 kilometres. **(6 marks)**

(Total: 13 marks)

42 PUBLIC TRANSPORT

The following information is available for a public transport business for a period:

	Service 1	Service 2	Service 3
Revenue from passengers (£'000)	146.2	293.5	271.9
Number of vehicles	7	12	10
Total vehicle usage (000s kilometres)	56	96	85
Variable operating costs (£ per kilometre)	0.60	0.60	0.56
Service fixed costs (£'000)	49.7	85.2	70.7

In addition to the above, general fixed costs are incurred. These include the costs of management, supervision, and administration and are absorbed into the cost of journeys at a predetermined rate per kilometre (to three decimal places of a £). The predetermined rate for the period was based upon:

Budgeted general fixed costs   £312,000

Budgeted vehicle usage   233,000 kilometres

Required:

Calculate the profitability of each of the services provided by the public transport business in terms of:

(a) Total net profit (to one decimal place of £'000).

(b) Contribution per kilometre (to two decimal places of £) net of variable costs.

(c) Contribution per vehicle (to one decimal place of £'000) net of all direct service costs.

(10 marks)

COSTING METHODS AND TECHNIQUES

ABSORPTION COSTING AND MARGINAL COSTING

43   OATHALL LTD

Oathall Limited, which manufactures a single product, is considering whether to use marginal or absorption costing to report its budgeted profit in its management accounts.

The following information is available:

	£/unit
Direct materials	4
Direct labour	15
	19
Selling price	50

Fixed production overheads are budgeted to be £300,000 per month and are absorbed on an activity level of 100,000 units per month.

For the month in question, sales are expected to be 100,000 units although production units will be 120,000 units.

Fixed selling costs of £150,000 per month will need to be included in the budget as will the variable selling costs of £2 per unit.

There are no opening stocks.

Required:

(a)   Prepare the budgeted profit and loss account for a month for Oathall Limited using absorption costing. Clearly show the valuation of any stock figures.   **(6 marks)**

(b)   Prepare the budgeted profit and loss account for a month for Oathall Limited using marginal costing. Clearly show the valuation of any stock figures.   **(4 marks)**

(Total: 10 marks)

44   SURAT

Surat is a small business which has the following budgeted marginal costing profit and loss account for the month ended 31 December 20X2:

	£'000	£'000
Sales		48.0
Cost of sales:		
Opening stock	3	
Production costs	36	
Closing stock	(7)	
		(32.0)
		16.0
Other variable costs:		
Selling		(3.2)
Contribution		12.8

Fixed costs
Production overheads   (4.0)
Administration   (3.6)
Selling   (1.2)

Net profit   4.0

The standard cost per unit is:

	£
Direct materials (1 kg)	8
Direct labour (3 hours)	9
Variable overheads (3 hours)	3
	20
Budgeted selling price per unit	30

The normal level of activity is 2,000 units per month. Fixed production costs are budgeted at £4,000 per month and absorbed on the normal level of activity of units produced.

Required:

(a) Prepare a budgeted profit and loss account under absorption costing for the month ended 31 December 20X2. **(6 marks)**

(b) Reconcile the profits under these two methods and explain why a business may prefer to use marginal costing rather than absorption costing. **(4 marks)**

(Total: 10 marks)

45 MARGINAL AND ABSORPTION

A company, which has been in existence for several years, manufactures a single product with a unit selling price of £34. Production and sales volumes of the product over a three-month period have been:

Month	1	2	3
Production (units)	12,000	10,500	10,000
Sales (units)	12,000	10,000	11,000

Total production costs per unit over the three-month period were £23.75, £25.00 and £25.50 respectively. Variable production costs per unit, and fixed production costs per month, were the same throughout the period. Selling and administration overheads totalled £87,000 in each month.

Required:

(a) Calculate the variable production costs per unit, and the fixed production costs per month, over the three-month period. **(4 marks)**

(b) Estimate the total cost that would be incurred in Month 4 if 12,500 units are manufactured. **(2 marks)**

(c) Prepare a profit statement for Month 2 using the absorption costing method. Assume that the fixed production overhead absorption rate is based upon normal production of 12,000 units per month. **(6 marks)**

(d)   Prepare a profit statement for Month 3 using the marginal costing method.   **(4 marks)**

(e)   Explain, with supporting figures, the profit difference in Month 2 if the marginal costing method had been used instead of the absorption method.   **(4 marks)**

(Total: 20 marks)

46   TRADING STATEMENT

A company sells a single product at a price of £14 per unit. Variable manufacturing costs of the product are £6.40 per unit. Fixed manufacturing overheads, which are absorbed into the cost of production at a unit rate (based on normal activity of 20,000 units per period), are £92,000 per period. Any over or under absorbed fixed manufacturing overhead balances are transferred to the profit and loss account at the end of each period, in order to establish the manufacturing profit.

Sales and production (in units) for two periods are as follows:

	Period 1	Period 2
Sales	15,000	22,000
Production	18,000	21,000

The manufacturing profit in Period 1 was reported as £35,800.

Required:

(a)   Prepare a trading statement to identify the manufacturing profit for Period 2 using the existing absorption costing method.   **(7 marks)**

(b)   Determine the manufacturing profit that would be reported in Period 2 if marginal costing was used.   **(4 marks)**

(c)   Explain, with supporting calculations:

(i)   the reasons for the change in manufacturing profit between Periods 1 and 2 where absorption costing is used in each period   **(5 marks)**

(ii)   why the manufacturing profit in (a) and (b) differs.   **(4 marks)**

(Total: 20 marks)

47   PERIODS 1 AND 2

A company manufactures a single product with the following unit costs:

Variable manufacturing	£4.50
Fixed manufacturing	£3.50
Variable selling and administration	£0.80
Fixed selling and administration	£3.00

Fixed manufacturing costs per unit are based on a predetermined absorption rate, established at normal activity of 90,000 production units per period. Fixed selling and administration costs are absorbed into the cost of sales at 20% of selling price. Under/over absorbed overhead balances are transferred to the profit and loss account at the end of each period.

The following information is available for two consecutive periods:

	Period 1		Period 2	
	units	£	units	£
Sales	85,000	1,275,000	90,000	£1,350,000
Production	80,000		92,000	
Variable manufacturing costs		360,000		414,000
Fixed manufacturing costs		320,000		315,000
Variable selling and administration costs		68,000		72,000
Fixed selling and administration costs		270,000		270,000

Required:

(a) Prepare the trading and profit and loss account for each of the two periods showing clearly both gross and net profit and any over/under absorbed overheads.   **(6 marks)**

(b) Explain how the profits would differ from those calculated in (a) above if a marginal costing system were employed.   **(4 marks)**

(Total: 10 marks)

48   MINOR AND MAJOR

XYZ Ltd currently produces two sizes of machines - the Minor and the Major. Various forecasts have been prepared for 20X5 which are summarised below.

Budgeted costs for 20X5:

	£
Direct materials	2,700,000
Direct labour	1,560,000
Variable overhead	3,120,000
Fixed overheads	4,200,000

The product details for 20X5 are as follows:

	Minor	*Major*
Forecast selling price/unit	£60	£95
Forecast sales volume (units)	120,000	70,000

Each unit of Major needs 1.5 times the amount of materials as a Minor and twice as much labour. Variable overheads are always absorbed in proportion to labour.

In the following year, 20X6, it is proposed to launch a luxury version of the Major to be called the Major Plus. The Major Plus is expected to sell at £125 per unit and to have estimated direct unit costs of £24 materials and £17 labour and to increase fixed costs by £600,000 per year.

The forecast sales volumes for 20X6 are:

	Units
Minor	120,000
Major	40,000
Major Plus	40,000

Required:

(a) Prepare a projected profit and loss account for **20X5** on marginal costing principles, showing the performance of the products.   **(6 marks)**

(b)   Prepare a projected profit and loss account for **20X6** on marginal costing principles, showing the performance of the products.   **(5 marks)**

(c)   Comment briefly on the position revealed by your statements.   **(4 marks)**

(Total: 15 marks)

49   DUO LTD

Duo Ltd makes and sells two products, Alpha and Beta. The following information is available:

	Period 1	Period 2
Production (units)		
Alpha	2,500	1,900
Beta	1,750	1,250
Sales (units)		
Alpha	2,300	1,700
Beta	1,600	1,250

Financial data	Alpha	Beta
	£	£
Unit selling price	90	75
Unit variable costs		
Direct materials	15	12
Direct labour (£6/hr)	18	12
Variable production overheads	12	8

Fixed costs for the company in total were £110,000 in period 1 and £82,000 in period 2. Fixed costs are recovered on direct labour hours.

Requirements:

(a)   Prepare profit and loss accounts for period 1 and for period 2 based on marginal cost principles.   **(5 marks)**

(b)   Prepare profit and loss accounts for period 1 and for period 2 based on absorption cost principles.   **(6 marks)**

(c)   Comment on the position shown by your statements.   **(4 marks)**

(Total: 15 marks)

STANDARD COSTING AND VARIANCE ANALYSIS

50   NEWCASTLE

Newcastle Limited uses variance analysis as a method of cost control. The following information is available for the year ended 30 September 20X3:

Budget	Production for the year	12,000 units
	Standard cost per unit:	£
	Direct materials (3 kg at £10/kg)	30
	Direct labour (4 hours at £6/hour)	24
	Overheads (4 hours at £2/hour)	8
		___
		62
		___
Actual	Actual production units for year	11,500 units
	Labour - hours for the year	43,350 hours
	- cost for the year	£300,000
	Materials - kg used in the year	37,250 kg
	- cost for the year	£345,000

Required:

(a)   Prepare a reconciliation statement between the original budgeted and actual prime costs.   **(7 marks)**

(b)   Explain what the labour variances calculated in (a) show and indicate the possible interdependence between these variances.   **(3 marks)**

(Total: 10 marks)

51   COMPANY M

The following standard costs apply in Company M which manufactures a single product:

Standard weight to produce one unit	12 kgs
Standard price per kg	£9
Standard hours to produce one unit	10
Standard rate per hour	£4

Actual production and costs for one accounting period were:

Material used	3,770 kgs
Material cost	£35,815
Hours worked	2,755
Wages paid	£11,571

The actual output was 290 units.

Required:

(a)   Calculate relevant material and labour cost variances, and present these in a format suitable for presentation to the management of the company.   **(5 marks)**

(b)   Explain how standard costs for material and labour might be compiled.   **(5 marks)**

(Total: 10 marks)

52   DEPARTMENT 7

Shown below is the previous month's overhead expenditure and activity, both budget and actual, for Department 7 in a manufacturing company:

	Month's budget	Month's actual
Activity:		
Standard hours	8,000	8,400
	£	£
Fixed overheads:		
Salaries	6,750	6,400
Maintenance	3,250	3,315
Variable overheads:		
Power	17,600	20,140
Consumable materials	6,000	5,960
Indirect labour	4,400	4,480
Total overheads	38,000	40,295

The budgeted overheads shown above are based upon the anticipated activity of 8,000 standard hours and it should be assumed that the department's budgeted overhead expenditure and activity occur evenly throughout the year. Variable overheads vary with standard hours produced.

Calculate the following variances incurred by the department during the previous month:

(i)   Fixed overhead volume variance.

(ii)   Fixed overhead expenditure variance.

(iii)   Variable overhead expenditure variance.   **(10 marks)**

53   GUNGE

The standard cost per gallon of Gunge, the only product manufactured by Chemit plc, is shown below:

	£
Direct material (4kg at £3/kg)	12
Direct labour (5 hours at £4/hour)	20
Variable overhead	5
Fixed overhead	15
Standard cost per gallon	52

The standard selling price of Gunge is £60/gallon and the budgeted quantity to be produced and sold in each period is 10,000 gallons. It may be assumed that variable overheads vary directly with the number of gallons produced.

The actual results achieved during period 4 were:

	£	£
Sales (9,500 gallons)		588,500
Cost of sales:		
Direct material (37,000 kg)	120,000	
Direct labour (49,000 hours)	200,000	
Variable overhead	47,000	
Fixed overhead	145,000	
		512,000
Profit		76,500

There were no stocks of work-in-progress or finished goods at the beginning or end of the period.

Required:

(a) Calculate the relevant manufacturing cost variances for period 4.   **(4 marks)**

(b) Calculate the appropriate sales variances for period 4, showing the effect on budgeted profit of actual sales being different from those specified, and prepare a statement reconciling the budgeted and the actual profit for the period.   **(6 marks)**

(Total: 10 marks)

54   FIXED PRODUCTION OVERHEAD

A company uses absorption costing for both internal and external reporting purposes as it has a considerable level of fixed production costs.

The following information has been recorded for the past year:

Budgeted fixed production overheads	£2,500,000
Budgeted (Normal) activity levels:	
Units	62,500 units
Labour hours	500,000 hours
Actual fixed production overheads	£2,890,350
Actual levels of activity:	
Units produced	70,000 units
Labour hours	525,000 hours

= 8hrs /unit

≈ 7.5

Required:

(a) Calculate the fixed production overhead expenditure and volume variances and briefly explain what each variance shows.   **(5 marks)**

(b) Calculate the fixed production overhead efficiency and capacity variances and briefly explain what each variance shows.   **(5 marks)**

(Total: 10 marks)

55   RECONCILIATION STATEMENT

SS Ltd makes and sells a single product 'PP'. The company uses a standard absorption costing system.

The budgeted production and sales for the year ended 31 October 20X1 were 59,500 units with a selling price of £2 each unit. The standard time for producing each unit was 3 minutes. The standard labour rate was £10 an hour. The standard material cost for one unit of PP was £0·75 per unit.

Production overhead absorption rates were based on direct labour cost and were as follows:

Variable overhead   35% of direct labour cost

Fixed overhead   40% of direct labour cost

For the year under review, the actual results were as follows:

Production and sales of PP   62,000 units

	£
Selling price for one unit	2.00
Labour cost incurred – for 3,500 hours	38,500
Material cost for each unit	0.75
Variable production overhead incurred	9,500
Fixed production overhead incurred	9,500

There were no changes in any stock levels during the period.

Required:

(a) Prepare a statement that reconciles budgeted profit with actual profit for the year ended 31 October 2001, showing the analysis of variances in as much detail as possible from the information given. **(14 marks)**

(b) Referring to your analysis in part (a), suggest two possible reasons for the labour efficiency variance and two possible reasons for the labour rate variance that you have calculated. **(4 marks)**

(c) Explain the factors that should be considered when selecting the most appropriate base to use for an overhead absorption rate. Your answer should include a discussion of the method used by SS Ltd. **(7 marks)**

(Total: 25 marks)

56 BB LTD

BB Ltd, a fast food restaurant, prepares and sells a meal called 'Yum Yum'. The meal consists of a burger, fries and a cold drink. BB Ltd uses a standard marginal costing system.

The budgeted meal sales for the quarter ended 31 March 20X2 were 100,000 meals with a selling price of £5 per meal. The standard labour cost for preparing each meal was £0.60. The standard labour time per meal was 6 minutes. The standard food and drink cost for each meal was £1.50. The budgeted fixed overheads for the year were estimated to be £500,000 and these are expected to be incurred evenly throughout the year.

For the quarter under review, the actual results were as follow:

Sales of 'Yum Yum'   90,000 meals

Selling price per meal	£4.75
Labour cost incurred – for 8,250 hours	£48,675
Food and drink cost incurred	£112,500
Fixed overhead incurred	£120,000

There was no stock of food or drink at the beginning or end of the quarter.

Required:

Complete the items labelled (a) to (f) on the reconciliation statement below. For all calculated variances, you must state whether they are favourable (F) or adverse (A).

Profit reconciliation statement for the quarter ending 31 March 20X2		£		£
(a)	Budgeted profit			?
(b)	Total sales margin contribution variance			?
(c)	Food and drink: total cost variance	?		
(d)	Labour efficiency variance	?		
(e)	Labour rate variance	?		
(f)	Fixed overhead expenditure variance	?		
	Total cost variances			
	Actual profit			146,325

(2 marks for each item (a) to (f))

(12 marks)

(g) If BB Ltd uses absorption costing, instead of marginal costing, state and briefly explain in no more than 25 words, another variance that would have to be included in the reconciliation statement. **(3 marks)**

(Total: 15 marks)

57 X LTD

X Ltd uses a standard absorption cost accounting system. The following details have been extracted from a standard cost card for one of its products:

	£
Direct materials	5.00
Direct labour	7.40
Variable overhead	2.30
Fixed overhead	3.80
	———
	18.50

The fixed overhead cost per unit is based on an estimated production of 1,000 units per month. During October 20X3 the actual number of units produced was 900 and the following variances arose:

	£
Direct materials	180 favourable
Direct labour	980 adverse
Variable overhead	240 adverse
Fixed overhead	200 adverse

You are required to calculate the actual cost of:

(a) direct materials

(b) direct labour

(c) variable overhead

(d) fixed overhead. **(10 marks)**

58   VARIANCES

XYZ Ltd is planning to make 120,000 units per period of a new product. The following standards have been set:

	Per unit
Direct material A	1.2 kgs at £11 per kg
Direct material B	4.7 kgs at £6 per kg
Direct labour	
Operation 1	42 minutes
Operation 2	37 minutes
Operation 3	11 minutes

Overheads are absorbed at the rate of £30 per labour hour. All direct operatives are paid at the rate of £8 per hour. Attainable work hours are less than clock hours, so the 500 direct operatives have been budgeted for 400 hours each in the period.

Actual results for the period were:

Production	126,000 units
Direct labour	cost £1.7m for 215,000 clock hours
Material A	cost £1.65m for 150,000 kgs
Material B	cost £3.6m for 590,000 kgs

Required:

(a)   Calculate the standard cost for one unit.   **(2 marks)**

(b)   Calculate the labour rate variance and a realistic efficiency variance.   **(5 marks)**

(c)   Calculate the material price and usage variances.   **(4 marks)**

(d)   Describe the manufacturing environment in which labour variances can provide useful information.   **(4 marks)**

(Total: 15 marks)

59   LABOUR-INTENSIVE PRODUCT

A labour-intensive production unit operating a standard absorption cost accounting system provides the following information for period 10:

Normal capacity, in direct labour hours	9,600
Budgeted variable production overhead	£3 per direct labour hour
Budgeted fixed production overhead per four-week financial period	£120,000

To produce one unit of output takes two hours of working.

Actual figures produced for the four-week period 10 were:

Production, in units	5,000
Variable production overhead incurred	£28,900
Fixed production overhead incurred	£118,000
Actual direct labour hours worked	9,300

You are required to calculate:

(a)   variable production overhead expenditure variance

(b)   variable production overhead efficiency variance

(c)   fixed production overhead expenditure variance

(d)   fixed production overhead volume variance.   **(8 marks)**

DECISION MAKING

COST BEHAVIOUR, TIME SERIES ANALYSIS

60   LINEAR FUNCTION

The following information is available for a company:

	Year 1	Year 2	Year 3	Year 4
Sales/production (units)	67,200	71,300	75,600	75,100
Total costs (£)	135,000	144,072	156,090	158,950
Cost inflation index	100	103.5	107.5	110.0

Required:

(a)   Determine a linear function for total costs per annum (at Year 1 prices) from the above data, using the high-low method (unit costs should be calculated to three decimal places of £).   **(5 marks)**

(b)   Using the function in (a) and the data above, evaluate and comment upon the accuracy of the function as a predictor of costs.   **(5 marks)**

(c)   Using the function in (a), forecast the total costs in Year 5 based on a volume of 77,200 units and a cost inflation index of 112.9.   **(2 marks)**

(d)   Selling prices in Year 5 are expected to be 15% higher than those in Year 1, when total sales revenue was £159,936.

Draw a profit-volume chart for Year 5, showing sales up to 90,000 units per annum.

(8 marks)

(Total: 20 marks)

61   TOTAL SURVEYS LTD

Total Surveys Limited conducts market research surveys for a variety of clients. Extracts from its records are as follows:

	20X5	20X6
Total costs	£6 million	£6.615 million

Activity in 20X6 was 20% greater than in 20X5 and there was general cost inflation of 5%.

Activity in 20X7 is expected to be 25% greater than in 20X6 and general cost inflation is expected to be 4%.

Requirements:

(a)   Derive the expected variable and fixed costs for 20X7.   **(6 marks)**

(b)   Calculate the target sales required for 20X7 if Total Surveys Limited wishes to achieve a contribution to sales ratio of 80%.   **(3 marks)**

(c)   Discuss briefly the problems in analysing costs into fixed and variable elements.

(6 marks)

(Total: 15 marks)

62   COST ANALYSIS

(a)   'The analysis of total cost into its behavioural elements is essential for effective cost and management accounting.'

Required:

Comment on the statement above, illustrating your answer with examples of cost behaviour patterns.   **(5 marks)**

(b)   The total costs incurred at various output levels, for a process operation in a factory, have been measured as follows:

Output (units)	Total cost (£)
11,500	102,476
12,000	104,730
12,500	106,263
13,000	108,021
13,500	110,727
14,000	113,201

Required:

Using the high-low method, analyse the costs of the process operation into fixed and variable components.   **(5 marks)**

(Total: 10 marks)

63   SOUTH

South has reported the following costs for the past four months:

Month	Activity level (units)	Total cost
1	300	£3,800
2	400	£4,000
3	150	£3,000
4	260	£3,500

Required:

(a)   Using regression analysis calculate the total cost equation.   **(6 marks)**

(b)   Calculate the total cost at the following activity levels:

(i)   200 units

(ii)   500 units

and comment on the usefulness of your equation with regard to these estimates.

(4 marks)

(Total: 10 marks)

64   SAPPHIRE

Sapphire recorded the following costs for the past 5 months of activity:

Month	Activity level (units)	Total cost
5	220	£4,500
6	400	£7,000
7	360	£5,500
8	380	£6,000
9	290	£5,000

Required:

(a)   Calculate the total cost equation for the above data using regression analysis.

(6 marks)

(b)   Calculate the total cost for the following activity levels:

(i)   300 units

(ii)   450 units

(4 marks)

(Total: 10 marks)

65   LINEAR RELATIONSHIP

A company is seeking to establish whether there is a linear relationship between the level of advertising expenditure and the subsequent sales revenue generated.

Figures for the last eight months are as follows:

Month	Advertising Sales £'000	Expenditure Revenue £'000
1	2.65	30.0
2	4.25	45.0
3	1.00	17.5
4	5.25	46.0
5	4.75	44.5
6	1.95	25.0
7	3.50	43.0
8	3.00	38.5
Total	26.35	289.5

Further information is available as follows:

(Advertising Expenditure × Sales Revenue) = £1,055.875

(Advertising Expenditure)^2 = £101.2625

(Sales Revenue)^2 = £11,283.75

All of the above are given in £ million.

Required:

(a)   On a suitable graph plot advertising expenditure against sales revenue or *vice versa* as appropriate. Explain your choice of axes.   **(5 marks)**

(b)   Using regression analysis calculate a line of best fit. Plot this on your graph from (a).

(5 marks)

(Total: 10 marks)

CVP ANALYSIS

66 TOOWOMBA

Toowomba manufactures various products and uses CVP analysis to establish the minimum level of production to ensure profitability.

Fixed costs of £50,000 have been allocated to a specific product but are expected to increase to £100,000 once production exceeds 30,000 units, as a new factory will need to be rented in order to produce the extra units. Variable costs per unit are stable at £5 per unit over all levels of activity. Revenue from this product will be £7.50 per unit.

Required:

(a) Formulate the equations for the total cost at:

   (i) less than or equal to 30,000 units;

   (ii) more than 30,000 units. **(2 marks)**

(b) Prepare a breakdown chart and clearly identify the breakeven point or points.

(6 marks)

(c) Discuss the implications of the results from your graph in (b) with regard to Toowomba's production plans. **(2 marks)**

(Total: 10 marks)

67 TRADING RESULTS

(a) A company has the following trading results for a period:

	£'000
Sales (3,150,000 units at £2.30 per unit)	7,245
Production costs	4,986
Gross profit	2,259
Selling and administration overhead	1,887
Net profit	372

Analysis of the market for the company's product has led to the following estimates of the impact on sales volume of a change in selling price:

Selling price	Sales volume
+20%	−33%
+10%	−15%
−10%	+14%
−20%	+25%

Production costs comprise:

Direct costs	£2,841,000
Overheads	£2,145,000

A reduction in sales volume would be expected to lead to a proportionate reduction in direct costs. An increase in sales volume would be expected to lead to economies of scale on direct costs as follows:

Sales volume	Direct costs
+14%	+12%
+25%	+20%

Overheads would be expected to decline or increase at a quarter of the rate of any sales volume decline or increase.

Required:

(i) Using the above estimates, form a table showing the company's sales, costs and profits for relevant sales volumes. **(5 marks)**

(ii) Prepare a graph of the company's sales revenue and cost functions over the relevant sales volume range. **(5 marks)**

(iii) Advise, based upon the results of your analysis, whether the selling price should be changed. **(2 marks)**

(b) Overhead costs and activity, for the above company, over the last five periods have been:

	Overheads	Sales volume
	£'000	000 units
Period 1	3,409	2,850
Period 2	3,559	2,750
Period 3	3,764	2,980
Period 4	3,913	3,105
Period 5	4,032	3,150

The inflation index over the five periods (base Period 1) has been:

Period 2	1.052
Period 3	1.091
Period 4	1.125
Period 5	1.154

Required:

(i) Adjust the overheads so that they are valued at Period 5 prices. **(3 marks)**

(ii) Demonstrate, using the high-low method, how the above data has been used to establish that overheads are expected to change at a quarter of the rate of any change in sales volume. **(5 marks)**

(Total: 20 marks)

68 BREAKEVEN

A company makes a range of products, which are sold through agents on a commission basis. Selling costs comprise the commission which is paid at 10% of selling price. The company is considering the introduction of its own sales force to replace the selling of products via agents.

Estimates of sales and costs (excluding selling costs) per period have been made at three different levels of activity as follows:

	Low	Medium	High
	£'000	£'000	£'000
Sales	600	700	800
Manufacturing costs	350	380	410
Administration costs	160	160	160

Sales and costs (excluding selling costs) are expected to be unaffected by the decision regarding method of selling. If the company's own sales force is introduced, selling costs per period would be expected to total £60,000.

Required:

(a) Calculate the break-even point per period if selling via agents is continued. **(5 marks)**

(b) Calculate the break-even point per period if the company introduces its own sales force. **(5 marks)**

Note: You do not have to provide a break-even chart. **(Total: 10 marks)**

69   PROFIT VOLUME

A company has the following summary results for two trading periods:

	Period 1 £'000	Period 2 £'000
Sales	742.7	794.1
Variable costs	408.3	409.0
Contribution	334.4	385.1
Fixed costs	297.8	312.7
Net profit	36.6	72.4

Required:

(a) Draw a profit volume chart, based on both periods, covering sales up to £1m per period. **(5 marks)**

(b) Calculate (to the nearest £'000) the sales required in Period 2 to achieve the same net profit as Period 1. **(3 marks)**

(c) Define the following terms (which are used in the context of CVP analysis):

   (i)   C/S ratio

   (ii) Margin of safety. **(2 marks)**

(Total: 10 marks)

70   PE LTD

PE Ltd produces and sells two products, P and E. Budgets prepared for the next six months give the following information:

	Product P per unit £	Product E per unit £
Selling price	10.00	12.00
Variable costs: production and selling	5.00	10.00

Common fixed costs: production and selling - for six months £561,600.

You are required, in respect of the forthcoming six months:

(a) to state what the break-even point in £s will be and the number of each product this figure represents if the two products are sold in the ratio 4P to 3E **(3 marks)**

(b) to state the break-even point in £s and the number of products this figure represents if the sales mix changes to 4P to 4E (ignore fractions of products)

(3 marks)

(c)   to advise the sales manager which product mix should be better, that in (a)(i) above or that in (a)(ii) above, and why   **(2 marks)**

(d)   to advise the sales manager which of the two products should be concentrated on and the reason(s) for your recommendation - assume that whatever can be made can be sold, that both products go through a machining process and that there are only 32,000 machine hours available, with product P requiring 0.40 hours per unit and product E requiring 0.10 hours per unit.   **(2 marks)**

(Total: 10 marks)

LIMITING FACTORS

71   CUCKFIELD

Cuckfield manufactures two products, the D and the H, which have the following standard costs per unit:

	D £	H £
Materials		
A (at £3/kg)	9.00	6.00
N (at £7/kg)	3.50	14.00
Labour		
Skilled (at £10/hour)	10.00	14.00
Semi-skilled (at £6/hour)	9.00	9.00
Fixed overheads	5.70	13.80
	37.20	56.80
Selling price	40.00	70.00
Profit	2.80	13.20

Unfortunately there is a problem obtaining some of the raw materials for production. Only 3,000kg of material A is available and only 1,000 litres of material N can be found for the week.

There are 45 semi-skilled workers who can only work a 40-hour week as there has been an overtime ban. Skilled workers are guaranteed a 35-hour week. There are 20 of these workers and there is no overtime ban for these employees.

The company's objective is to maximise contribution.

Required:

(a)   Formulate the constraint equations for this problem excluding the non-negativity constraint.   **(4 marks)**

(b)   Plot the constraints on a graph and suggest possible points for the optimal solution. (Note: calculations for the optimal solution are NOT required).   **(6 marks)**

(Total: 10 marks)

72 T LIMITED

T Limited manufactures two products, X and Y. Details for each product are given below.

Per unit	X	Y
	£	£
Selling price	158	129
Raw materials (£6 per kilogram)	30	24
Labour		
Skilled (£7 per hour)	56	35
Semi-skilled (£4 per hour)	20	20
Variable overheads	28	20
(£2 per labour hour, both skilled and semi-skilled)		
Contribution per unit	24	30

The supply of skilled labour is limited to 1,200 hours each month, and the supply of semi-skilled labour is limited to 900 hours each month.

The maximum sales demand for product X is 100 units each month and the maximum demand for product Y is 150 units each month. The company aims to maximise total contribution from monthly sales.

Required

(a) State the objective function for maximising contribution. **(1 mark)**

(b) State the constraints on achieving this objective. **(3 marks)**

(c) Draw a graph to show these constraints and indicate the feasible area for a solution on the graph. **(3 marks)**

(d) Calculate the quantities of product X and product Y that should be made and sold each month so as to maximise the objective function. **(3 marks)**

(Total: 10 marks)

73 OPTIMAL PRODUCTION PLAN

A company uses linear programming to establish an optimal production plan in order to maximise profit.

The company finds that for the next year materials and labour are likely to be in short supply.

Details of the company's products are as follows:

	A	B
	£	£
Materials (at £2 per kg)	6	8
Labour (at £6 per hour)	30	18
Variable overheads (at £1 per hour)	5	3
Variable cost	41	29
Selling price	50	52
Contribution	9	23

There are only 30,000 kg of material and 36,000 labour hours available. The company also has an agreement to supply 1,000 units of product A which must be met.

Required:

(a)   Formulate the objective function and constraint equations for this problem. **(4 marks)**

(b)   Plot the constraints on a suitable graph and determine the optimal production plan.

(6 marks)

(Total: 10 marks)

74   PRODUCTION PLANNING

A company manufactures two products in one of its factories. Information concerning the two products is as follows:

	Product A	Product B
Selling price per unit	£5.00	£3.50
Variable costs per unit	£2.80	£1.40
Machine hours per 1,000 units	80	70
Direct labour hours per 1,000 units	125	62.5

The following graph shows the production possibilities in June given that direct labour hours and machine hours will be in limited supply:

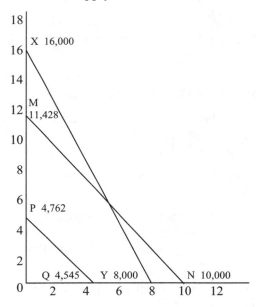

MN represents production possibilities fully utilising the available machine hours. XY represents production possibilities fully utilising the available direct labour hours. It may be assumed that any combination of products A and B can be sold at the selling prices prevailing.

Required:

With reference to the graph:

(i)   Identify the feasible region and establish the equations for lines MN and XY.

(5 marks)

(ii)   Explain fully the line PQ using any relevant information provided.   **(5 marks)**

(Total: 10 marks)

RELEVANT COSTS, DECISIONS WITH UNCERTAINTY, PRICING DECISIONS

75   MIKE LIMITED

Mike Limited has been asked to quote a price for a one off contract. Management have drawn up the following schedule:

		£
Contract price	(Cost plus 20%)	60,780
Costs:		
Materials:	V (300 kg at £10/kg)	3,000
	I (1,000 litres at £7/litre)	7,000
	C (550 kg at £3/kg)	1,650
Labour:	Department 1 (1,500 hours at £8/hour)	12,000
	Department 2 (2,000 hours at £10/hour)	20,000
Overheads:	Absorbed on a budgeted labour hour basis	
	3,500 hours at £2/labour hour)	7,000
Total costs		50,650

The following is also relevant:

Material V. The cost of £10 is the original purchase cost incurred some years ago. This material is no longer in use by the company and if not used in the contract then it would be sold for scrap at £3/kg.

Material I. This is in continuous use by the business. £7 is the historic cost of the material although current supplies are being purchased at £6.50.

Material C. Mike Limited has 300 kg of this material in stock and new supplies would cost £4/kg. If current stocks are not used for the contract then they would be used as a substitute for material Y in another production process costing £7/kg. 2 kg of C replaces 1 kg of Y.

Department 1. This department has spare labour capacity sufficient for the contract and labour would be retained.

Department 2. This department is currently working at full capacity. Mike Limited could get the men to work overtime to complete the contract paid at time and a half, or they could divert labour hours from the production of other units that currently average £3 contribution per labour hour.

Overheads. These are arbitrarily absorbed at a pre-determined rate. There will be no incremental costs incurred.

Required:

Calculate the minimum contract price that Mike Limited could accept to breakeven using relevant costing techniques.   **(10 marks)**

76   ALBANY

Albany has recently spent some time on researching and developing a new product for which they are trying to establish a suitable price. Previously they have used cost plus 20% to set the selling price.

The standard cost per unit has been estimated as follows:

		£
Direct materials		
Material 1	(4 kg at £2.50/kg)	10
Material 2	(1 kg at £7/kg)	7
Direct labour	(2 hours at £6.50/hour)	13
Fixed overheads	(2 hours at £3.50/hour)	7
		———
		37
		———

Required:

(a)   Using the standard costs calculate two different cost plus prices using two different bases and explain an advantage and disadvantage of each method.   **(6 marks)**

(b)   Give two other possible pricing strategies that could be adopted and describe the impact of each one on the price of the product.   **(4 marks)**

(Total: 10 marks)

77   NORTHSHIRE HOSPITAL TRUST

The Northshire Hospital Trust operates two types of specialist X-ray scanning machines, XR1 and XR50. Details for the next period are estimated as follows:

Machine:	XR1	XR50
Running hours	1,100	2,000
	£	£
Variable running costs (excluding plates)	27,500	64,000
Fixed costs	20,000	97,500

A brain scan is normally carried out on machine type XR1: this task uses special X-ray plates costing £40 each and takes 4 hours of machine time. Because of the nature of the process, around 10% of the scans produce blurred and therefore useless results.

Requirement:

(a)   Calculate the cost of a satisfactory brain scan on machine type XR1.   **(7 marks)**

(b)   Brain scans can also be done on machine type XR50 and would take only 1.8 hours per scan with a reduced reject rate of 6%. However, the cost of the X-ray plates would be £55 per scan.

Advise which type should be used, assuming sufficient capacity is available on both types of machine.   **(8 marks)**

(Total: 15 marks)

78   JETPRINT LTD

Jetprint Ltd specialises in printing advertising leaflets and is in the process of preparing its price list. The most popular requirement is for a folded leaflet made from a single sheet of A4 paper. From past records and budgeted figures, the following data have been estimated for a typical batch of 10,000 leaflets:

Artwork	£65
Machine setting	4 hours at £22 per hour
Paper	£12.50 per 1,000 sheets
Ink and consumables	£40
Printers' wages	4 hours at £8 per hour

Note: Printers' wages vary with volume.

General fixed overheads are £15,000 per period during which a total of 600 labour hours are expected to be worked.

The firm wishes to achieve 30% profit on sales.

Requirements:

(a)   Calculate the selling prices (to the nearest pound) per thousand leaflets for quantities of 10,000 and 20,000 leaflets.   **(7 marks)**

(b)   Calculate the profit for a period, assuming that during the period the firm sold 64 batches of 10,000 and 36 batches of 20,000, and that all costs and selling prices were as expected.   **(4 marks)**

(c)   Comment critically on the results achieved for the period.   **(4 marks)**

(Total: 15 marks)

79   TP LTD

TP Ltd is a small company that specialises in servicing computers. The company operates a standard costing system and details of the standard cost of servicing a computer are shown below.

The figures were based on servicing 20,000 computers during the year.

Standard cost to service one computer:

		£
Material	One unit of X	10.00
	One unit of Y	5.00
Labour (service engineers)	2 hours at £15 per hour	30.00
Variable overheads	2 hours at £7.50 per hour	15.00
Fixed overheads	2 hours at £15 per hour	30.00
		———
Total service cost		90.00
Profit mark up	50%	45.00
		———
Service price per computer		135.00
		———

The majority of work that TP Ltd undertakes is based on three-year service contracts. However, PP Ltd, a new local company, has asked TP Ltd to quote for an urgent stand-alone job of servicing 150 computers. TP Ltd wants to win this order because it has some spare capacity, but knows that the standard price per service is more than PP Ltd is willing to pay.

The accountant of TP Ltd has ascertained the following information:

- Material X is regularly used. There is sufficient stock of Material X held, with a book value of £10 per unit. The replacement cost of Material X is £11 per unit.

- Material Y is regularly used. There are 100 units held in stock, with a book value of £5 per unit. The replacement cost of Material Y is £5.50 per unit.

- No additional engineers would be required to do this job. The service engineers are paid for a 35-hour week. 70% of the time required to complete this job can be undertaken within normal working hours; however, the remainder would have to be completed during overtime. Overtime is paid at time plus a half.

- There will be no additional fixed costs incurred by this job.

Required:

TP Ltd is preparing a quote for the PP Ltd job based on relevant costing.

(a)   The total relevant cost of Material X for this job would be   **(2 marks)**

(b)   The total relevant cost of Material Y for this job would be   **(2 marks)**

(c)   The total relevant cost of the labour for this job would be   **(2 marks)**

(d)   The total relevant cost of the variable overheads for this job would be   **(2 marks)**

(e)   Explain in no more than 20 words how you would calculate the relevant cost of the fixed overheads for this job.   **(2 marks)**

TP Ltd is now planning for next year. The budgeted demand next year is expected to be 20,000 services. Because of changes in technology, Material X and Material Y will be replaced by a new component that will cover both of their functions. Labour costs, variable overhead costs and fixed overhead costs are expected to remain at the same level as the previous year. The new component will cost £14.40 per service. TP Ltd will keep the standard service charge at £135 for each computer.

Required:

(f)   The breakeven output for next year will be   **(2 marks)**

(g)   If the fixed costs were to increase to £650,000, the sales revenue required in order to achieve a profit of £673,000 next year will be   **(3 marks)**

(Total: 15 marks)

Section 3

ANSWERS TO
OBJECTIVE TEST QUESTIONS

ACCOUNTING FOR MANAGEMENT AND COST ACCOUNTING

1   D

All three *could* be true, but are not necessarily true in specific cases.

2   D

Items of data are discrete when they have unique values, such as 1, 2, 3 and so on. Continuous data is for items that can have a value anywhere in a continuous range, such as heights and weights of individuals. Qualitative data is normally *non-numerical*. Information comes from both internal and external sources. Operational information is usually short-term (current) in nature.

3   C

Budgeting is 'tactical' medium-term planning, which is used for planning operations, typically one year ahead. It can also be used to motivate managers to achieve certain targets. Budgeting is not planning for longer-term or strategic matters.

4   C

Short-term objectives are set out in detail not in very general terms.

5   A

The Board of Directors is responsible for major decisions affecting the company, including strategic planning. Tactical planning is usually the responsibility of middle management, and operational planning is the responsibility of managers dealing with day-to-day issues.

6   B

A management information system provides information to managers. Managers need information for planning and controlling the business, and for making decisions and co-ordinating activities and plans.

7   C

Item B describes the costs of an activity or cost centre. Item A describes cost units. Item D describes budget centres. A cost centre is defined as 'a production or service location, function, activity or item of equipment for which costs are accumulated'.

8   A

Cost accounting can be used for stock/inventory valuation to meet the requirements of both internal reporting and external financial reporting.

9   A

Higher-level management could be involved with all levels of decision-making within an enterprise, in short-term decisions as well as longer-term decisions.

10   D

All the techniques listed in the question could be used to monitor and control costs.

ELEMENTS OF COST

11   B

Direct costs are those attributable to a cost unit, which can be economically identified with the unit.

12   C

A stores requisition note is a request by a department for goods to be delivered from the stores. On the assumption that items are in stock when a stores requisition is made (so there is no need for a purchase requisition), the sequence is:

(1)   Raise a purchase order to buy goods from a supplier.

(2)   On receipt of the goods from the supplier, prepare a goods received note.

(3)   Update the stores ledger account from the goods received note.

(4)   Raise a stores requisition to obtain items from the stores.

13   B

$$400 = \sqrt{\frac{2 \times £20 \times 24,000}{H}}$$

Square both sides of the equation:

$(400 \times 400) = (2 \times £20 \times 24,000)/H$

$160,000 = £960,000/H$

$160,000H = £960,000$

$H = £6$

14   C

Profit = £60/3

Selling price = total cost + profit = £60 + £20 = £80

15   A

Stock valuation = £(10 + 29 + 3 + 7 + 5) = £54. Non-manufacturing expenses are not included in the stock valuation. It could also be argued that £49 is a valid answer, but only if the organisation uses a marginal costing system.

16   C

Variable cost = £(10 + 29 + 3 + 7 + 2) = £51. The total variable cost includes non-manufacturing variable costs.

17   C

Prime cost = £(10 + 29 + 3) = £42. Prime costs are direct costs, and exclude all overheads.

18   A

Date			Balance units	Value £
12 August	Received	(4,000 × £5)	4,000	20,000
15 August	Issued	(3,900 × £5)	(3,900)	(19,500)
		(100 × £5)	100	500
19 August	Received	(1,200 × £6)	1,200	7,200
			1,300	7,700
21 August	Issued	(100 × £5) + (1,000 x £6)	(1,100)	(6,500)
		(200 × £6)	200	1,200
24 August	Received	(2,800 × £7.5)	2,800	21,000
			3,000	22,200

19   C

Date			Balance units	Value £
12 August	Received	(4,000 × £5)	4,000	20,000
15 August	Issued	(3,900 × £5)	(3,900)	(19,500)
		(100 × £5)	100	500
19 August	Received	(1,200 × £6)	1,200	7,200
		(1,300 × £5.9231)	1,300	7,700
21 August	Issued	(1,100 × £5.9231)	(1,100)	(6,515)
		(200 × £5.9231)	200	1,185
24 August	Received	(2,800 × £7.5)	2,800	21,000
			3,000	22,185

20   A

Purchases in the period were (300 × £25) + (400 × £22) = £16,300.

Issues = 700 units, receipts = 700 units and closing stock = 400 units.

Therefore opening stock = 400 units.

Let the unit value of opening stock be £A.

Value of materials issued:

On 10July: $(300 \times £25) + (200A) = £7,500 + 200A$.

On 20 July: $200 \times £22 = £4,400$

Total value of issues $= £7,500 + 200A + £4,400 = £11,900 + 200A$.

Opening stock + Purchases = Issues + Closing stock

$400A + 16,300 = (11,900 + 200A) + 10,000$

$200A = 5,600A = £5,600/200 = £28$.

Opening stock $= 400A = 400 \times £28 = £11,200$.

21   D

Opening stock 200 units + Purchases 1,000 units – Issues 1,000 units = Closing stock 200 units.

With FIFO, the closing stock units are valued as the units purchased on 29 May.

Closing stock $= 200$ units $\times £7 = £1,400$

22   C

Date			Units	Stock £	Issues £
1 May	Opening	200 at £5	200	1,000	
5 May	Receipts	300 at £4.50	300	1,350	
			500	2,350	
7 May	Issues	300 at £4.50 + 100 at £5	(400)	(1,850)	1,850
			100	500	
12 May	Receipts	100 at £6	100	600	
22 May	Receipts	400 at £5.50	400	2,200	
			600	3,300	
23 May	Issues	400 at £5.50	(400)	(2,200)	2,200
			200	1,100	
29 May	Receipts	200 at £7	200	1,400	
			400	2,500	
30 May	Issues	200 at £7	(200)	(1,400)	1,400
			200	1,100	5,450

23   A

FIFO means that the value of closing stock reflects the most recent prices paid.

24   C

This should be a straightforward question. The economic batch quantity/economic order quantity formulae are for deciding the order quantity that will minimize the combined costs of stockholding and stock ordering.

25   C

		£
Purchase costs	(20,000 units × £40)	800,000
Order costs	(20,000/500 orders × £25/order)	1,000
Holding costs	(500/2 average units × £4/unit)	1,000
Total costs		802,000

26   B

Re-order when level of stock held = (maximum usage in maximum lead time)

Maximum usage:	175 per day
Maximum lead time:	16 days

Re-order level = 175 × 16 = 2,800 units.

27   C

	Tyres
Number in stock when order placed	2,800
Received in minimum lead time	3,000
Minimum usage in minimum lead time (90 × 10)	(900)
Maximum stock level	4,900

28   D

The carriage costs have to be paid for, and so are part of the cost of placing an order.

$$\text{EOQ} = \sqrt{\frac{2CoD}{Ch}} = \sqrt{\frac{2 \times (50+5) \times 4,000}{(15 \times 0.1)+0.2}}$$
$$= 509 \text{ units}$$

29   C

D is the rate of demand for the item and R is the rate of production. The (1 − D/R) adjustment applies when the re-ordered item is manufactured in-house, and is delivered into stores as units of the item come off the production line. Maximum stock levels are Q (1 − D/R), rather than Q. (1 − D/R) is therefore a measure of the rate at which stock levels decrease.

30   D

Authorisation should be obtained, if the stores function is to be properly maintained. Answer A ignores both stores issues and returns and also price data (which might have to come from the purchase invoice). A stores requisition must detail other information, such as quantities required. The lead time is the time from ordering to delivery from the supplier.

31   B

It would be appropriate to use the costs for a batch of cakes, since the cost for an individual cake might be too small. The cost per kilogram might not relate to the same number of cakes, and the cost per production run might relate to different quantities of output.

32   A

	Units	Unit cost £	Total £
Opening stock	100	3.00	300
3 March receipt	200	3.50	700
	300		1,000
8 March issue	(250)	200 at 3.50	(700)
		50 at 3.00	(150)
	50	3.00	150
15 March receipt	300	3.20	960
17 March receipt	200	3.30	660
	550		1,770
21 March issue	(500)	200 at 3.30	(660)
		300 at 3.20	(960)
	50	3.00	150
23 March receipt	450	3.10	1,395
	500		1,545
27 March issue	(350)	3.10	1,085
Closing balance	150		460

The closing balance in stock represents 50 units at £3 and 100 units at £3.10.

33   B

	Units	Unit cost £	Total £
Opening stock	100	3.00	300
3 March receipt	200	3.50	700
	300	3.333	1,000
8 March issue	(250)	3.333	(833)
	50	3.333	167
15 March receipt	300	3.20	960
17 March receipt	200	3.30	660
	550	3.249	1,787
21 March issue	(500)	3.249	(1,625)
	50	3.249	162
23 March receipt	450	3.10	1,395
	500	3.114	1,557
27 March issue	(350)	3.114	(1,090)
Closing balance	150	3.114	467

Issues = £833 + £1,625 + £1,090 = £3,548.

34   A

Both holding costs and demand are shown in the formula as monthly amounts. The same answer is obtained if annual holding costs and annual demand figures are used.

$$EOQ = \sqrt{\frac{2 \times 10 \times 1,250}{0.10}} = 500 \text{ units}$$

35   D

Statements (i) and (ii) should fairly obviously seem correct. In a stock control system, the reorder level might be set as maximum usage per day/week × maximum supply lead time in days or weeks; therefore Statement (iii) is also correct.

36   B

20X6 wages at 20X1 prices are

$$£315 \times \frac{117}{157} = £235$$

37   C

		£
Product A	1,750 units × 3 hours/unit × £7 /hour	36,750
Product B	5,000 units × 4 hours/unit × £7 /hour	140,000
		176,750

38   A

Statement (i) is correct, because extra spending would be incurred to pay the temporary additional staff. Statement (ii) is incorrect, because total spending on labour is unaffected when spare capacity is utilised and idle time reduced. Statement (iii) is also incorrect, because total labour costs will not be increased by switching labour from working on one product to working on another product. However, there is an opportunity cost in switching labour. This is the total contribution forgone by no longer producing and selling the original product. This opportunity cost would be a relevant cost in evaluating a decision to switch the labour from one product to the other. Even so, as worded, statement (iii) is incorrect.

39   B

Unless the overtime can be traced to a specific product or job, it will be treated as an indirect production cost and absorbed into units using the normal absorption basis.

40   B

62,965 + 13,600 = £76,565. The only direct costs are the wages paid to direct workers for ordinary time, plus the basic pay for overtime. Overtime premium and shift allowances are usually treated as overheads. However, if and when overtime and shift work are incurred specifically for a particular cost unit, they are classified as direct costs of that cost unit. Sick pay is treated as an overhead and is therefore classified as an indirect cost.

41   D

When overtime is worked by direct labour on a specific job and for a specific purpose, the full cost of the labour, including the overtime premium, is treated as a direct cost. When overtime is worked as a general requirement, the overtime premium of direct labour workers is treated as a production overhead. In this situation, the overtime cost of the semi-skilled workers will probably be treated as a direct cost of the order, because the work was done specifically for the order. (In other words, in this case it is appropriate to disregard the normal treatment of semi-skilled labour costs as indirect costs.)

		Direct cost £	Indirect cost £
Skilled workers:			
Specific overtime	(10 × £10 × 1.50)	150	
General overtime	(20 × £10)	200	
	(20 × £10 × 0.50)		100
Semi-skilled workers			
Specific overtime	(15 × £6 × 1.50)	135	
General overtime	(30 × £6 × 1.50)	–	270
Total		485	370

42   B

Working conditions, pension provisions and welfare are all costs associated with *retaining* labour, not *replacing* labour. The learning curve effect describes the way in which employees learn a job and reduce the time they need to complete the work as they gain familiarity and experience. When new staff are taken on, they are likely to take longer to do the work to begin with, but then gain speed and efficiency as they 'learn' their work. Costs will therefore be higher until the 'learning curve effect' has occurred.

43   D

Paid hours including idle time = 2,400 × 100/80 = 3,000.
Budgeted labour cost = 3,000 hours × £10 = £30,000.

44   D

Efficiency compares the standard hours produced with the hours actively worked
(9,300 hrs ÷ 9,200 hrs) × 100% = 101%.

45   B

Unless the overtime has been incurred specifically for a particular product or job, it will be treated as an indirect production cost.

46   A

Productive hours	3,300
Idle time (3,300 × 25/(100 – 25))	1,100
Total paid hours	4,400
Total labour cost	£36,300
Labour rate per hour	£8.25

47   18%

Employees	
At start of year	4,600
Recruited during the year	1,800
	6,400
At end of year	5,500
Therefore leavers during the year	900

Average number of employees = (4,600 + 5,500)/2 = 5,050.

Labour turnover rate = (900/5,050) × 100% = 17.8%, or 18% to the nearest percentage figure.

48   C

	Hours
Active time required	2,520
Lost time (× 10/(100 − 10))	280
Budgeted hours (paid hours)	2,800
Labour rate per hour	£4
Budgeted labour cost	£11,200

49   B

The costs of a stores department in a factory are an overhead cost. This includes all labour costs in the stores department. The other examples of labour costs in the question are all direct labour costs for the particular businesses in which they work.

50   B

Managers are not usually classified as direct labour.

51   B

£24,600 × 278/255 = £26,819. £26,800 to the nearest £100.

COSTING METHODS – OVERHEADS, ABSORPTION COSTING AND MARGINAL COSTING

52   C

	£
Actual overheads	500,000
Over-absorbed overhead	50,000
Absorbed overheads	550,000

Units produced: 110,000

Absorption rate = £550,000/110,000 = £5 per unit.

53 A

Under- or over-absorption is determined by comparing the actual overhead expenditure with what has been absorbed.

54 C

Total fixed costs	= £25,000	
Budgeted units	= 2,000	
Fixed cost per unit	= £25,000/2,000	= £12.50.

Since the company makes only one product, the unit fixed cost can be calculated simply by dividing total fixed costs by the production volume in units. It is unnecessary to calculate an absorption rate per hour for each department.

55 A

In the process of apportioning overheads and re-apportioning service centre overheads, only production overhead costs are considered. Allocation is where *all* an overhead expense is assigned to a cost centre (so Statement B is incorrect). Costs are re-apportioned from service centres to production centres, not the other way round (so Statement C is incorrect). Statement D is nonsense – allocated overheads are not ignored!

56 B

	Total £	Dept 1 £	Dept 2 £	Maint'ce £	Basis
Heating/lighting	12,000	4,500	5,625	1,875	
Welfare costs	7,000	2,500	3,750	750	(20:30:6)
Power	42,000	24,500	17,500	–	(35:25)
	61,000	31,500	26,875	2,625	

57 B

	Dept 1 £	Dept 2 £	Maint'ce £	Basis
Apportioned	31,500	26,875	2,625	
Maintenance	1,050	1,575	(2,625)	(2:3)
	32,550	28,450		

Department 1 appears to be a machining department, with more machine hours worked than labour hours. A machine hour absorption rate therefore seems appropriate.

Absorption rate per machine hour = £32,550/40,000 hours = £0.814.

58 D

Answer A is incorrect because it refers to controllability. Answer B is incorrect because it is describing absorption of costs. Answer C is incorrect because it is describing allocation of costs. Only answer D refers to the sharing of common costs.

59   A

Department 1 recovery rate = 2,400,000 ÷ 240,000 = £10 per hour

Department 2 recovery rate = 4,000,000 ÷ 200,000 = £20 per hour

Fixed overhead cost per IC = (3 × £10) + (2 × £20) = £70

60   D

Cutting department:

Budgeted hours = (6,000 × 0.05) + (6,000 × 0.10) = 900 hours

Absorption rate for the cutting department = £120,000/900 = £133.33.

Stitching department:

Budgeted hours = (6,000 × 0.20) + (6,000 × 0.25) = 2,700 hours

Absorption rate for the cutting department = £72,000/2,700 = £26.67.

Fixed overhead cost of a Bomber = (0.10 × £133.33) + (0.25 × £26.67) = £20.

61   D

This is a simple definition question.

62   C

An absorption rate is used to determine the full cost of a product or service. Answer A describes overhead allocation and apportionment. Absorption does not control overheads, so answer D is not correct.

63   A

Since each machine receives exactly the same amount of servicing time, regardless of its cost, usage or floor space occupied, apportionment between the two production centres on the basis of the number of machines (i.e. the same apportionment of cost to each machine) would seem fairest.

64   A

The overhead absorption rate would be based on budgeted figures:

$$\frac{£258,750}{11,250} = £23 \text{ per hour}$$

Since actual hours were 10,980, this means that overheads absorbed were 10,980 × £23 = £252,540. Actual overheads were £254,692, which means that overheads were under-absorbed by £2,152.

65   D

	£
Actual overhead	138,000
Over-absorbed overhead	23,000
Therefore amount of overhead absorbed	161,000

Hours worked = 11,500.

Therefore absorption rate per hour = £161,000/11,500 hours = £14 per hour.

66   B

As stocks decrease over the period, the cost of sales will be higher with absorption costing, since they will include fixed overhead in the opening stock now sold. The extra cost of sales (and thus reduction in profit) = $(8,500 - 6,750) \times £3 = £5,250$. This means that since profit will be lower with absorption costing by £5,250, the absorption costing profit will be £$(62,100 - 5,250) = £56,850$.

67   A

Over/(under) absorption = Absorbed overheads − Incurred overheads

Since variable overhead costs were as budgeted (£5 per unit), there was no under- or over-absorption of variable overheads.

Budgeted fixed overhead = 3,000 units × £9 = £27,000.

Actual production volume = 3,500 units − 300 units = 3,200 units.

	£
Fixed overhead absorbed (3,200 × £9)	28,800
Fixed overhead incurred (£27,000 × 1.05)	28,350
Over-absorbed fixed overheads	450

68   C

Budgeted fixed overhead cost per unit = £48,000/4,800 units = £10.

	£	
Budgeted fixed overhead	48,000	
Expenditure variance	2,000	(A)
Actual fixed overhead	50,000	

	£
Actual fixed overhead	50,000
Under-absorbed	8,000
Absorbed overhead	42,000

Units produced = Absorbed overhead/Absorption rate per unit
= £42,000/£10 = 4,200 units.

69   D

Fixed production overhead cost per unit = £72,000/7,200 units = £10.

	£	
Budgeted fixed overhead	72,000	
Expenditure variance	3,000	(A)
Actual fixed overhead	75,000	

	£
Actual fixed overhead	75,000
Over-absorbed	12,000
Absorbed overhead	87,000

Units produced = Absorbed overhead/Absorption rate per unit
= £87,000/£10 = 8,700 units.

70   B

	£
Actual fixed overhead	694,075
Under-recovered overhead	35,000
Absorbed fixed overhead	659,075

Actual consulting hours: 32,150

Absorption rate = £659,075/32,150 hours = £20.50 per hour.

71   B

Machine hour rate = £180,000/10,000 machine hours = £18 per machine hour.

Machine hours are more appropriate than labour hours as a basis for recovering/absorbing overhead costs, because the enterprise has a machine-intensive operation, with more machine hours of operation than direct labour hours worked. A unit basis for absorbing overhead is inappropriate because the enterprise makes a wide range of different products.

72   C

Using the simultaneous equations/reciprocal method, let the total overheads apportioned from the Stores department be S, and let the total overheads apportioned from the Maintenance department be M.

(i)   S = 6,300 + 0.05M

(ii)   M = 8,450 + 0.10S

Substitute (2) in (1):

S = 6,300 + 0.05 (8,450 + 0.10S)

S = 6,300 + 422.5 + 0.005S

0.995S = 6,722.5

S = 6,722.5/0.995 = 6,756

Substitute in (2)

M = 8,450 + 0.10 (6,756) = 9,126.

Total apportionment to production department 1

= 17,500 + 0.60S + 0.75M

= 17,500 + 0.60 (6,756) + 0.75 (9,126)

= 17,500 + 4,054 + 6,844

= 28,398

Using the repeated distribution method

	P1	*P2*	*S*	*M*
Allocated and apportioned	17,500	32,750	6,300	8,450
Apportion M	6,338	1,690	422	(8,450)
			6,722	–
Apportion S	4,033	2,017	(6,722)	672
Apportion M	504	134	34	(672)
Apportion S	21	10	(34)	3
Apportion M	2	1	–	(3)
Final allocation and apportionment	28,398	36,602		

73   **B**

Contribution per unit = £(10 – 6) = £4.

	£
Total contribution (250,000 × £4)	1,000,000
Fixed overheads (200,000 × £2)	400,000
Profit	600,000

74   **C**

There was an increase in stock in the period; therefore the absorption costing profit is higher than the marginal costing profit (because a larger amount of fixed overhead is carried forward in the closing stock value).

	£
Marginal costing profit	72,300
Less: fixed costs in opening stock (300 units × £5)	(1,500)
Add: fixed costs in closing stock (750 units × £5)	3,750
Absorption costing profit	74,550

75   **B**

The difference in profit between absorption and marginal costing is attributable to the fixed overhead in opening stock (a cost to the current period) and the fixed overhead in closing stock (a cost deferred to the next accounting period).

	£
Profit with absorption costing	47,500
Add: fixed costs in opening stock (400 units × £12)	4,800
Subtract: fixed costs in closing stock (600 units × £12)	(7,200)
Profit with marginal costing	45,100

When closing stock is higher than opening stock, reported profits will be higher with absorption costing than with marginal costing.

76   A

Unit fixed overhead costs are based on normal production of 10,000 units.

Budgeted fixed overheads (10,000 units × £12)	£120,000
	£
Actual fixed overheads (same as budget)	120,000
Absorbed overheads (= 11,500 units × £12)	138,000
Over-absorbed fixed overheads	18,000

77   B

Production volume exceeded sales volume, so the profit with absorption costing is higher than the profit with marginal costing. Fixed overheads in stock = £30,000/750 = £40 per unit, therefore total fixed overhead in closing stock (absorption costing) = 250 units × £40 = £10,000. Profit with marginal costing is therefore lower by £10,000.

78   D

	£
Sales (600 × (£90,000/500 per unit))	108,000
Production cost of sales (600 × (£75,000/750))	60,000
	48,000
Under-absorbed overhead (750 – 700 units) × £40	2,000
	46,000
Variable selling costs (600 × (£5,000/500))	6,000
Fixed selling costs	25,000
Profit	15,000

79   C

	£	£
Sales (9,000 × £20 per unit)		180,000
Production cost of sales (9,000 × £(2 + 3 + 3 + 4))		108,000
		72,000
Production overhead absorbed (11,000 × £4)	44,000	
Production overhead incurred (10,000 × £4)	40,000	
Over-absorbed overhead		4,000
		76,000
Variable selling costs (9,000 × £1)		9,000
Fixed selling costs (10,000 × £2)		20,000
Profit		47,000

80 B

With marginal costing, profit will be lower than with absorption costing because closing stock is higher than opening stock.

The production overhead cost in the stock increase = 2,000 units × £4/unit = £8,000.

Marginal costing profit = £47,000 − £8,000 = £39,000.

Alternatively:

	£
Sales (9,000 × £20 per unit)	180,000
Variable cost of sales (9,000 × £(2 + 3 + 3 + 1))	81,000
Total contribution	99,000
Fixed production costs (10,000 × £4)	40,000
Fixed selling costs (10,000 × £2)	20,000
Profit	39,000

81 C

During the period, stocks increased by 34,000 − 31,000 = 3,000 units.

Fixed overhead in the additional closing stock = £(955,500 − 850,500) = £105,000.

Fixed overhead per unit = £105,000/3,000 = £35 per unit.

Budgeted fixed costs = £1,837,500

Budgeted production volume = £1,837,500/£35 per unit = 52,500 units.

82 A

Increase in stock level in the period = (10,000 − 8,000) = 2,000 units.

Fixed overhead cost per unit = $\dfrac{£2,000}{2,000 \text{ units}}$ = £1/unit.

Contribution per unit = Profit per unit + Fixed cost per unit
= £5 + £1 = £6/unit.

83 B

In an absorption costing system, the fixed cost per unit would be £3,000/15,000 units = £0.20 per unit.

Budgeted profit with marginal costing = Contribution − Fixed costs
= £26,000 − £3,000 = £23,000.

By switching to absorption costing, in a period when stock levels increase by 2,000 units, absorption costing profit would be higher by 2,000 units × fixed cost per unit, i.e. by 2,000 × £0.20 = £400.

Absorption costing profit = £23,000 + £400 = £23,400.

COSTING SYSTEMS

84   B

The information about material lost in production should be ignored, because the raw material quantities are for the materials input to production. The input quantities allow for losses during production.

	kg
Materials to produce 450 units of Pye (× 10)	4,500
Materials to produce 375 units of Combe (× 4)	1,500
Add: opening stock of materials	400
Minus: closing stock of materials	(300)
Budgeted material purchases	6,100

85   D

	units
Sales	10,000
Less: opening stock	(600)
Add: closing stock (5% × 10,000)	500
Good production required	9,900

Good production = 90% of total production, therefore

Total production = $\dfrac{9,900}{90\%}$ = 11,000 units.

86   D

Process account

	Units	£		Units	£
Input	3,000	9,000	Normal loss	300	450
Conversion costs		11,970	Output	2,900	???
Abnormal gain	200	???			
	3,200			3,200	

Equivalent units of output =

Expected output for the given input = 3,000 – normal loss 300 = 2,700 equivalent units.

(Alternatively, it is actual output 2,900 units minus the abnormal gain 200 units = 2,700 equivalent units.)

Total costs = £(9,000 + 11,970 – 450*) = £20,520.

(* Scrap value of the normal loss.)

Cost per equivalent unit = £20,520/2,700 equivalent units = £7.60.

Cost of output = 2,900 units × £7.60 = £22,040.

87   C

Don't be misled by the wording of answer D, which refers to 'ignoring the opening stock units'. Equivalent units are not the total number of whole units started. (For example, normal loss counts as zero equivalent units.) Equivalent units are the number of effective whole units worked on in the period, allowing for the level of completion in opening stock and in closing stock.

88   D

	kg
Opening stock	3,000
Input	5,000
	8,000
Closing stock	2,000
Finished output	6,000

With FIFO, of the 6,000 units of finished output, 3,000 kg are the opening stock now completed, and the remaining 3,000 kg must be units started and finished in the period.

	Total units		Equivalent units
Opening stock completed	3,000	(60%)	1,800
Other finished output	3,000		3,000
Total finished output	6,000		4,800
Closing stock	2,000	(75%)	1,500
	8,000		6,300

Total cost of work done in this period = £10,000 + £19,925 = £29,925.

Cost per equivalent unit of work in this period = £29,925/6,300 = £4.75.

Cost of finished output with FIFO =

	£
Opening stock b/f	6,750
Costs this period (4,800 equiv. units × £4.75)	22,800
Total cost of finished output	29,550

89   C

Total sales revenue	= (18 × 10,000) + (25 × 20,000) + (20 × 20,000)
	= 1,080,000
Joint costs to be allocated	= 277,000 − (2 × 3,500)
	= 270,000
Allocation rate = (270,000/1,080,000)	= 0.25 of sales revenue.
Joint costs allocated to product 3	= 0.25 × (20 × 20,000)
	= £100,000
	= (£100,000/20,000 units) £5 per unit

90   C

Normal loss = 25% of 3,500 units = 875 units. Value of normal loss (at £8 per unit) = £7,000.

Process account

	Units	£		Units	£
Materials	3,500	52,500	Normal loss	875	7,000
Labour		9,625	Output	2,800	???
Abnormal gain	175	???			
	3,675			3,675	

$$\text{Cost/unit} = \frac{52,500+9,625-7,000}{3,500-875} = \frac{55,125}{2,625} = £21$$

Valuation of output = £21 × 2,800 = £58,800.

91   A

Process

	Units		Units
Opening stock	400	Losses	400
Input	3,000	Output (balancing figure)	2,800
		Closing stock	200
	3,400		3,400

92   D

This can be calculated as a balancing figure in the process account.

Process account

	kg		£		kg		£
Input (balance)	3,000		21,150	Output	2,800	(× 7.50)	21,000
Abnormal gain	100	(× 7.50)	750	Normal loss	300	(× 3)	900
			21,900				21,900

Alternatively:

	£
Cost of output (2,800 × 7.50)	21,000
Scrap value of normal loss (300 × 3)	900
	21,900
Less: Value of abnormal gain (100 × 7.50)	(750)
Cost of input	21,150

93   A

	kg
Material input	2,500
Normal loss (10%)	(250)
Abnormal loss	(75)
Good production achieved	2,175

94   B

	Equivalent units
Opening stock completed (400 × 70%)	280
Units started and finished in the period (2,000 – 200)	1,800
Closing stock (200 × 60%)	120
Total equivalent units produced in the period	2,200

Cost per equivalent unit (labour and overhead) = £3,300/ 2,200 units = £1.50.

(Note: It is assumed that the FIFO method of stock valuation applies.)

95   C

	Materials equivalent units
Opening stock completed (400 × 0%)	0
Units started and finished in the period (800 – 400)	400
Closing stock (600 × 75%)	450
Total equivalent units produced in the period	850

96   B

	units
Input	13,200
Normal loss (13,200 × 10/110)	1,200
Expected output	14,400

	£
Process costs	184,800
Less: scrap value of normal loss (1,200 × £4)	4,800
Cost of good output	180,000

Cost for each expected unit of output = £180,000/12,000 = £15.

Finished units of output, and also abnormal loss and abnormal gain units will be valued at this amount.

97   £19,050

	Total units	Equivalent units	
		Materials	Conversion costs
Opening stock	2,000		
Input materials	8,000		
	10,000		
Closing stock	3,000	3,000	1,500

Finished output	7,000	7,000	7,000
		10,000	8,500
Costs (£9,400 + £41,600)		£51,000	
(£4,800 + £16,450)			£21,250
Cost/equivalent unit		£5.10	£2.50

Valuation of closing stock	£
Direct materials (3,000 × £5.10)	15,300
Conversion costs (1,500 × £2.50)	3,750
	19,050

98   C

By convention, normal loss is attributed to material costs, not labour costs (or conversion costs).

	Total units		Labour equivalent units
Opening WIP	250	(250 × 60%)	150
Units started and finished	3,850		3,850
	4,100		4,000
Normal loss	225		0
Abnormal loss	275		275
Closing WIP	150	(150 × 30%)	45
	4,750		4,320

99   D

	Job 1	Job 2	Total
	£	£	£
Opening WIP	8,500	0	8,500
Material in period	17,150	29,025	46,175
Labour for period	12,500	23,000	35,500
Overheads (see working)	43,750	80,500	124,250
	81,900	132,525	214,425

Working

Total labour cost for period = £(12,500 + 23,000 + 4,500) = £40,000

Overhead absorption rate = £140,000/£40,000 = 3.5 times the direct labour cost.

100   C

	Job 3
	£
Opening WIP	46,000
Labour cost for period	4,500
Overheads (3.5 × £4,500)	15,750
Total production costs	66,250
Profit (50%)	33,125
Selling price of 2,400 boards	99,375

Selling price of one board = £99,375/2,400 = £41.41

101   C

	£
Sales price	1,690
Profit (× 30/130)	390
Total cost	1,300
Overhead	694
Prime cost	606

102   C

Revenue is most likely to be based on the quantity delivered and the distance travelled. In addition, costs are likely to relate to both distance travelled and weight of load. Cost per tonne mile gives a measure of both quantity and distance.

103   D

	units
Opening work in progress	2,000
Input of new materials	42,300
	44,300
Transfer to finished goods	(40,100)
Normal loss	(400)
Closing work in progress	(1,500)
Abnormal loss	2,300

104   B

Finished output = (20,000 + 110,000 – 40,000) = 90,000 units.

Closing WIP = 40,000 units 50% complete, = 20,000 equivalent units.

Cost per equivalent unit (in £000) = £132,000/(90,000 + 20,000)

= £1,200 per equivalent unit/finished car.

105 C

Actual labour costs = budgeted labour costs = £14,500 + £3,500 + £24,600 = £42,600.

Absorption rate = £126,000/£42,600 = 2.957746 times labour costs.

Overhead for job CC20 = £24,600 × 2.957746 = £72,761.

106 D

	£
Opening WIP value	42,790
Added material	0
Labour in period	3,500
Overhead (£3,500 × 2.957746)	10,352
Total cost	56,642
Profit (1/3 on sales = 50% on cost)	28,321
Sales price	84,963

107 D

	AA10 £	CC20 £	Total
Opening WIP	26,800	0	
Materials added	17,275	18,500	
Labour	14,500	24,600	
Overhead (= labour cost × 2.957746)	42,887	72,761	
	131,336	85,987	£217,323

(Exclude BB15 as it was completed and delivered during the period.)

108 D

The equivalent units for closing WIP, and so total equivalent units (EUs) produced in the period, will be lower. If there are fewer EUs, the cost per EU will be higher and so the cost of finished goods will be higher.

109 D

Statement A is correct. Job costs are identified with a particular job, whereas process costs (of units produced and work in process) are averages, based on equivalent units of production.

Statement B is also correct. The direct cost of a job to date, excluding any direct expenses, can be ascertained from materials requisition notes and job tickets or time sheets.

Statement C is correct, because without data about units completed and units still in process, losses and equivalent units of production cannot be calculated.

Statement D is incorrect, because the cost of normal loss will usually be incorporated into job costs as well as into process costs. In process costing this is commonly done by giving normal loss no cost, leaving costs to be shared between output, closing stocks and abnormal loss/gain. In job costing it can be done by adjusting direct materials costs to allow for normal wastage, and direct labour costs for normal reworking of items or normal spoilage.

110 D

	Units
Opening WIP	2,000
Input	24,000
	26,000
Output	(19,500)
Normal loss	(2,400)
Closing WIP	(3,000)
Abnormal loss	1,100

Equivalents units

	Total units	Materials		Conversion costs	
		%	EUs	%	EUs
Output	19,500	100	19,500	100	19,500
Abnormal loss	1,100	100	1,100	100	1,100
Closing WIP	3,000	100	3,000	45	1,350
			23,600		21,950

111 B

Net realisable value:	£
Product X: $8,000 \times £(12 - 3)$	72,000
Product Y: $6,000 \times £6$	36,000
	108,000

Joint processing costs should be apportioned in the ratio 72,000 : 36,000 or 2:1 between X and Y.

	£
Direct materials cost	40,000
Labour and overhead cost	44,000
	84,000
Less: Sale value of by-product $(3,000 \times £0.50)$	(1,500)
Costs of output from process	82,500
Apportioned to Product Y (1/3)	27,500
Cost/unit of Product Y (27,500/6,000)	£4.58

112 D

A service industry is an industry not involved in agriculture, mining, construction or manufacturing. Transport industries are service industries.

COSTING METHODS AND TECHNIQUES – STANDARD COSTING AND VARIANCE ANALYSIS

113   B

		Iron sheets units		Copper spools units	Total
800 units should use	(× 5)	4,000	(× 3)	2,400	
Did use		3,900		2,600	
Usage variance		100 F		200 A	
Price per unit		£2		£3	
Usage variance in £		£200 F		£600 A	£400 A

114   A

Actual cost of labour = 2,000 hours at £7 per hour plus 1,400 hours at £7.20 per hour = £24,080.

	£
3,400 hours should cost (× £7)	23,800
Did cost	24,080
Labour rate variance	280 A

A quicker way to the answer is to identify that the rate variance is adverse by 1,400 hours at £7.20 – £7 per hour.

115   A

	£
3,400 hours should cost (× £3)	10,200
Did cost	10,000
Variable overhead expenditure variance	200 F

116   C

	£
Budgeted fixed overheads (4,000 hrs × £2)	8,000
Actual fixed overheads	8,800
Fixed overhead expenditure variance	800 A

117 D

Fixed overhead volume = 8 × (800 − [4,000 ÷ 4]) = £1,600 A

	Units	
Budgeted production volume	1,000	
(4,000 hours/4 hours per unit)		
Actual production volume	800	
Volume variance	200	A
Budgeted fixed overhead cost per unit	£8	
Fixed overhead volume variance	£1,600	A

118 B

Standard material cost per unit = £125,000/25,000 units = £5 per unit.

Standard price per kg of materials = £5 per unit/2 kg per unit = £2.50 per kg.

	£	
53,000 kg of materials should cost (× £2.50)	132,500	
They did cost	136,000	
Material price variance	3,500	Adverse

119 A

	Kg	
27,000 units of product should use (× 2 kg)	54,000	
They did use	53,000	
Material price variance (in kg)	1,000	Favourable
Standard price per kg	£2.50	
Material price variance (in £)	£2,500	Favourable

120 C

Fixed production overhead cost per unit = £120,000/20,000 units = £6 per unit.

	Units	
Budgeted output	20,000	
Actual output	21,000	
Volume variance in units	1,000	F
Fixed overhead cost per unit	£6	
Fixed overhead volume variance	£6,000	F

121 A

Efficiency variance in hours = £11,250 (F) /£6 per hour = 1,875 hours (F).

	Hours	
12,500 units did take	41,000	
Efficiency variance	1,875	F
12,500 units should take	39,125	

Standard time per unit = 39,125/12,500 = 3.13 hours per unit.

122 B

Efficiency variance in hours = £8,250 (A) /£7.50 per hour = 1,100 hours (A).

	Hours	
Actual hours worked	25,600	
Efficiency variance	1,100	A
Standard hours produced	24,500	

123 D

Standard price of materials = £76,500/1,500 kg = £51/kg.
Standard materials usage = 1,500/600 = 2.5 kg per unit.

	Kg	
580 units should use (× 2.5)	1,450	
Did use	1,566	
Usage variance in kg	116	(A)

Standard price per kg	£51	
Usage variance in kg	£5,916	(A)

124 D

Usage variance = £300 (A)
Usage variance in kg = £300 (A)/£2 per kg = 150 kg (A)

	Kg	
500 units should use (× 3)	1,500	
Usage variance in kg	150	(A)
500 units did use	1,650	
Increase in stock (400 – 100)	300	
Material purchases in kg	1,950	

125　A

Standard price per kg = £25,500/1,500 kg = £17

	£
1,566 kg should cost (× 17)	26,622
Did cost	25,839
Material P price variance	783　F

126　B

	£	
Actual labour cost	117,600	
Rate variance	8,400	(A)
Standard cost of hours worked	109,200	

Hours worked	28,000
Standard rate per hour	£3.90

Efficiency variance in hours = £3,900 (F)/£3.90 per hour = 1,000 hours (F)

	hours	
Actual hours worked	28,000	
Efficiency variance in hours	1,000	F
Standard hours produced	29,000	

127　D

Standard cost per kg = £46,248/11,280 kg = £4.10

Usage variance in kg = £492(A)/£4.10 per kg = 120 kg (A).

(The usage variance is adverse, so actual materials used were more than the standard usage quantity.)

	kg	
Materials used	11,280	
Usage variance in kg	120	(A)
Standard usage	11,160	

128　D

Efficiency variance in hours = £7,800 (F)/£6.50 per hour = 1,200 hours (F).

(Note: The efficiency variance is favourable, so actual hours worked were less than the standard number of hours for the work done.)

	Hours	
Actual hours worked	17,500	
Efficiency variance in hours	1,200	(F)
Standard hours produced	18,700	

129 C

	£	
6,800 units purchased should cost (× £0.85)	5,780	
Purchase price variance	544	(A)
6,800 units purchased did cost	6,324	

Purchase cost per unit = £6,324/6,800 = £0.93.

130 C

	Kg	
Standard material usage for actual production (500 ×3)	1,500	
Usage variance in kg (£200 (F)/£2 per kg)	100	(F)
Actual materials used in production	1,400	
Increase in stocks (300 – 100)	200	
Actual purchases	1,600	

131 A

Since material stocks are valued using standard purchase price, the price variance would be calculated using the quantity **purchased**. Therefore:

	£
Actual cost of 7,800 kg	16,380
Price variance	1,170 (A)
Standard cost of 7,800 kg	£15,210

$$\text{Standard price per kg} = \frac{£15,210}{7,800 \text{ kg}} = £1.95/\text{kg}$$

132 B

	£	
6,850 kg purchased did cost	21,920	
Material price variance	1,370	(F)
6,850 kg did cost	20,550	

Purchase cost per unit = £20,550/6,850 = £3.00

133 C

Efficiency variance in hours = £4,400 (A)/£8 per hour = 550 hours (A).

(Note: The efficiency variance is adverse, so actual hours worked were more than the standard number of hours.)

	Hours	
Standard hours produced (850 × 24)	20,400	
Efficiency variance in hours	550	(A)
Actual hours worked	20,950	

134   A

Standard cost of purchases = Actual cost – Adverse price variance

= £43,250 – £3,250 = £40,000.

Standard cost per kg = £2.

Quantity purchased = £40,000/£2 per kg = 20,000 kg.

135   B

Budgeted fixed overhead cost per unit = £100,000/20,000 units = £5.

	Units	
Budgeted production	20,000	
Actual production	19,500	
Volume variance	500	(A)

Fixed overhead cost per unit	£5	
Fixed overhead volume variance	£2,500	(A)

136   B

Standard contribution per unit = £10 – £5.60 = £4.40.

Sales volume variance in units = Actual sales – Budgeted sales

= 4,500 – 5,000 = 500 units (A).

Sales volume variance in £ = 500 units × £4.40 per unit = £2,200 (A)

137   B

	£	
Budgeted fixed overhead for the month = £120,000/12	10,000	
Actual fixed overhead	9,800	
Fixed overhead expenditure variance	200	(F)

138 B

Standard variable overhead cost per hour = £180,000/90,000 hours = £2.

	£
82,650 hours should cost (× £2)	165,300
Did cost	173,800
Variable overhead expenditure variance	8,500 (A)

139 C

The standard labour rate should be the expected rate/hour, but allowing for standard levels of idle time. For example, if the work force is paid £9 per hour but idle time of 10% is expected, the standard labour rate will be £10 per hour, not £9.

140 C

This is simply a description of a variance that you should know how to calculate.

141 B

Overhead absorption rate	= Budgeted fixed overhead/budgeted labour hours
	= £135,000/9,000 hours = £15 per direct labour hour.

Actual hours worked	9,750	hours
Budgeted hours worked	9,000	hours
Capacity variance	750	hours (F)
Variance in £ (× £15)	£11,250	F

142 D

Expenditure variance

Monthly budgeted production (10,800/12) = 900 units

Monthly budgeted expenditure

(Flexed budget)	£
Fixed costs (900 × £4)	3,600
Variable costs (800 × £6)	4,800
Total expected expenditure	8,400
Actual expenditure	8,500
Expenditure variance	100 (A)

Volume variance

This only applies to fixed overhead costs:

Volume variance in units	100 units (A)
Standard fixed overhead cost per unit	£4
Fixed overhead volume variance	£400 (A)

143 C

$$\text{Absorption rate/unit} = \frac{£48,000}{4,800} = £10\text{/unit.}$$

	£	
Under absorption	8,000	
Expenditure variance	2,000	(A)
Volume variance	6,000	(A)

Volume variance in units = £6,000 (A)/£10 per unit = 600 units (A).

	Units	
Budgeted units	4,800	
Volume variance	600	(A)
Actual units	4,200	

144   A

The standard contribution per unit is £(50 – 4 – 16 – 10 – 1) = £19.

Budgeted sales volume	3,000	units
Actual sales volume	3,500	units
Sales volume variance in units	500	units (F)

Standard contribution per unit	£19
Sales volume variance in £	£9,500 (F)

SHORT-TERM DECISION MAKING

145   C

Total costs continue to rise as more quantities are bought. However, the rate of increase slows down above the point where the discount starts to be earned. This is where the 'kink' occurs in the cost line.

146   D

Although total fixed costs are the same at all levels of activity, the fixed cost per unit falls as the activity level increases. The unit cost does not fall in a straight line, but in a curved line, as shown in the question.

147   B

The cost of rental of property is a fixed period cost. Direct material costs are variable costs. Telephone costs consist of some fixed costs and some variable costs (e.g. fixed rental charge and variable call charges). Supervisory costs are fixed within a certain level of output, but a large increase in activity is almost certain to result in a requirement for additional supervision.

148   A

	£
Total cost of 15,100 square metres	83,585
Total cost of 12,750 square metres	73,950
Variable cost of 2,350 square metres	9,635

Variable cost is £9,635/2,350 square metres = £4.10 per square metre.

Fixed costs can be found by substitution:

	£
Total cost of 12,750 square metres	73,950
Variable cost of 12,750 square metres (× £4.10)	52,275
Fixed costs	21,675

So for 16,200 square metres:

Overheads   =   £21,675 + (16,200 × £4.10)

=   £88,095

149   C

In the formula C = 1,000 + 250P, 1,000 represents the weekly fixed costs and 250 the variable cost per unit.

150   A

The high-low method identifies the expected variable and fixed elements within a total cost, and so can be used to estimate the budgeted or expected costs (fixed plus variable) at any given activity level.

151   D

High = 20X6 output, and low = 20X5 output.

20X5 costs re-stated at 20X5 prices = £93,500 x 352/340 = £96,800.

	£
Cost of 8,000 at 20X6 prices	112,000
Cost of 6,400 at 20X6 prices	96,800
Variable cost of 1,600 at 20X6 prices	15,200

Variable cost/unit at 20X6 prices = £15,200/1,600 = £9.50.

	£
Total cost of 8,000 at 20X6 prices	112,000
Variable cost of 8,000 at 20X6 prices (× £9.50)	76,000
Fixed costs at 20X6 prices	36,000

	£
Fixed costs at 20X6 prices	36,000
Variable cost of 7,500 at 20X6 prices (× £9.50)	71,250
Total cost of 7,500 units at 20X6 prices	107,250
Total cost at 20X7 prices (× 370/352)	**£112,734**

(£112,700 to the nearest £100).

152   A

As advertising will hopefully generate sales, advertising is the independent variable and sales the dependent; i.e. advertising is x and sales is y.

		£
High	Sales from £6,500 of advertising	225,000
Low	Sales from £2,500 of advertising	125,000
	Marginal sales from £4,000 of advertising	100,000

Marginal sales for each £1 of advertising = £100,000/£4,000 = £25.

	£
Sales from £6,500 of advertising	225,000
Marginal sales from £6,500 of advertising (× £25)	162,500
Fixed sales (even with no advertising)	62,500

This gives a function of sales = £62,500 + £25x, where x is the spending on advertising.

153   C

	£
Total cost of 18,500 hours	251,750
Total cost of 17,000 hours	246,500
Variable cost of 1,500 hours	5,250

Variable cost per hour = £5,250/1,500 hours = £3.50.

	£
Total cost of 17,000 hours	246,500
Less variable cost of 17,000 hours (× £3.50)	59,500
Balance = fixed costs	187,000

154   C

The contribution/sales ratio is 20%.

If fixed costs go up by £8,000, the breakeven point will go up by £8,000/20% = £40,000.

Since the sales price is £40 pr unit, the breakeven point would rise by 1,000 units.

155 C

Product	Budgeted sales £	C/S ratio	Budgeted contribution £
J	105,000	40%	42,000
K	315,000	50%	157,500
	420,000		199,500

Weighted average C/S ratio = 199,500/420,000 = 47.5%.

Breakeven point = £120,000/0.475 = £252,632, say £253,000.

156 D

	£
Target profit	150,000
Fixed costs	75,000
Target contribution	225,000
C/S ratio	0.75

Sales required to achieve target contribution (in £) £225,000/0.75 = £300,000.

Sales required to achieve target contribution (in units) = £300,000/£10 per unit = 30,000 units.

157 B

	£
Direct materials	2,500
Direct labour	5,000
Variable production overhead (50% × 1,000)	500
Variable selling costs (80% × 1,250)	1,000
Total variable costs for 500 units	9,000
Sales revenue for 500 units	17,500
Total contribution for 500 units	8,500
Total contribution for 1,000 units (8,500 × 2)	17,000
Fixed production overhead (50% × 1,000)	(500)
Fixed selling costs (20% × 1,250)	(250)
Profit for 1,000 units of sale	16,250

SR – CONT = VBLG.

158 D

	£
Total cost of 350 units	2,800
Subtract increase in fixed costs above 200 units	(500)
Adjusted total cost of 350 units	2,300

	£
Adjusted total cost of 350 units	2,300
Total cost of 150 units	1,500
Variable cost of (350 – 150) 200 units	800

Variable cost per unit = £800/200 = £4

	£
Total cost of 150 units	1,500
Variable cost of 150 units (× £4)	600
Variable cost of (350 – 150) 200 units	900

Cost of 180 units = £900 + (180 × £4) £1,620.

159   **A**

Period 2 overhead costs at period 1 price levels = £321,880/1.04 = £309,500.

	£
Total cost of 18,000 hours at Period 1 prices	309,500
Total cost of 14,000 hours	277,500
Variable cost of 4,000 hours	32,000

Variable cost is £32,000 /4,000 hours = £8 per hour.

160   **A**

Where y = a + bx, we know that:

$$a = \frac{\sum y}{n} - \frac{\sum x}{n}$$

$$= \frac{200}{4} - \frac{17.14(5.75)}{4}$$

$$= 50 - 24.64 = 25.36$$

161   **£10**

x	y	xy	x^2
5	132	660	25
4	127	508	16
6	139	834	36
4	119	476	16
7	153	1,071	49
$\sum x = 26$	$\sum y = 670$	$\sum xy = 3,549$	$\sum x^2 = 142$

Using the formula for regression analysis:

$$b = \frac{5\,(3,549) - (26)(670)}{5\,(142) - (26)(26)}$$

$$= \frac{17,745 - 17,420}{710 - 676}$$

$$= 325/34 = 9.5588, \text{ which is £10 to the nearest £1.}$$

162 £84,000

$$a \quad = \quad \frac{670}{5} - \frac{9.5588(26)}{5}$$

$$= \quad (670 - 249)/5 = (\text{in } £000) \; 84.2 \text{ approximately.}$$

To the nearest £1,000, a = £84,000.

163 £7

x	y	xy	x^2	y^2
1.0	16	16.0	1.00	256
1.5	21	31.5	2.25	441
0.5	14	7.0	0.25	196
1.0	17	17.0	1.00	289
$\Sigma x = 4.0$	$\Sigma y = 68$	$\Sigma xy = 71.5$	$\Sigma x^2 = 4.50$	$\Sigma y^2 = 1,182$

Using the formula for regression analysis:

$$b \quad = \quad \frac{n\Sigma y - \Sigma x \Sigma y}{n\Sigma x^2 - (\Sigma x)^2} = \frac{4(71.5) - 4(68)}{4(4.5) - 4^2}$$

$$= \quad \frac{286 - 272}{18 - 16}$$

$$= \quad 14/2 = £7$$

164 £10

$$a \quad = \quad \frac{68}{4} - \frac{7(4)}{4}$$

$$= \quad 17 - 7 = 10$$

165 0.97

$$r = \frac{4(71.5) - (4)(68)}{\sqrt{[4(4.5) - (4)(4)][4(1,182) - (68)(68)]}}$$

$$= \quad \frac{286 - 272}{\sqrt{(2)(4,728 - 4,624)}}$$

$$= 14/ \sqrt{(2 \times 104)}$$

$$= 14/14.42$$

$$= 0.97$$

A correlation coefficient close to 1.0 indicates a high degree of correlation, suggesting that the formula for estimating fixed and variable costs is likely to be reliable.

166 C

	Before	*After*
Sales price	100	110
Variable cost	60	60
Contribution	40	50

The increase in contribution from 40 to 50 is an increase of 25%.

167   B

Current year:

Variable cost per unit = £50

Sales price = £50 × (100/(100 − 75)) = £200

Contribution per unit = £150.

	£
Total contribution (5,000 units × £150)	750,000
Fixed costs (5,000 units × £70)	350,000
Profit	400,000

Next year:

Sales price = £200 × 1.08 = £216

Variable cost per unit = £50 × 1.12 = £56

Contribution per unit = £160.

	£
Target profit (minimum)	400,000
Fixed costs (350,000 × 1.12)	392,000
Target contribution	792,000

Contribution per unit	£160
Minimum sales required (£792,000/£160)	4,950 units

168   C

	£
Net profit	56,400
Fixed costs	30,000
Contribution	86,400

Contribution/sales ratio	30%
Sales (£86,400/30%)	£288,000
Variable costs (70% of £288,000)	£201,600
Direct wages cost (20% of £201,600)	£40,320

169   C

Answer A would appear as a curve. Answer B would cause an increase in the cost per unit. Answer D is irrelevant as far as the standard costs per unit are concerned, since this would not affect the overheads.

170 C

$$\text{C/S ratio} = \frac{£125,000}{£300,000} = 0.416666$$

$$\text{Break-even revenue} = \frac{£100,000}{0.416666} = £240,000$$

$$\text{Margin of safety} = \frac{300,000 - 240,000}{300,000} = 20\%$$

171 C

Point C is where total revenue exceeds total costs by the largest amount, i.e. where profit is maximised.

172 D

Total fixed cost = £137,500 + £27,500 = £165,000.
Contribution/sales ratio = 275/500 = 55%.
Breakeven sales revenue = Fixed costs/C/S ratio
= £165,000/55% = £300,000.

173 A

Breakeven = 80% of 5,000 units = 4,000 units.
Total contribution at 4,000 units = (4,000 × £25) = £100,000.
Profit at 4,000 units = £0.
Fixed costs are therefore £100,000.

174 B

	£
High: Total cost of 3,000 units	74,000
Low: Total cost of 1,500 units	69,500
Variable cost of 1,500 units	4,500
Variable cost per unit (4,500/1,500)	£3
	£
Total cost of 3,000 units	74,000
Variable cost of 3,000 units (× £3)	9,000
Fixed costs	65,000

Total costs = £65,000 + (£3 × quantity produced)

175 B

Contribution per unit = £26 – £10 = £16.
Break-even point = £50,000/£16 per unit = 3,125 units.

176   B

Materials are a limiting factor (workings not shown).

	Product I	Product II	Product III
Contribution per unit	£35	£25	£48
Materials/unit (kg)	8	5	6
Contribution per kg	£4.75	£5	£8
Priority	3rd	2nd	1st

	Quantity	Materials needed
	units	kg
Product I (special contract)	1,000	8,000
Product III	2,000	12,000
		20,000
Product II (balance)	3,000	15,000
		35,000

177   A

Original contribution = $48 \times 10 + 100 \times 22.50 = £2,730$

Contribution/Labour hour   X : $10 \div 0.5 = £20$ (make first)

Y : $22.50 \div 1.5 = £15$

New contribution = $(48 \times 10) + \dfrac{(150-24)}{1.50} \times 22.50 = £2,370$

Therefore reduction = $£2,730 - £2,370 = £360$.

178   D

Materials requirements for maximum demand

= $(1.5 \times 3,000) + (1 \times 2,000) + (1.25 \times 1,500) + (2 \times 2,500)$

=   13,375 kg of direct materials. There is enough material to meet maximum demand, so materials are not a limiting factor.

Labour requirements for maximum demand

= $(1 \times 3,000) + (1 \times 2,000) + (1.5 \times 1,500) + (1.5 \times 2,500)$

=   11,000 hours.

Labour is a limiting factor, since there are only 10,250 hours available.

Product	L	E	W	S
Contribution per unit	£10	£15	£12	£20
Labour hours per unit	1	1	1.5	1.5
Contribution per labour hour	£10	£15	£8	£13.33
Ranking	3rd	1st	4th	2nd

Production schedule to maximise profit

Product	Hours per unit	Units	Total hours
E	1.0	**2,000**	10,250 (2,000)
			8,250
S	1.5	**2,500**	(3,750)
			4,500
L	1.0	**3,000**	(3,000)
			1,500
W	1.5	**1,000**	(1,500)
			0

179 C

Using the regression analysis formula to find b:
$$\frac{(6 \times 447,250,000) - (13,500 \times 192,000)}{(6 \times 32,125,000) - 13,500^2} = 8.714$$

180 C

Budgeted fixed costs = 1,000 × (£5.80 + £4.60) = £10,400.

Contribution per unit = £(24.90 – 5.60 – 3.40) = £15.90

Breakeven point = £10,400/£15.90 per unit = 654 units.

181 C

$$\text{Break-even number of units} = \frac{\text{Fixed costs}}{\text{Contribution per unit}}$$

If the selling price per unit and the variable cost per unit both rise by 10%, then the contribution per unit also rises by 10%.

Given no change in fixed costs, the break-even number of units will therefore decrease.

182 A

Breakeven point in sales revenue= Fixed costs / Contribution to sales ratio

= £48,000 / 40% = £120,000.

If actual sales = £140,000, then the margin of safety is £20,000 (£140,000 –£120,000) in terms of sales revenue.

Since the selling price is £10 per unit, this is equivalent to 2,000 units.

183 B

		kg
Product I	(2,000 units × 36/6 kg/unit)	12,000
Product II	(1,500 units × 24/6 kg/unit)	6,000
Product III	(4,000 units × 15/6 kg/unit)	10,000
Total materials required		28,000

184 C

$$\text{Break-even number of units} = \frac{\text{Fixed costs}}{\text{Contribution per unit}}$$

If selling price per unit and variable cost per unit fall by 5%, the contribution per unit also falls by 5%.

Given no change in total fixed costs, the break-even number of units will therefore be higher.

185 D

If a sales value of £100 per unit is assumed then the original and revised situations will be:

	Original	Revised
	£	£
Selling price	100	110
Variable cost/unit	60	60
Contribution/unit	40	50

Fixed costs do not affect contribution and if sales volume is unchanged then the overall change in contribution can be measured using the contribution per unit:

$$\frac{(50-40)}{40} = 25\%$$

186 C

Since the company has an objective of **minimising** costs, the potential optimal solutions are those corner points of the feasible area that are closest to the origin of the graph, i.e. D and E.

187 D

Finishing process hours required for production to meet maximum demand

	Units	Minutes per unit	Total minutes
X	4,500	45	202,500
Y	4,500	36	162,000
Z	4,500	25	112,500
			477,000

477,000 minutes = 7,950 hours.

Time is therefore a limiting factor.

	X	Y	Z
Contribution per unit	£10	£9	£6
Minutes per unit	45	36	25
Contribution per minute	£0.222	£0.25	£0.24
Ranking	3rd	1st	2nd

Optimal plan

Product	Units	Minutes
Y	**4,500**	162,000
Z	**4,500**	112,500
		274,500
X (balance: 85,500/45)	**1,900**	85,500
		360,000

188 C

Scarce resource – 7,000 labour hours

	A	B	C
Labour hours per unit	2.5	6	7.5
Contribution per unit	£7	£8	£15
Contribution per labour hour	£2.80	£1.33	£2
Ranking	1st	3rd	2nd

Optimal production plan

Product	Units	Hours
A	**1,000**	2,500
C	**200**	1,500
		4,000
B (balance: 3,000/6)	**500**	3,000
		7,000

189 C

Materials required to meet sales demand = $1,000 \times (1 + 0.5 + 2) = 3,500$ square metres.

Labour required = $1,000 \times (3 + 1 + 1) = 5,000$ hours.

Labour is a limiting factor but materials are not.

	Kilts	Skirts	Dresses
Contribution per unit	£12	£5.50	£7
Contribution per labour hour	£4	£5.50	£7
Ranking	3rd	2nd	1st

Since only 1,000 hours are available, profit will be maximised by making 1,000 dresses.

190 C

Current costs *may* be relevant but only if they are indicative of future costs. Estimated future costs are only relevant if they are cash flows and are expected to occur as a direct consequence of the decision being taken.

191 B

The original cost is irrelevant. The material could be sold now for scrap for £12,500. If reworked, it could be sold for a net £10,000. The incremental effect of reworking is therefore a loss of £2,500.

192 D

Since material R is in regular use and is readily available in the market, its relevant cost is the replacement price of £6 per kg.

The relevant cost of 1,000 kg = 1,000 × £6 per kg = £6,000.

193 D

Only buy those components where the buying price is less than the variable manufacturing cost. This applies only to component T, which has an 'in-house' variable cost of £8, but would cost only £7 to buy in from outside.

194 B

Sunk costs include costs already incurred and committed costs that will be incurred whatever happens. Answer A is therefore not a complete definition of sunk costs, and answer B is correct.

195 B

The manager who would be used as supervisor will be paid his full salary whatever the decision, so the manager's salary is not a relevant cost.

Cost of hiring skilled employees = 4 × £40,000 = £160,000.

Cost of using internal staff = Replacement cost + Training cost = £100,000 + £15,000 = £115,000.

The lower-cost option would be selected, so the relevant cost of the labour for the contract is £115,000 (rather than £160,000).

196 B

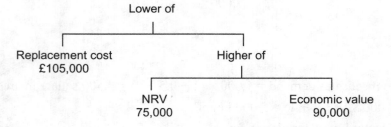

You might prefer to reach the answer logically. The machine will not be replaced, because the net income it can earn is less than its cost. Replacement cost cannot therefore be deprival value. If the machine is used for any other purpose, the company would forgo the net income of £90,000 it would otherwise generate (which is more than it would earn if it were sold for scrap).

197 C

Ignoring the time value of money, the (net) relevant cost before the purchase of the machine is £150,000 + £25,000 – £10,000 = £165,000. However, the relevant cost was £175,000 in year 0 with a scrap value income of £10,000 at the end of year 5. It can also be argued that as the machine has already been purchased, the purchase cost is a sunk cost and so not relevant to any current decision. The question is therefore unsatisfactory, but answer C is the best of the available options.

198 A

The company has no other use for the component. It would cost £50 to modify. Alternatively, the company could buy a new component for £280. It is cheaper to modify the existing component, and the relevant cost (i.e. the future cash flow arising as a consequence of using the component) is the cost of modification.

199 A

Since the materials have no alternative use, they will not be replaced, thus the relevant cost is the scrap proceeds forgone.

200 C

The opportunity cost per unit of material is:

(1)   Replacement cost for material S, since S is in common use

(2)   Scrap value for material T, since T is not in common use and its scrap value is the opportunity cost of using existing stocks to make the new product.

Relevant cost per unit of product:	£
Material S (2 kg × £4.20)	8.40
Material T (3 kg × £0.40)	1.20
	9.60

201 B

Relevant cost of:	£
250 skilled labour hours	
Basic pay (× £10)	2,500
Opportunity cost, contribution forgone (× £12)	3,000
750 semi-skilled hours*	0
	5,500

* Paid anyway, so not a relevant cost.

202 B

The deprival value of a fixed asset is the lower of:

• its replacement cost (£37,000) and

• the higher of its net realisable value from disposal (£11,000) and its economic value in use (£17,500).

Essentially, the deprival value of the asset is its relevant cost. The historical cost is irrelevant. The asset would not be replaced, because replacement cost is more than the asset is worth to the business. The opportunity cost of the asset is the value of its most profitable alternative use, which is on the project to earn £17,500.

203 C

Hours required to meet demand = $(5,000 \times 0.4) + (5,000 \times 0.5) + (2,000 \times 0.75) = 6,000$ hours. Labour is therefore a limiting factor, since only 3,600 hours are available.

	X	Y	Z
Contribution per unit	£24	£25	£30
Hours per unit	0.40	0.50	0.75
Contribution per hour	£60	£50	£40
Ranking	1st	2nd	3rd

Optimal plan	Units	Hours
X	5,000	2,000
Y (balance: 1,600/0.50)	3,200	1,600
		3,600

204 A

A future cost is a relevant cost provided that it is a cash flow arising as a direct consequence of the decision under consideration. Avoidable costs, opportunity costs and differential costs are all examples of relevant costs (relevant future cash flows).

205 B

	X	Y	Z
	£	£	£
Variable cost of manufacture	5	16	10
Cost of external purchase	8	14	11
Gain/(loss) from external purchase	(3)	2	(1)

On the assumption that fixed overhead costs would be unaffected by a decision to switch to external purchasing, WW should consider buying only Product Y externally.

206 D

If you start up in business on your own, you will have to forgo your current salary with the insurance company. Your salary is therefore an opportunity cost of starting up in business.

207 B

Relevant costs	£
Skilled workers: basic pay	
Basic pay	900
Opportunity cost of lost contribution 100 × £7/2 per hour)	350
Semi-skilled: basic pay	1,000
Management cost (zero, as there is spare capacity)	0
Total relevant cost of labour	2,250

208 C

The historical cost of N is irrelevant. The relevant cost of N is its replacement cost, because if units of N are used, they will be replaced.

Relevant costs	£
N: 100 kg × £4 (replacement cost)	400
T:	
Lost scrap proceeds: 200 kg × £4	800
New stocks of T to be purchased: 100 kg × £8	800
Total relevant cost of materials	2,000

209 B

Unavoidable costs are not relevant for decision making, because they will be incurred anyway, regardless of the decision that is taken.

210 B

Specific fixed overheads of the three divisions = 60% of 262,500 = 157,500.

Divided equally between the three divisions, specific fixed overheads of each division are 157,500/3 = 52,500.

	Division A	Division B	Division C	Total
	£000	£000	£000	£000
Contribution	70.0	210.0	30.0	310.0
Specific fixed costs	(52.5)	(52.5)	(52.5)	(157.5)
Profit after specific costs	17.5	157.5	(22.5)	152.5

On the basis of the information given, Division C should be closed down because the contribution it earns is insufficient to cover its specific fixed costs, and total profits would increase by £22,500 as a consequence of its closure.

211 B

Quantity produced = Q

Marginal cost (MC) = variable cost per unit = 5.

Marginal revenue = $30 - 0.5Q$

Profits are maximised when MC = MR:

$5 = 30 - 0.5Q$

$0.5Q = 25$

$Q = 50.$

At this output and sales level:

$P = 30 - 0.25Q$

$P = 30 - 0.25(50) = £17.50.$

212   £22,475

Marginal cost (MC) = variable cost = £2.
Profits are maximised where MC = MR
$2 = 60 - 0.08Q$
$0.08Q = 58$
$Q = 725$.
When Q = 725, the sales price/unit is:
$60 - 0.04Q$
$= 60 - 0.04(725) = 31$.

Profits will be maximised by selling 725 units at £31 each.
Sales revenue will be **£22,475**.

213   C

Target *costing* attempts to achieve a target cost for an item. It is not a pricing strategy. It might be used when developing a new product, for example, when a target cost for the product is set. Achieving a target cost might also be a necessary requirement for having a target *pricing* strategy, but target costing and target pricing are not the same thing.

214   D

Absorption rate = £250,000/12,500 = £20 per direct labour hour.

	£
Variable cost of job	125
Production overhead absorbed (3 hours × £20)	60
	185
Selling and distribution and administration	15
Total cost of the job (= 80/100 of sales)	200
Profit margin (= 20/80 of cost)	50
Sales price	250

215   D

The cost of other products is not normally relevant, although the selling prices of other products is often very relevant.

216   B

A low-price strategy aimed at acquiring a large share of a new target market is known as a penetration pricing strategy.

217   D

Price discrimination is most effective when the two 'markets' in which the two price structures operate can be kept totally separate. Price discrimination on the basis of time, with higher prices at some times of the day or week than at others, is just one example.

218 C

	£
Target profit	150,000
Fixed costs	240,000
Target contribution	390,000
Units to be sold	32,500
	£
Contribution/unit (390,000/32,500)	12
Variable cost/unit	16
Sales price/unit	28

Section 4

ANSWERS TO PRACTICE QUESTIONS

ACCOUNTING FOR MANAGEMENT AND COST ACCOUNTING

1 SWAINSTHORPE LTD

Report

To: Ms Swainsthorpe

From: AN Accountant

Re: **Computerised accounts and stock control**

Date:

The following report addresses the advantages and disadvantages of implementing a computer system. It also explains what a management information system is and how it can be used. Finally it addresses your current stock control procedures.

Computer system

The advantages of a computer system is that it will be quicker to input entries to the accounting system and easier to extract management information. Another advantage is that fewer errors are likely to occur as the computer can check that all the debits equal the credits.

The disadvantages are the expense of the new system. Also the training costs involved may be high and you may also experience some resistance from the employees to this new way of working. Finally you would not be able to switch over immediately as you would have a cost of running two parallel systems for a short time to check that everything is working correctly.

Management Information System (MIS)

A MIS is an accounting system that will provide management with appropriate information both routine and non-routine as required by the organisation. It is expected that management will be able to effectively utilise the output from the system to make efficient use of the resources of the business.

The MIS will help you run the business as it will provide you with relevant information. This information will help with decision-making, planning and control and coordination of the organisation. The type of information extracted will depend on the needs of you, the user.

Stock

The current stock-take procedures seem onerous as they require the business to be closed once a month. This results in a loss of a day's production and so will eventually impact on profit.

If the bin card system is working effectively then an entire stock-take should only be necessary once or twice a year. Instead of a complete stock-take spot checks could be carried High value or high usage items could be checked more often than slower moving stock. In this way the business need not close so often.

ACCA marking scheme	
	Marks
Report format	½
Introduction to report	½
Three advantages of computer system (½ each point)	1½
Three disadvantages of computer system (½ each point)	1½
Definition of an MIS	2
How could it be useful	1
Critical comment on current stock control methods	1½
Suggestion for improvement	1½
Total	10

2 PLANNING

(a) Operational planning

This is often referred to as short term budgeting and looks at the resources, production etc for a financial period, usually a year. It provides a detailed plan of what the organisation hopes will be achieved within the next financial year.

Strategic planning

This is often referred to as the long-term plan and looks at where the organization is heading over a number of years, for example a five-year plan would be a long-term plan. It presents the organisation with an idea of the broad direction that it hopes to be heading in.

The strategic plan will incorporate the operational plans of the organisation. The operational plan translating the strategic plan into achievable short-term goals.

(b) 1   Identify objectives – defines what the organisation hopes to achieve.

2   Look at alternative courses of action – looks at different ways that the goals might be achieved.

3   Evaluate the alternatives using relevant data – look at the information that has been obtained.

4   Select the most appropriate course of action – from information make the best choice to achieve corporate goals.

5   Implement the long term plan in the form of a budget – prepare detailed budget.

6   Monitor actual results – collect data regarding what is actually happening with the organization.

7   Compare actual to planned results – look at actual versus budget and see whether control action needs to be taken.

3 CHOICE OF COST CENTRES

A cost centre is 'a location, function or item(s) of equipment in respect of which costs may be ascertained, and related to cost units, for control purposes.'

The key objective in establishing cost centres is cost control.

The factors influencing the choice of cost centres within a business in order to facilitate cost control are:

(1)   The responsibility of individuals for parts of the organisation. The manager of a cost centre should have control over the operations and costs for which he/she is held responsible.

(2)   The extent to which costs can be attributed to particular areas of activity. Cost centres have traditionally been departments within an organisation. However, if two departments share a large amount of joint costs, it would be inappropriate to establish each department as a cost centre. In activity based costing, cost centres might be based on activities that span several departments.

(3)   The size of the organisation. As a general rule, smaller organisations will have fewer cost centres than larger organisations.

(4)   The effect on the 'accuracy' of apportioning indirect costs to production cost centres/production units. When cost centres are overhead operations, the costs of each cost centre will be apportioned to production departments/revenue-earning departments, and the choice of cost centres could affect the 'accuracy' of the overhead apportionment.

4   COMPUTER PACKAGES

Key answer tips

Discuss packages first and then their uses – try and be general rather than writing all you know about a particular computer package – the question is looking for their use in general.

Computerised financial planning packages provide mathematical statements of the relationships between all operating and financial activities within an organisation, as well as other major internal and external factors that may affect financial performance. Packages come in varying degrees of sophistication. The most simple are used to produce standard financial statements and supporting schedules from specific company data input. These packages are applicable to companies in general. At the other end of the spectrum are specially-written financial models designed for the specific company in question. Sophisticated models include interactive capabilities and integrate the detailed activities of all sub-units of an organisation. They also provide for probabilistic/risk analysis and sensitivity analysis to be carried out.

An obvious application for computerised financial planning packages is in the preparation of budgets. The quotation states that the packages have 'revolutionised the process of budget preparation'. Whether they have revolutionised or merely 'helped' is a subjective argument, but nobody can deny that they have made a difference. The packages can make computations, based on data input such as product selling prices, variable cost, type of expense, etc, very quickly and produce a number of different statements from the database. The packages will also greatly assist in budget revisions and assessment of the effects (financial) resulting from the various courses of action that may be open to management. Statistical techniques such as sensitivity analysis may also be easily incorporated into the budget preparation.

Packages therefore speed up the budgeting process and provide information for risk analysis and the assessment of alternative planning options.

These packages can certainly help with tasks that are time-consuming when undertaken manually, but to say they have 'revolutionised' budgeting may be an unfair assessment.

5   **COST INFORMATION**

Key answer tips

Note the different requirements of this question and be sure you answer them all.

Cost accounting information serves three main purposes.

1   *To help with planning decisions*

Planning for the future is a vital management function. Cost accounting can provide information about estimated future costs and revenues which will form the basis of financial planning. Cost information may be provided about operating at different volumes of output; or the costs and revenues resulting from acceptance of a special contract may be provided. Without this cost accounting information, budgets could not be prepared.

2   *To facilitate control*

Financial control is typically exercised by means of a comparison between budgeted costs and revenues and actual costs and revenues; significant differences between the two ('variances') are investigated and appropriate control action is taken. Cost accounting information will provide both the actual figures and the budgeted figures against which actuals are compared. For example, the actual cost and usage of raw materials in production may be compared with budget, and the reasons for any significant differences in price and usage investigated.

3   *To facilitate performance measurement*

Cost accounting information also forms an important element of performance evaluation procedures. For example, we may wish to know whether a particular cost centre has achieved its budgeted output for the period; or whether the business as a whole has exceeded budgeted profit.

Two differences between cost and financial accounting are that:

- Cost accounting information may be future orientated. For example, plans and decisions relate to the future, so information for these purposes must be forward-looking. Financial accounting is predominantly historical in nature.

- Financial accounting is concerned with the stewardship of assets and with external reporting of the organisation's financial results, whereas cost accounting is concerned with 'internal' management information, to assist management with planning and control decisions, and with monitoring performance.

6   **CHARACTERISTICS**

Key answer tips

Name the characteristic – but then fully explain it to maximise your marks – bullet points only gain a few marks.

(a)   Three characteristics of useful information are:

1   **Objective**. There should not be any bias in the information due to the way it has been produced or presented. For example, use of absorption costing to calculate profit for a period during which sales are constant but production is rising, may

give a misleading impression of profitability simply because of the method of calculation.

2   **Timely**. The information must be produced in time for some action to be taken on it. If it is too late, it is worthless. For example, it would be of little value in the context of controlling costs if a business used year-end published accounts for comparison with budget: by the time published accounts are available, it will be too late for any effective control action to be taken.

3   **Appropriate to the purpose**. Information must be suitable for the purpose for which it is produced. The level of detail, for example, can vary according to the user's needs. The Managing Director will not require a detailed analysis of direct labour booked to individual jobs - a summary of direct labour costs will be sufficient; however, production scheduling and supervision would be particularly interested in such information.

Note: Other characteristics could be quoted.

(b)   Non-financial information, such as the number of idle direct labour hours, or kilograms of material lost in a process, is important for two main reasons:

•   It supplements financial information: the number of idle hours may be as important as their cost.

•   It may have more immediate relevance to certain staff: reporting the number of kilograms lost in a process above normal may have more meaning to workers directly involved with operating that process than the cost of the abnormal loss.

7   COST CLASSIFICATIONS

Key answer tips

Easy marks are available from learning key definitions such as those given in this question.

(a)   '**Avoidable**' costs are costs that would not be incurred if a particular decision is taken, but would be incurred otherwise. Whether or not avoidable costs will arise therefore depends on the course of action chosen from alternatives which are under consideration. '**Unavoidable**' costs are costs that will be incurred regardless of the course of action chosen.

For example, a manufacturing company may be considering whether to continue to manufacture, or instead to buy-in, one of the many components that it currently produces in its factory.

Many of the costs incurred in the factory will be unavoidable whichever of the alternatives is chosen because the factory will continue to be used for the production of many other components. Examples of such costs would be rent and rates of the factory and the factory manager's salary.

However, other costs may be avoidable (or at least partly avoidable) according to the alternative chosen. Examples of completely avoidable costs in such a situation are the bought-in cost of the component and the material costs incurred in its manufacture. Avoidable costs are relevant to the decision between alternatives, whereas unavoidable costs are not.

(b)   A **cost centre** is an area of a business (a department, location, or item of equipment) in relation to which costs may be ascertained for the purposes of cost control and product costing. Separate production and service departments in a factory may each be a cost centre for example. Alternatively, a department may consist of more than one cost centre where costs may be separately ascertained for each cost centre and an individual held responsible for the costs in each case.

A **cost unit** is a quantitative unit of product or service in relation to which costs are ascertained. In manufacturing, cost units will be units of output produced within production cost centres. If the manufacturing unit is operating on a job order basis, the cost unit will be individual jobs for particular customers. If the manufacturing unit is a continuous production process with output of homogeneous product, the cost unit will be a standardised quantity of output expressed in terms of units, weight or volume (e.g. cost per kg of manufactured output). Similarly, in a service environment (business or cost centre) costs may be related either to individual jobs or per unit of service (e.g. cost per hour of service).

ELEMENTS OF COST

MATERIALS

8 WIVELSFIELD

(a) (***Tutorial note***: The current (pre-discount) EOQ is 200, and with the discount the EOQ will be higher than this. This means that the calculation of the new EOQ should be made using the assumption that there will be a 3% discount.)

$$EOQ \text{ new} = \sqrt{\frac{2 \times 2 \times 15,000}{15 \times 97\% \times 10\%}} = 203 \text{ units}$$

The optimal reorder level that minimises total costs is either the EOQ or the minimum order quantity required to obtain a higher bulk purchase discount, which in this problem is 500 units or 700 units. The total costs of ordering 203 units, 500 units and 700 units should therefore be compared.

Total costs are the sum of purchasing costs, order costs and stock holding costs.

Order quantity Q	Purchase costs pD	Order costs $Co \times D/Q$	Holding costs $Q \times Ch/2$
203	$15 \times 97\% \times 15,000$	$\dfrac{2 \times 15,000}{203}$	$(15 \times 97\% \times 10\%) \times \dfrac{203}{2}$
	$= £218,250$	$= £148$	$= £148$
500	$15 \times 95\% \times 15,000$	$\dfrac{2 \times 15,000}{500}$	$(15 \times 95\% \times 10\%) \times \dfrac{500}{2}$
	$= £213,750$	$= £60$	$= £356$
700	$15 \times 93\% \times 15,000$	$\dfrac{2 \times 15,000}{700}$	$(15 \times 93\% \times 10\%) \times \dfrac{700}{2}$
	$= £209,250$	$= £43$	$= £488$

Total cost of ordering in batches of 203 units = £218,250 + £148 + £148 = £218,546.

Total cost of ordering in batches of 500 units = £213,750 + £60 + £356 = £214,166.

Total cost of ordering in batches of 700 units = £209,250 + £43 + £488 = £209,781.

The best option is to order 700 units at a time, as this results in the lowest total cost.

(b)   The discount band of 0 – 199 units has been ignored as this is below the current EOQ. The EOQ was recalculated as it is now subject to a discount. For all the other discount bands the revised stock costs were calculated taking into account the new purchase price.

ACCA marking scheme		
		Marks
(a)	Recalculation of EOQ with discount	1.0
	Calculation of:	
	- Purchase cost at 203 units	0.5
	- Order cost at 203 units	0.5
	- Holding cost at 203 units	0.5
	- Purchase cost at 203 units	0.5
	- Order cost at 203 units	0.5
	- Holding cost at 203 units	0.5
	- Purchase cost at 203 units	0.5
	- Order cost at 203 units	0.5
	- Holding cost at 203 units	0.5
	Conclusion regarding best option	0.5
(b)	Statement regarding lowest price band ignored	2.0
	Statement regarding upper price bands	2.0
Total		10.0

9   MATERIAL Z

(a)   **Stockholding costs include the costs of:**

- Insurance of items held in stock

- Interest on the investment in stocks held

- Stores handling costs

- The cost of storage space

- The costs of damage to inventory

- The costs of deterioration and obsolescence.

These costs might be controlled in the following ways:

- Insurance costs could be controlled by seeking quotations from different insurance companies to find the cheapest quotation, and also by controlling the losses that give rise to insurance claims (since a lower history of losses should result in lower insurance premiums).

- Minimising stock levels, subject to ordering stock in economic order quantities and holding the required buffer stock).

- Careful planning of stores locations, to minimise stores handling and damage.

- Setting targets for expenditure in relation to the level of stock held, and monitoring actual costs with reference to target costs.

- Maximising the use of stores space through investment in appropriate storage equipment (e.g. storage units, fork-lift trucks and so on).

(b) **Production requirements**

	Product A	Product B
Sales (units)	24,600	9,720
Stock increase	447	178
Production net of rejects (units)	25,047	9,898
	/0.99	/0.98
Production before rejects (units)	25,300	10,100
Material usage (net of wastage)	1.8 kg per unit	3.0 kg per unit
Total materials used (net of wastage)	45,540 kg	30,300 kg
	/0.95	/0.89
Total material Z required (before wastage)	47,937 kg	34,045kg

Total material Z required (before wastage) = (47,937 + 34,045)kg = 81,982 kg.

Economic order quantity

$$\sqrt{\frac{2 \times 30 \times 81,982}{18\% \,of\, £3.50}}$$

$$\sqrt{7,799,238}$$

= 2,793 kg.

(c) Average stock investment (in kg) = (2,793/2) + 1,000 buffer stock

= 2,397 kg.

Cost per kg = £3.50

Value of average stock investment = 2,397 × £3.50 = £8,390.

Annual stock-holding costs = £8,390 × 18% = £1,510

10 EOQ

Key answer tips

Beware of confusing units and boxes, and don't adjust the purchase quantity for safety stock. The EOQ must not be stated in £s or number of orders.

Economic order quantity (EOQ) formula:

$$EOQ = \sqrt{\frac{2CD}{H}}$$

Order cost (C) = $\frac{5,910}{30}$ × 1.02 = £200.94 per order

Demand (D) = 90,800 units

Holding cost (H) = £20 per unit × 15% = £3.00 per unit

$$EOQ = \sqrt{\frac{2 \times 200.94 \times 90,800}{3.0}} = 3,488 \text{ units (349 boxes)}$$

Number of orders each year = 9,080 boxes/349 = 26 orders.

Ordering frequency = 52 weeks ÷ 26 (annual orders) = every two weeks.

11 MATERIALS ISSUED

Key answer tips

The question asks you to discuss stocktaking (a physical activity) and inventory – a written record – be careful not to confuse the two. The layout for (b) is important – be sure your table shows the changes in the stock level, valuation per kg and total value. You can show receipts, issues and balance of physical quantities in one column or in separate columns. The important thing is to be able to show after each receipt, the total quantity and value of stock held. This is used to calculate the new weighted average value, which should also be shown in the table. This will then be used to value all subsequent issues, until the next receipt arises.

(a)   (i)   **Continuous stocktaking** refers to a system whereby stocktaking is carried out on an ongoing rota basis throughout the year, so that every stock item is checked at least once. Items of greater value or importance may be counted several times during the year. As a result, stocktaking effort can be directed so as to maximise control and minimise costs. In contrast to periodic stocktaking it also avoids disruption to production.

(ii)   **Perpetual inventory** is a system of entering details of all stock receipts and issues for each individual raw material/finished product onto a record card, thus enabling the stock quantity on hand to be known at any time. The stock quantity provides the necessary information for stock re-ordering and for verifying/reconciling physical stock counts.

(b)

	3,040 kgs	×	£0.765/kg	=	£2,325.60
Day 1	1,400 kgs	×	0.780/kg	=	1,092.00
	4,440 kgs*	×	0.770/kg	=	3,417.60
Day 2	(1,700) kgs	×	0.770/kg	=	(1,309.00)
	2,740 kgs	×	0.770/kg	=	2,108.60
Day 3	60 kgs	×	0.770/kg	=	46.20
Day 4	(220) kgs	×	0.780/kg	=	(171.60)
Day 4	1,630 kgs	×	0.778 /kg	=	1,268.14
	4,210 kgs*	×	0.772/kg	=	3,251.34
Day 5	(1,250) kgs	×	0.772/kg	=	(965.00)
	2,960 kgs	×	0.772/kg	=	£2,286.34

* Calculate a new weighted average price with each new purchase or each return to the supplier.

12 RETAIL STOCK CONTROL

Tutorial note: The maximum control level is the stock level that should never be exceeded.

Re-order level = Maximum usage × Maximum lead time.

Maximum control level = [Re-order level + EOQ – (Minimum usage × Minimum lead time)]

(i)   Cost of sales % = 100% - gross margin %.

Weekly cost of sales (£000)

Item		Minimum		Maximum
14/363	(58% × 26,000)	15,080	(58% × 30,000)	17,400
11/175	(54% × 130,000)	70,200	(54% × 160,000)	86,400
14/243	(63% × 60,000)	37,800	(63% × 128,000)	80,640

Weekly sales units

Item		Minimum		Maximum
		units		units
14/363	(£15,080/£2.25)	6,702	(£17,400/£2.25)	7,733
11/175	(£70,200/£0.36)	195,000	(£86,400/£0.36)	240,000
14/243	(£37,800/£0.87)	43,448	(£80,640/£0.87)	92,690

(ii)   **Re-order level**

Since the re-order lead time of two weeks can be relied on, the reorder level to avoid stock-outs is twice the maximum weekly usage quantities.

Item 14/363: = 7,733 × 2 = 15,466 units

Item 11/175: = 240,000 × 2 = 480,000 units

Item 14/243: = 92,690 × 2 = 185,380 units

(iii) **Maximum control level**

Item 14/363: = [15,466 + 25,000 – (6,702 × 2)] = 27,062 units

Item 11/175: = [480,000 + 500,000 – (195,000 × 2)] = 590,000 units

Item 14/243: = [185,380 + 250,000 – (43,448 × 2)] = 348,484 units.

13   EOQ OF COMPONENT

(a)   **EOQ formula**:

$$EOQ = \sqrt{\frac{2C_oD}{C_H}}$$

$$= \sqrt{\frac{2 \times 65 \times 2,600}{4 \times 0.2}}$$

= 650 units

(b)   (i)   **Weighted average price (periodic weighted average):**

Units	Price (£/unit)	Value (£)
228		401.810
320	1.778	568.960
275	1.785	490.875
823		1,461.645

£1,461.645/823 units = £1.776 per unit.

Amount charged to production:

= Usage 494 units × £1.776/unit

= £877.34

(ii) *FIFO*:

With FIFO, the 494 units used are assumed to consist of the opening stock at the start of the period (228 units) and the remainder (266 units) are units purchased on Day 4. Closing stock is therefore the remaining 54 units purchased on Day 4 and all 275 units purchased on Day 15.

Closing stock value =

	£
54 units × £1.778/unit	96.01
+ 275 units × £1.785/unit	490.88
Closing stock value (329 units*)	**£586.89**

*228 + 320 + 275 – 494 = 329

LABOUR

14 LABOUR COSTS

(a) (i) **Idle time** is time paid for that is non-productive time. It can be important for management to monitor the amount of idle time, to find out why it might be excessive, and take any suitable measures to keep idle time under control. A system for recording the amount of idle time incurred should be in place.

There are several possible causes of idle time, such as machine breakdowns, poor scheduling of work flow and lack of production orders/sales demand. Idle time could be either avoidable or unavoidable, depending on its cause.

- If idle time is unavoidable, the cost of idle time is usually treated as an overhead cost and so apportioned to all production output as apart of the normal cost.

- If idle time is avoidable, its cost might be charged directly to the profit and loss account as a loss for the period, instead of treated as an overhead and added to product costs.

(ii) **Overtime** is time worked in excess of normal basic hours of work, and it is usually paid for at a rate above the normal basic rate of pay. The difference between the overtime rate of pay and the basic rate of pay is called the overtime premium. Overtime could be worked either for a specific job/customer order (to complete the job as quickly as possible), or because the volume of demand is so high that overtime is necessary to met the demand.

The basic rate of pay for hours worked in overtime by direct labour employees should be treated as a direct labour cost. Overtime premium will generally be treated as an overhead cost, on the assumption that the overtime hours are worked to meet a high volume of demand. In exceptional cases, where overtime is worked for a specific customer, the overtime premium might be charged as a direct cost of the order/job. In very exceptional cases, where overtime hours should have been avoided, the cost of overtime premium might be charged directly to the profit and loss account as a special charge (i.e. loss) for the period.

(b) (i) *Wages paid (before share of group bonus)*

	Direct labour employees		Indirect labour employees	
Normal hours	(12 × 37)	444	(3 × 37)	111
Therefore overtime hours	(488 – 444)	44	(121 – 111)	10
		£		£
Hours at basic rate	(488 × £7.50)	3,660	(121 × £6)	726
Overtime premium	(44 × £2.50)	110	(10 × £2)	20
		3,770		746

(ii) *Analysis of wages*

The idle time and training time for direct labour workers are treated as an indirect labour cost.

	Direct labour cost		Indirect labour cost	
		£		£
Direct workers:				
Hours at basic rate	(432 hrs × £7.50)	3,240	(56 hrs × £7.50)	420
Overtime premium				110
Indirect workers:				
Hours at basic rate				726
Overtime premium				20
Group bonus				520
		3,240		1,796

(iii) It is assumed that the efficiency ratio includes idle time within the measure of efficiency/inefficiency.

$$\text{Efficiency ratio} = \frac{\text{Expected hours to produce actual output}}{\text{Actual hours taken}} \times 100\%$$

$$\text{Efficiency ratio} = \frac{470}{(470 + 32)} \times 100\% = 101\%$$

15 EARNINGS

(a) **Earnings**

2000 = £150 (given in the question)

2001 = £150 ×1.05 = £157.5

2002 = £157.5 ×1.03 = £162.2

2003 = £162.2 ×1.04 = £168.7

(b)

Year	(i) RPI	(ii) AEI
2000	162.2 = 150 × (170.3/157.5)	172.8 = 150 × (124.4/108)
2001	164.7 = 157.5 × (170.3/162.9)	172.6 = 157.5 × (124.4/113.5)
2002	167.0 = 162.2 × (170.3/165.4)	169.6 = 162.2 × (124.4/119)
2003	168.7 = 168.7 × (170.3/170.3)	168.7 = 168.7 × (124.4/124.4)

(c) Using the RPI shows that Jim has had a real increase in his wages over the four-year period.

Using the AEI shows that Jim has actually seen a reduction in his earnings compared to the average wages earned by workers generally.

(d) 1998 is the base year for the Average Earnings Index. This means that all figures are compared to the average earnings in that year.

ACCA marking scheme		
		Marks
(a)	Noting Jim's wages for 2000	0.5
	Calculating the figure for 2001	0.5
	Calculating the figure for 2002	0.5
	Calculating the figure for 2003	0.5
		2
(b)	Calculating the wage figures adjusted for the RPI for:	
	2000	0.5
	2001	0.5
	2002	0.5
	2003	0.5
	Calculating the wage figure adjusted for the AEI for:	
	2000	0.5
	2001	0.5
	2002	0.5
	2003	0.5
		4
(c)	Comment on Jim's wages compared to the:	
	RPI	1.0
	AEI	1.0
		2
(d)	Mentioning the words 'base period'	1.0
	Explaining what this means	1.0
		2
Total		10

16 KL LTD

Key answer tips

Be sure to use the formula given and don't forget that marks can be obtained for comments even if you have not done the calculations.

(a)   Employee 0035/A took 44 hours to perform 94 operations. The standard time allowed per operation is 37.5 minutes, giving a standard time of $(94 \times [37.5/60]) = 58.75$ hours to perform 94 operations. The time saved is therefore $(58.75 - 44) = 14.75$ hours. The bonus payable will be:

(time taken/time allowed) $\times$ time saved $\times$ hourly rate

$= (44/58.75) \times 14.75 \times £6.50 = £71.80$ (rounded).

The gross wage for Week 24 will therefore be:

(44 hours $\times$ £6.50) + £71.80 = £357.80.

(b)   In Week 23, Employee 0035/A took 41 hours to perform 87 operations. The standard time per operation is 37.5 minutes, so the standard time allowed for 87 operations is $(87 \times [37.5/60]) = 54.375$ hours.

Efficiency ratio = (time allowed/time taken) $\times$ 100%.

For Week 23, this is $(54.375/41) \times 100\% = 133\%$ (rounded).

For Week 24: $(58.75/44) \times 100\% = 134\%$ (rounded).

Alternatively, the efficiency ratios could have been calculated as:

(actual units/target units) $\times$ 100%.

In this example, 'units' will equate with operations. Target units per hour = $(60/37.5)$ = 1.6. So target units in Week 23 were (41 hours $\times$ 1.6) = 65.6; and in Week 24, target units were (44 $\times$ 1.6) = 70.4.

Efficiency ratio: Week 23 $(87/65.6) \times 100\% = 133\%$.

Week 24 $(94/70.4) \times 100\% = 134\%$.

Tutorial note: You should take care in calculating efficiency ratios. Make sure numerator and denominator are correct.

Comment

There has been little improvement in efficiency between the two weeks (133% in Week 23 rising to 134% in Week 24). It may be that some time will be required for the incentive aspect of the bonus scheme to improve efficiency. Or perhaps the standard time per operation has been set so tight that little room for real improvement exists. It may even be that employees are concerned about the implications for future employment of the new bonus system: if productivity improves markedly, will redundancies result?

(c)   One advantage of a piece rate coupled with a lower rate per hour might be:

- It will avoid the necessity to calculate standard timings for tasks: the output-related part of pay under this type of approach would be linked solely to the volume of output, rather than to volume and time taken. Setting standard timings which the workforce will agree to may be problematic, so such a system may avoid potential disputes over standard timings and may be easier to administer.

One disadvantage might be:

- Quality of output may suffer. As employees try to increase output volume, the quality of work might suffer as a consequence. If this is likely to happen, the company may incur extra 'quality costs' associated with additional inspection of output, additional wastage and (possibly) higher returns of goods by customers.

OVERHEADS

17   SERVICE AND PRODUCTION CENTRES

A service centre is a department that does not directly produce units but is required to support the other departments. Examples include maintenance departments, stores or a canteen.

A production centre is a centre where units are actually made, examples being a machining department or a welding department.

Although a service will have overheads allocated and apportioned to it, these will be reapportioned to the production centers so that, at the end of a period, all overheads are included in the production centres only. Once all the overheads are included in the production centres they can be absorbed into production.

ACCA marking scheme	
Definition of a service centre	1
Example of a service centre	1
Definition of a production centre	1
Example of a production centre	1
Explanation of the differing treatments of overheads:	2
Total	6

18   WARNINGLID

(a)

	Basis of apportionment	Total cost	Dept 1	Dept 2	S	M
		£	£	£	£	£
Rent	floor space	12,000	8,850	2,100	600	450
Heat and light	cubic capacity	6,000	4,320	1,200	240	240
Welfare	employee numbers	2,000	1,120	480	240	160
Supervisors	direct allocation	2,500	1,500	1,000	-	-
		22,500	15,790	4,780	1,080	850

(b)   Let the total amount of overheads apportioned from the Stores division be S.

Let the total amount of overheads apportioned from the Maintenance division be M.

(1) $S = 1,080 + 0.05M$

(2) $M = 850 + 0.10S$

Substitute equation (2) in equation (1)

(3) $S = 1,080 + 0.05(850 + 0.10S)$

$S = 1,080 + 42.5 + 0.005S$

$0.095S = 1,122.5$

$S = 1,128$

Substitute in equation (2)

$M = 850 + 0.10(1,128)$

$M = 963$

Apportion to Production Department 1

$15{,}790 + 0.50S + 0.45M$

$= 15{,}790 + 0.50(1{,}128) + 0.45(963)$

$= 15{,}790 + 564 + 433$

$= £16{,}787$.

Apportion to Production Department 2

$4{,}780 + 0.40S + 0.50M$

$= 4{,}780 + 0.40(1{,}128) + 0.50(963)$

$= 4{,}780 + 451 + 482$

$= £5{,}713$.

Note: The repeated distribution method would also be acceptable as a method of reaching the same answer.

(c) **Production department 1** is a labour-intensive department and overheads should therefore be absorbed on a direct labour hour basis.

Tutorial note: Overheads would normally be absorbed on the basis of budgeted overheads and budgeted activity levels, but the question here clearly expects your answer to be based on actual costs and actual hours.

Absorption rate = Overheads/Labour hours

= £16,787/2,400 = **£6.995/direct labour hour (round to £7 /direct labour hour)**..

Production department 2 is a machine-intensive department, and overheads are therefore it is more appropriate to absorb overheads on the basis of machine hours worked.

Absorption rate = Overheads/Machine hours

= £5,713/4,570 = **£1.25/machine hour**.

ACCA marking scheme		
		Marks
(a)	Stating basis of allocation and apportionment	1.0
	Allocation/apportionment of:	
	- Rent	0.5
	- Heat and light	0.5
	- Welfare	0.5
	- Supervisors	0.5
(b)	Equation for the total cost apportioned from Stores	0.5
	Equation for the total cost apportioned from Maintenance	0.5
	Solution of simultaneous equations	2.0
	Re-apportionment	1.0
(c)	Labour hour basis for department 1	0.5
	Calculation of overhead absorption rate	1.0
	Machine hour basis for department 2	0.5
	Calculation of overhead absorption rate	1.0
Total		10.0

19   TWO PRODUCTION COST CENTRES

(a)

	Department A £	Department B £
Allocated overhead costs	217,860	374,450
Apportioned overhead costs	45,150	58,820
Total production overhead costs	263,010	433,270
Budgeted machine hours	13,370	16,110
Absorption rate per machine hour	£19.16	£26.89

(b)   70% of Department C costs = £72,278. These are apportioned between departments A and B in the ratio 13,672:16,953 (i.e. at £2.36 per machine hour).

30% of Department C costs = £30,976. These are apportioned between departments A and B in the ratio 16,402:27,568 (i.e. at £0.70448 per direct labour hour).

	Department A £	Department B £
Allocated overhead costs	219,917	387,181
70% of C costs apportioned =	32,267	40,011
30% of C costs apportioned =	11,555	19,421
Total overhead costs	263,739	446,613

		Dept A £		Dept B £
Overhead absorbed	(13,672 × £19.16)	261,956	(16,953 × £26.89)	455,866
Overhead incurred	(see above)	263,739		446,613
Overhead over/(under) absorbed		(1,783)		9,253

(c)   The repeated distribution method might be applied when there is more than one service department, and each service department provides services to other service departments as well as to production departments. In other words, the service departments provide reciprocal services.

The repeated distribution method of service department overhead cost apportionment to production centres is intended to provide a more fair allocation of the service department costs.

The costs of each service department are apportioned in turn (and on a fair basis) to every other department that uses its services, including other service departments. This will leave some overhead costs re-apportioned to service departments. Taking each service department in turn again, their re-apportioned overheads are apportioned once more. This process of overhead distribution is repeated over and over again until no more costs are apportioned to the service departments, and all the costs have been apportioned to the production departments.

20   COST CENTRES

(a)

	£
Budget	
Apportioned costs	74,610
Directly incurred costs	98,328
Budgeted fixed overhead expenditure	172,938
Budgeted machine hours	1,900
Budgeted absorption rate per machine hour (£172,938/1,900 hours)	£91.02

(b)

	£	
Budgeted fixed overhead expenditure	172,938	
Fixed overhead volume variance	4,551	(F)
Absorbed fixed overheads	177,489	
Absorption rate per machine hour	£91.02	
Machine hours actually worked	1,950 hrs	

(c)

	£
Actual fixed overhead expenditure	173,732
Absorbed fixed overheads	177,489
Over-absorbed fixed overheads	3,757

21   A, B AND C

Key answer tips

When this was set in the exam the main areas where marks were lost were:

- the balancing overheads were ignored, incorrectly calculated, or not apportioned as instructed in the question
- service department overheads were not reapportioned
- labour and machine hours were calculated incorrectly.

(a)

	Production department			Service dept	Total
	A	*B*	*C*		
	£	£	£	£	£
Direct	261,745	226,120	93,890	53,305	635,060
Apportioned *	135,400	118,475	67,700	16,925	338,500
Service dept apportionment	23,410	23,410	23,410	(70,230)	-
	420,555	368,005	185,000	0	973,560

(* Total apportioned = £973,560 – 635,060 = £338,500).

Activity level (see note)	÷ 17,760	÷ 5,760	÷ 148,000
Absorption rate	= £23.68	= 63.89	= £1.25
	per direct labour hour	per machine hour	per unit

Note: Activity levels for calculating the overhead absorption rates

Department A direct labour hours = $10 \times 37 \times 48 = 17,760$.

Department B machine hours = $5 \times 24 \times 48 = 5,760$.

Department C units = 148,000.

(b)

		£
Dept A	9 direct labour hours at £23.68	213.12
Dept B	3 machine hours at £63.89	191.67
Dept C	100 units at £1.25	125.00
Manufacturing overhead for 100 units		529.79
		÷ 100 units
Manufacturing overhead per unit		£5.30

22   SOLICITORS' COSTING

Key answer tips

(a)   Here, you are asked to unravel the existing system, working back from actual data to budgeted – this requires a good grasp of the computation of absorption rates and over/under absorption. Note, however, that the remaining parts of the question do not rely on you having done this part, and are more straightforward. So if you struggled with this, good exam technique would tell you to move on and get the easier marks in later parts.

(b)   A little thought is needed here to account for the 40% premium on the senior staff rate - it is easy to end up with rates that don't achieve the right overall absorption. But you would certainly get some marks for ignoring this premium and carrying out the normal calculation.

(a)   (i)   Budgeted professional staff hours (year to 31.3.X6):

Actual overheads	£742,600
+ Overheads over-absorbed	4,760
Overheads absorbed	£747,360
Divide by absorption rate per hour = £7.50/hr	
= Actual professional staff hours worked	99,648
Hours over budget	(1,360)
Budgeted professional staff hours	98,288

(ii)   Budgeted overhead expenditure (year to 31.3.X6);

      Budgeted professional staff hours   98,288

      × £7.50 (absorption rate per hour)

      = **Budgeted overhead expenditure**   £737,160

(b)   **Overhead absorption rates (year to 31.3.X7):**

Budgeted hours	Weighting	Adjusted hours
21,600	1.4	30,240
79,300	1.0	79,300
		109,540

Split of overheads:

$$\text{Senior staff} = 784,000 \times \frac{£30,240}{109,540} = \qquad £216,434$$

$$\text{Junior staff} = 784,000 \times \frac{£79,300}{109,540} = \qquad £567,566$$

$$£784,000$$

Absorption rates:

$$\text{Senior staff:} \ \frac{216,434}{21,600} = £10.020 \text{ per hour}$$

$$\text{Junior staff:} \ \frac{567,566}{79,300} = £7.157 \text{ per hour}$$

23   DIVISIONS A AND B

(a)   (i)   **Overhead absorption rates**:

$$\text{Machining} = \frac{£256,200}{4,200 \text{ m/ch}} = £61.00 \text{ per machine hour}$$

$$\text{Welding} = \frac{£168,100}{15,500 \text{ dlh}} = £10.85 \text{ per direct labour hour}$$

	£	£
Job No 1763:		
Materials (16,740 + 264)		17,004
Direct labour		
440 × £8 =	3,520	
726 × £10 =	7,260	
		10,780
Production overhead:		
293 machine hours × £61.00 =	17,873	
726 d. labour hours × £10.85 =	7,877	
		25,750
		53,534

(ii) **Plant-wide overhead absorption rate**:

Total plant-wide budgeted overheads = £256,200 + £168,100 = £424,300.

Plant-wide budgeted direct labour hours = 8,100 + 15,500 = 23,600 hours.

Plant-wide absorption rate = $\dfrac{£424,300}{23,600 \text{ dlh}}$ = £17.98 per direct labour hour

Job number 1763:	£
Materials (as above)	17,004
Direct labour (as above)	10,780
Production overhead: 1,166 hours × 17.98 =	20,965
	48,749

(b) Total direct labour hours worked = 8,296 + 15,109 = 23,405 hours.

Overhead absorbed = 23,405 hours × £17.98/hr

= £420,822.

Overhead expenditure incurred = £47,440 + £203,740 + £172,838 = £424,018.

Under-absorbed overhead = £424,018 – £420,822 = **£3,196.**

(Tutorial note: Overhead is under-absorbed because absorbed overhead is less than actual overhead expenditure incurred.)

24 HOTEL

Tutorial note: The repeated distribution method is used to answer part (a), although you might prefer to use the reciprocal method (simultaneous equations). This should give you the same answer.

(a) **Overhead cost apportionment**

	Bedrooms	Catering	Meetings	Gen Admin	Dom. Serv.
	£	£	£	£	£
Hotel occupancy	657,172	78,861	113,910	17,525	8,762
Allocated costs				167,255	155,108
				184,780	163,870
Apportion:					
General Admin (1)	55,434	55,434	55,434	(184,780)	18,478
					182,348
Dom Services (2)	109,409	25,529	41,940	5,470	(182,348)
General Admin (3)	1,641	1,641	1,641	(5,470)	547
Dom Services (4)	338	79	130		(547)
	823,994	161,544	213,055		

Notes:	1	Apportionment	30 : 30 : 30 : 10
	2	Apportionment	60 : 14 : 23 : 3
	3	Apportionment	30 : 30 : 30 : 10
	4	Apportionment	60 : 14: 23 (rounded)

(b)   **Trading performance**

	Bedrooms £	Catering £	Meetings £	Total £
Sales	1,125,718	601,180	293,100	2,019,998
Direct costs	120,979	448,479	63,228	632,686
Overheads	823,994	161,544	213,055	1,198,593
Total costs	944,973	610,023	276,283	1,831,279
Profit/(loss)	180,745	(8,843)	16,817	188,719
Sales less direct costs (= margin)	1,004,739	152,701	229,872	
Margin as % of sales	89.3%	25.4%	78.4%	

(c)   **Comments on trading performance**

- The Catering operations made a loss and failed to achieve the target margin (sales less direct costs) of 30% of sales revenue. If the margin could have been increased by 4.6 points, from 25.4% to 30%, the Catering profits would have been higher by about £28,000 (4.6% × £601,180).

- There seems to be a need for better cost control over Catering operations. The below-target margin could be due to poor staff planning or high food wastage (or both).

- Most of the profit is generated by Bedrooms, but the direct costs of these operations are very low, and the measurement of profitability depends largely on the 'accuracy' or 'fairness' of the overhead apportionment.

- It is not possible to look at the three revenue-generating operations in isolation in terms of sales revenue. In particular, although Catering made a loss, the Bedrooms and Meetings areas of operation could not function properly without offering catering services to customers.

- Meetings made a small profit, but again, as with Bedrooms, profitability depends largely on overhead cost apportionment.

- All three areas of operation made a positive margin, i.e. sales revenue from the operations exceeded direct costs.

25   PTS LTD

Key answer tips

You need to choose an appropriate allocation method for each type of overhead and produce a table which allows you to calculate total overheads for each department.

(a)   **Overhead analysis sheet for 20X2**

Expense	Basis of apportionment	Machining	Assembly	Finishing	Total
		£	£	£	£
Indirect wages	allocated	120,354	238,970	89,700	449,024
Factory rent	floor space	5,708,475	4,439,925	2,537,100	12,685,500
Rates	floor space	1,552,905	1,207,815	690,180	3,450,900
Heat/light	floor space	443,408	344,872	197,070	985,350
Machine power	horse power	1,878,890	72,265	939,445	2,890,600
Plant dep'n	machine value	375,000	45,000	180,000	600,000
Canteen sub'y	no of employees	100,000	120,000	36,000	256,000
		10,179,032	6,468,847	4,669,495	21,317,374

(b)   **Overhead absorption rates**

Machining $\dfrac{£10,179,032}{200,000}$ = £50.90 per machine hour

Assembly $\dfrac{£6,468,847}{140,000}$ = £46.21 per direct labour

Finishing $\dfrac{£4,669,495}{90,000}$ = £51.88 per machine hour

26   UTOPIAN HOTEL

(a)

Item	Basis	Total	Residential	Catering	House-keeping	Mainten-ance
		£	£	£	£	£
Consumable materials	Allocated	73,000	14,000	23,000	27,000	9,000
Staff costs	Allocated	46,500	16,500	13,000	11,500	5,500
Rent/rates	Floor area	37,500	20,625	10,125	4,500	2,250
Insurance	Equipt value	14,000	6,533	4,667	1,400	1,400
Heat/light	Floor area	18,500	10,175	4,995	2,220	1,110
Dep'n	Equipt value	37,500	17,500	12,500	3,750	3,750
		227,000	85,333	68,287	50,370	23,010
Apportion	Maint'ce	-	11,505	6,903	4,602	(23,010)
Apportion	H'keeping	-	38,480	16,492	(54,972)	-
		227,000	135,318	91,682	Nil	Nil

(b)   **Absorption rates**

Residential (per guest-night):

$\dfrac{\text{Costs}}{\text{Guest - nights}} = \dfrac{£135,318}{2,800} = £48.33$

Catering (per meal):

$\dfrac{\text{Costs}}{\text{Meals}} = \dfrac{£91,682}{16,000} = £5.73$

(c)   **Residential**

	£
Amount absorbed (3,050 × £48.33)	147,406.50
Cost incurred	144,600.00
Over absorption	2,806.50

Catering

	£
Amount absorbed (15,250 × £5.73)	87,382.50
Cost incurred	89,250.00
Under absorption	1,867.50

(d)   The hotel might consider the use of alternative methods of accounting for its overhead costs by trying to identify them with particular activities. They may also consider the introduction of a standard costing system for some parts of their organisation (where there are clearly definable common tasks involved).

27   QRS LTD

Key answer tips

Note that while you are asked to calculate the over/under absorption of overheads for each department in part (b), you should only discuss the casting department in this section. Dressing and Assembly are discussed in part (c). Any investigation of fixed overheads should be into the individual cost elements.

(a)   **Absorption rates**

Department	Casting	Dressing	Assembly
Overhead	225,000	175,000	93,000
Hours	7,500	7,000	6,200
Rate	= £30/hour	= £25/hour	= £15/hour

(b)   **Department**

	Casting	Dressing	Assembly
	£	£	£
Actual overhead	229,317	182,875	94,395
Absorbed overhead (Working)	238,500	182,000	100,440
(Over)/under-absorbed	(9,183)	875	(6,045)

Working

Department	Casting	Dressing	Assembly
Actual hours	7,950	7,280	6,696
× Absorption rate	£30	£25	£15
= Absorbed	£238,500	£182,000	£100,440

The casting department has over absorbed overheads by £9,183 - actual overheads incurred are less than expected for the number of production hours worked. The original absorption rate assumed overheads of a total value of £225,000 would be incurred in the period, and would be spread over 7,500 hours, based on budgeted production of 110,000 units.

The overheads, and thus the absorption rate, are likely to contain both fixed and variable elements.

Possible causes of the over-absorption of overheads include:

(i) Over-absorption of fixed costs due to the actual production hours being greater than budgeted (used to set the rate)

(ii) The variable and/or fixed cost estimates built into the original budget for 110,000 units being over-estimated (giving too high an absorption rate)

(iii) The number of hours required for production of 110,000 units being under-estimated (again giving too high an absorption rate) - although the given data does not support this, as the actual time per unit was less than budgeted.

(c) **Dressing department (£875 under-absorbed)**

The actual total number of hours exceeds budgeted, thus the fixed element of the cost would in fact be over-absorbed.

Under-estimation of the fixed and variable cost elements of the overheads may be one cause of the under-absorption, although this cannot be analysed without further information.

One identifiable contributory factor to the overall under-absorption is that the hours per unit is lower than expected (just under 62 hours per 1,000 units against a budgeted level of over 64 hours). Thus the costs have been absorbed over fewer hours than expected for the level of production.

Assembly department (£6,045 over-absorbed)

The overhead costs have only increased by 1.5% against a production increase of 6.8%. This may indicate a high proportion of fixed costs, which will be over-absorbed over the higher actual hours than budgeted.

The actual number of hours per unit in this department is in fact slightly greater than expected (just under 57 per 1,000 units against just over 56); this inefficiency will also contribute to over absorption.

Again, over-estimation of cost elements may also be relevant.

Under/over absorption of overheads arises purely from estimation errors in arriving at the elements for the absorption rate - the total amounts of costs incurred and the level of activity that will be achieved. Certainly the reasons why costs and activity levels were different from expected need to be investigated, but this will be done far more usefully by looking at expenditure and efficiency variances for the separate costs, rather than looking at the overall effect on the amount of overheads absorbed into production.

COSTING SYSTEMS

28 PRINTING

Key answer tips

Be sure you can calculate material losses and selling price correctly.

	£	£
Photography: 64 sessions at £150 per session		9,600
Set-up		
Labour		
64 plates × 4 hours per plate at £7.00 per hour	1,792	
Materials		
64 plates at £35 per plate	2,240	
Overhead (64 × 4 hours × £9.50)	2,432	
		6,464
Printing		
Paper		
100,000 catalogues × 32 ÷ 0.98 sheets × (£12/1,000)	39,184	
Other materials: (100,000/500) × £7	1,400	
Labour and overheads		
(100,000/1,000) machine hours at £62 per hour	6,200	
		46,784
Binding		
Labour and overheads		1,720
(100,000/2,500) machine hours at £43 per hour		
Total costs		64,568
Profit margin (10/90 of cost)		7,174
Selling price: £64,568 ÷ 0.9		71,742

29 JOB COST

(a) (i) A materials requisition is a request for the transfer of materials from stores to a job. When it has been authorised, it is a formal order for materials for the job, and it acts as a source document for posting the transfer of materials, for both the bin card and the stores ledger (i.e. the physical stores records and the accounting records). The details required in a materials requisition include the type of material (description and stores code) and the job number. The requisition form also needs a section for pricing the materials issued, for charging to the cost of the job.

(ii) In a job costing system, there is a job cost card for each job. It is used to record all the direct costs of the job, such as direct materials costs and direct labour costs (hours worked and cost per hour). Production overhead costs are also added, using the appropriate overhead absorption rate or rates. If the job is unfinished at the end of an accounting period, the total costs so far recorded on the card are used to establish the value of closing work in progress. Job costs recorded for a completed job can be compared with the original estimate of the cost for the job.

(b)   (i)   **Job XYZ: 'normal' material costs**

'Normal' wastage and rectification = 2% + 3% = 5% of actual input materials. Normal costs are therefore × 100/95 of actual costs after allowing for normal (rather than actual) losses.

	£
Materials initially allocated to the job	17,560
Less:	
Actual wastage	(620)
Actual rectification	(756)
Net cost of output	16,184
Normal cost of wastage (16,184 × 2/95)	341
Normal cost of rectification (16,184 × 3/95)	511
'Normal' material cost of output	17,036

(ii)   Efficiency with respect to wastage and rectification is measured as the actual cost of wastage/rectification as a percentage of the (initially allowable) raw material cost.

	Job XYZ		*All jobs*	
Wastage	(620/17,560) × 100%	= 3.5%	(5,164/234,720)	= 2.2%
Rectification	(756/17,560) × 100%	= 4.3%	(6,105/234,720)	= 2.6%

30   JOB Y COSTS

Key answer tips

Your read through of the question should have identified the basic categories of costs to be charged to Job Y: Direct labour (two grades), direct materials and overheads (including indirect labour and materials). So draw up a pro-forma statement with these headings to focus your thinking.

Now use the information to cost up the different elements in your proforma. Take care to use quantity information specific to Job Y (you are also given total information for the quarter). Direct labour is straightforward; direct materials requires a calculation of weighted average cost from the total stock receipts in the period, and overheads requires a computation of the absorption rate using the *total* cost/ hours information for the quarter.

(1)   **Production overhead absorption rate =**

$$\frac{\text{overheads incurred}}{\text{direct labour hours worked}} \text{ in the last calendar quarter}$$

Production overheads incurred:

	£000	£000
Indirect materials		85
Indirect labour:		
Grade M	135	
Grade N	180	
		315
General expenses		325
Depreciation		370

Rent and rates	249
	1,344

Direct labour hours worked 210,000

Production overhead absorption rate =

$$\frac{£1,344,000}{210,000 \text{ hours}} = £6.40 \text{ per direct labour hour}$$

(2) **Weighted average cost price of Material X for the week** (calculated at the end of the week)

	kilos	£
Opening stock	962	2,532.16
+ Receipts	660	1,745.70
	1,622	4,277.86

Weighted average $\dfrac{£4,277.86}{1,622 \text{ kilos}} = £2.6374$ per kilo

(3) **Production costs charged to Job Y in the week:**

	£	£
Direct materials		
- 362 kilos × £2.6374/kilo =		955
Direct labour		
- 105 hours × £6/hour =	630	
- 192 hours × £5/hour =	960	
		1,590
Production overhead		
- 297 hours × £6.40/hour =		1,901
		4,446

31   ADAM

(a)

Process account					
	Units	£		Units	£
Opening WIP	100		Normal loss	150	
Input (balancing figure)	1,500		Output	1,250	
			Closing WIP	200	
	1,600			1,600	

(b)

Statement of equivalent units

	Total units	Materials		Conversion costs
Opening WIP (to complete)	100	—	(= 100 × 70%)	70
Units started and finished	1,150	1,150		1,150
Output	1,250			1,220
Normal loss	150	-		-
Closing WIP	200	200	(= 200 × 40%)	80
Total	1,600	1,350		1,300

(c)

Input costs incurred in period

	Materials £		Conversion costs £
Cost per equivalent unit (given)	2.60		1.50
Cost in period (= 1,350 × 2.60)	3,510	(= 1,300 × £1.50)	1,950
Add scrap proceeds from normal loss (= 150 × £2)	300		—
	3,810		1,950

Tutorial note: the cost per equivalent unit for materials is calculated after deducting the scrap value of normal loss. Therefore to calculate the cost of material input, we need to add back this normal loss process account for the period.

ACCA marking scheme		
		Marks
(a)	Calculation of input units	1.0
	Stating the input units	1.0
		2.0
(b)	Equivalent units for opening WIP	1.0
	Calculation of units started and finished	0.5
	Equivalent units for started and finished units	0.5
	Equivalent units for normal loss	1.0
	Equivalent units for closing WIP	1.0
		4.0
(c)	Calculation of costs for materials	1.0
	Adjusting for scrap proceeds	1.0
	Calculation of costs for conversion costs	1.0
	Stating the input costs	1.0
		4.0
Total		10.0

32   TWO PROCESSES

(a)

Output:	Units	Units
Opening WIP, Process 2		12,000
Transfers from Process 1		95,000
		107,000
Closing WIP, Process 2	10,000	
Normal loss (= actual loss)	200	
		10,200
Output from Process 2		96,800

Tutorial note: The question states that there is no abnormal loss or abnormal gain in the process.

Equivalent units for Process 2

		Process 1 materials		Added materials		Conversion costs
	(%)		(%)		(%)	
Output from Process 1		96,800		96,800		96,800
Closing WIP	(100)	10,000	(90)	9,000	(70)	7,000
		106,800		105,800		103,800
Costs		£		£		£
Opening stock		13,440		4,970		3,120
Costs in the period		107,790		44,000		51,480
		121,230		48,970		54,600
Cost per equivalent unit		£1.135		£0.463		£0.526

Total cost per equivalent unit = £1.135 + £0.463 + £0.526 = **£2.124**.

(b)

Process 2 account

	Units	£		Units	£
Opening WIP	12,000	21,530	Finished goods (W1)	96,800	205,603
From Process 1	95,000	107,790	Normal loss	200	0
Added materials		44,000	Closing WIP (W2)	10,000	19,197
Conversion costs		51,480			
		224,800			224,800

Workings

(W1) Cost of finished output = 96,800 equivalent units × £2.124 = £205,603.

(W2) Value of closing WIP

= (10,000 × £1.135) + (9,000 × £0.463) + (7,000 × £0.526) = £19,199.

This is adjusted to £19,197 in the process account above to allow for a rounding error in the calculations.

(c)   If there is no allowance for normal rejects, there would be no normal loss. As a consequence, all rejected units would be given a full share of product costs. The cost of these losses would be credited to the process account and debited to an abnormal loss account. From the abnormal loss account, they would be transferred to the profit and loss account as a loss for the period.

In contrast, under the current system, normal loss is given no cost, and the cost of output will consequently be higher. Only abnormal loss (or abnormal gain) is given a value.

(d)   If the FIFO method of stock valuation is used, the calculation of equivalent units and cost per equivalent units will be different. Equivalent units in the period will exclude the equivalent units brought forward in the opening stock, and the cost per equivalent unit for the period will ignore the cost of the opening WIP. The cost of completed production is then calculated as the value of opening WIP brought forward plus the cost to complete the opening WIP, plus the cost of units started and finished in the period.

ACCA marking scheme		
		Marks
(a)	Output	2.0
	Equivalent units	2.0
	Costs	1.0
	Cost per equivalent unit	2.0
(b)	Transfer to finished goods	1.0
	Closing WIP	1.0
	Process account: debit entries	1.5
	Process account: credit entries	1.5
(c)	Why	2.5
	How	2.5
(d)	Equivalent units	1.5
	Costs	1.5
Total		20.0

33   FINAL PROCESS

(a)

Process account

	£		£
Opening work-in-progress	1,527	Finished goods	23,545
Input from previous process	14,625	Closing work-in-progress	1,975
Added materials	5,760		
Conversion costs	3,608		
	25,520		25,520

Workings

	Total units	Equivalent units		
		Previous process materials	*Added materials*	*Conversion costs*
Opening WIP completed	500	0	100	300
Other finished output	5,900	5,900	5,900	5,900
	6,400	5,900	6,000	6,200
Closing WIP	600	600	480	360
	7,000	6,500	6,480	6,560
Costs in the period		£14,625	£5,760	£3,608
Cost per equivalent unit		£2.25	£0.88	£0.55

Cost of finished output from the process

		£
Opening WIP		1,527
Previous process materials	(5,900 × £2.25)	13,275
Added materials	(6,000 × £0.88)	5,333
Conversion costs	(6,200 × £0.55)	3,410
		23,545

Value of closing WIP

		£
Previous process materials	(600 × £2.25)	1,350
Added materials	(480 × £0.88)	427
Conversion costs	(360 × £0.55)	198
		1,975

(b)   (i)

	Product M	Product N	Total
Sales price	£11.00	£4.80	
Further processing costs	£1.20	£0.90	
Net realisable value per kilogram	£9.80	£3.90	
Production (kilograms)	2,760 kg	6,640 kg	
NRV of production	£27,048	£25,896	£52,944
Apportioned joint costs:			
£44,730 × (27,048/52,944)	£22,852		
£44,730 × (25,896/52,944)		£21,878	

(ii) As illustrated in the answer above, joint products are charged with a full share of the joint costs of production. This is because each joint product is financially significant, and it is therefore appropriate to apportion a share of costs to each to establish product costs and profitability.

In contrast, by-products are financially insignificant, and unlike joint products, they have very little sales value. It is therefore considered inappropriate to charge a share of joint process costs to these products. By-products are accounted for in either of two ways.

- The revenue from sales of the by-product is treated as incidental sales income.

- Alternatively, the revenue from sales of the by-product is deducted from the costs of the main process (by crediting the process account with the amount of the sales revenue earned).

34   MANUFACTURING PROCESS

Key answer tips

Do note the layout of the suggested answer and take care to check your equivalent units calculations.

Workings

Normal loss = 5% × 10,000 = 500 units.

Actual loss = 420 units, therefore abnormal gain = (500 – 420) = 80 units. This is valued as 80 equivalent units of materials and (60%) 48 equivalents of labour as overhead.

	Total units	Equivalent units	
		Materials	*Labour and overhead*
Good output (10,000 – 420)	9,580	9,580	9,580
Abnormal gain	(80)	(80)	(48)
Total equivalent units		9,500	9,532
		£	£
Costs		16,445	28,596
Less: Scrap value of normal loss (500 × £0.40)		(200)	–
		16,245	28,596
Cost per equivalent unit		£1.71	£3.00

Total cost per equivalent unit = £1.71 + £3 = £4.71.

Cost of good output = 9,580 units × £4.71 = £45,122.

Value of abnormal gain = (80 × £1.71) + (48 × £3) = £281.

Process account

	£		£
Materials	16,445	Finished goods	45,122
Labour and overhead	28,596	Normal loss: scrap account	200
Abnormal gain	281		
	45,322		45,322

Scrap account

	£		£
Process account: normal loss	200	Abnormal gain (note)	32
		Bank (note)	168
	200		200

Note: The actual units of scrap for which cash is received is the actual loss of 420 units × £0.40 = £168. The difference between the scrap value of expected (normal) loss and actual scrap is the scrap value of the abnormal gain. This is debited to the normal gain account and credited to the scrap account.

Abnormal gain account

	£		£
Scrap account	32	Process account	281
Profit and loss account	249		
	281		281

35 EQUIVALENT UNITS

(a)

	Previous process/ materials		Labour/overhead	
	%	equiv units	%	equiv units
Output: (8,250 – 1,600 = 6,650)	100	6,650	100	6,650
Closing WIP (1,600)	100	1,600	60	960
Equivalent units produced		8,250		7,610

(b) *Cost per equivalent unit*

Materials: $\dfrac{£478,500}{8,250} = £58.00$

Labour and overhead: $\dfrac{£350,060}{7,610} = £46.00$

(c)

Process account

	Units	£		Units	£
Previous process	8,250	453,750	Output	6,650	691,600
Materials		24,750	Closing WIP	1,600	136,960
Labour/overhead		350,060			
	8,250	828,560		8,250	828,560

(d)   A joint product is produced when two or more products arise simultaneously from the operation of a single process. Each joint product is of significant value to the producer.

A by-product arises in the same way as a joint product except that its value is small and NOT considered to be significant.

When accounting for joint products the common (or pre-separation) costs are apportioned between the products either on a value or output basis. Accounting for by-products requires that its realisable value be used to reduce the cost of the other product(s) from the same common process.

36   PROCESS MANUFACTURING LTD

(a)   **Process 1**

Process account

	kg	£		kg	£
Materials	24,000	168,000	Process 2	19,000 (W)	190,000
Labour		52,800	Work in progress	5,000 (W)	44,000
Overheads		13,200			
	24,000	234,000		24,000	234,000

Workings

Calculation of cost per equivalent unit

	Total	Materials	Labour + Overhead
Finished goods	19,000	19,000	19,000
Closing work in progress	5,000	5,000	3,000
Total equivalent units	24,000	24,000	22,000
Costs (£)		168,000	66,000
Cost per equivalent unit (£)		7.0	3.0

Valuation		£
Finished goods	$19,000 \times £(7 + 3)$	190,000
Work in progress	$5,000 \times £7$	
	$3,000 \times £3$	44,000
		234,000

(b) **Process 2**

Process account

	kg	£		kg	£
Labour		45,752	Finished goods	15,200 (W)	228,000
Overhead		27,353	Work in progress	2,850 (W)	35,105
From Process 1	19,000	190,000	Normal loss (W2)	950	–
	19,000	263,105		19,000	263,105

Workings

(W1) Calculation of cost per equivalent unit

	Total	Materials	Labour + Overhead
Finished goods	15,200	15,200	15,200
Work in progress	2,850	2,850	1,140
Total equivalent units	18,050	18,050	16,340
Costs (£)		190,000	73,105
Cost per equivalent unit (£)		10.53	4.47

Valuation		£
Finished goods	$15,200 \times £(10.53 + 4.47)$	228,000
Work in progress	$2,850 \times £10.53$	
	$1,140 \times £4.47$	35,106
	Rounding error	(1)
		35,105

(W2) Output = 95% of input

Normal loss = $5\% \times 19,000$ kg = 950 kg

Therefore: Work in progress = $19,000 - (950 + 15,200) = 2,850$

(c) A process gain is where expected normal process losses exceed actual process losses. Thus, if normal process losses were expected to be 5% of input, (i.e. 950 kgs in Process 2 above), but actual losses turned out to be 4% of input, (i.e. 760 kgs in Process 2 above), then there would have been a process gain of 1% of input (i.e. 190 kgs in Process 2 above).

37   CHEMICAL COMPOUND

Key answer tips

Calculate the cost per kg for each process before completing the T accounts.

(i)   Process A

$$\text{Cost/kg} = \frac{\text{Total costs - scrap value of normal loss}}{\text{Expected output}}$$

Total costs	£
Direct material (2,000kg at £5/kg)	10,000
Direct labour	7,200
Process plant time (140hrs at £60/hr)	8,400
Departmental overhead (60% × £7,200) (W1)	4,320
	29,920
Scrap value of normal loss (20% × 2,000kg × £0.50/kg)	200
	29,720

$$\text{Cost/kg} = \frac{£29,720}{2,000\text{kg} \times 80\%} = £18.575/\text{kg}$$

Process A

	Kg	£		Kg	£
Direct material	2,000	10,000	Normal loss	400	200
Direct labour		7,200	Process B	1,400	26,005
Process plant hire		8,400	Abnormal loss	200	3,715
Departmental overhead		4,320			
	2,000	29,920		2,000	29,920

(ii) **Process B**

Total costs	£
Transfer from Process A	26,005
Direct material (1,400kg at £12/kg)	16,800
Direct labour	4,200
Process plant time (80hrs at £72.50/hr)	5,800
Departmental overhead (60% × £4,200)	2,520
	55,325
Scrap value of normal loss (10% × 2,800kg × £1.825)	511
	54,814

$$\text{Cost/kg} = \frac{54,814}{2,800\text{kg} \times 90\%} = 21.751587$$

say £21.75

Process B

	Kg	£		Kg	£
Process A	1,400	26,005	Normal loss	280	511
Direct material	1,400	16,800	Finished goods	2,620	56,989
Direct labour		4,200			
Process plant time		5,800			
Departmental overhead		2,520			
Abnormal gain	100	2,175			
	2,900	57,500		2,900	57,500

(iii)

Normal loss/gain

	Kg	£		Kg	£
Process A	400	200	Abnormal gain - B	100	182.5
Abnormal loss - A	200	100	Bank (Bal)	780	628.5
Process B	280	511			
	880	811		880	811

(iv)

Abnormal loss/gain

	Kg	£		Kg	£
Process A	200	3,715	Normal loss/gain	200	100
Normal loss/gain	100	182.5	Process B	100	2,175
			P&L a/c (Bal fig)		1,622.5
	300	3,897.5		300	3,897.5

(v)

Finished goods

	£		£
Process B	56,989		

(vi)

Profit and loss account (Extract)

	£		£
Abnormal loss/gain	1,622.5		

Working

Departmental overhead absorption rate:

$$= \frac{£6,840}{£7,200 + £4,200} = 60\% \text{ of direct labour cost}$$

38   NET REALISABLE VALUE

(a)   The cost of output from the process is after deducting the scrap value of normal loss. (This is the usual treatment of the scrap value of loss in process costing. Abnormal loss or abnormal gain is given a full cost/value per unit of loss)

	£
Materials cost	45,625
Labour cost	29,500
Overheads	26,875
	102,000
Less: scrap value of normal loss (20% × 12,500 units × £4/unit)	10,000
Total cost of output from the process	92,000

Alternative method

Process

	units	£		units	£
Materials	12,500	45,625	Normal loss	2,500	10,000
Labour	-	29,500			
Overheads	-	26,875	Output (balance)	10,000	92,000
	12,500	102,000		12,500	102,000

(b)

	£
Cost of output from joint process	92,000
Less: sale value of by-product C (10% × 10,000 units × £2/unit)	2,000
Costs to share between joint products	90,000

	Product A 5,000 units £	Product B 4,000 units £
Sales value	100,000	100,000
Further processing costs	50,000	0
Net realisable value at split-off point	50,000	100,000
Apportion joint costs (£90,000 in proportion 50,000:100,000)	30,000	60,000
Profit	20,000	40,000
Profit per unit	**£4**	**£10**

The profit per unit for product A is £4 and for B is £10.

	ACCA marking scheme	
(a)	Calculating the total cost of output to include:	
	material cost	0.5
	labour cost	0.5
	overhead cost	0.5
	deduct normal loss scrap proceeds	1.0
	Calculation of 92,000	1.5
(b)	Calculating joint costs less by-product proceeds	1.0
	Calculating number of units of A, B and C from output	1.0
	NRV at split-off for A	0.5
	NRV at split-off for B	0.5
	Total NRV calculation, 0.5 marks each A and B	1.0
	Joint cost allocation, 0.5 marks each A and B	1.0
	Profit per unit, 0.5 marks each A and B	1.0
	Total	10.0

39   JOINT PRODUCT PROCESS

Key answer tips

(a)   Product C is a by-product and so is given no share of the joint costs. The most common treatment of by-product sales revenue is to deduct it from the joint process costs before allocation between joint products. (An alternative treatment is simply to credit it to the profit and loss account with the by-product revenue). Following the first treatment, you need to first deduct the revenues expected from the sale of C from the joint manufacture costs.

You are told to apportion joint costs by market values. This is another term for sales *revenue*, not unit selling prices. Don't forget to exclude the by-product, C, from this exercise.

Finally, you are required to calculate the cost per kg - so divide the total costs apportioned in Step 4 by the total weight, and give your answer to 3 decimal places, as required.

(b)   This part switches to process costing with only one product and process losses. To write up the process account, you first need the quantities and costs (materials and conversion) coming into the account on the debit side, using the cost and price information given in the question. To complete the credit side, you need to identify where the costs are being attributed. You should use the normal loss information to determine that there is also an abnormal loss; the costs will thus be attributed to both actual output and abnormal loss units (but not normal loss units)

(a)   Costs to apportion   =   Joint process costs − Revenue from by-product C

=   £272,926 − (2,770kgs × £0.80/kg)

=   £272,926 − £2,216

=   £270,710

Market value of output:

Product A − 16,000 kgs × £6.10/kg =   £97,600

Product B − 53,200 kgs × £7.50/kg =   £399,000

£496,600

Apportionment of joint process costs:

$$\text{Product A} = 270{,}710 \times \frac{97{,}600}{496{,}600} = £53{,}204$$

$$\text{Product B} = 270{,}710 \times \frac{399{,}000}{496{,}600} = £217{,}506$$

Cost per kg:

$$\text{Product A} = \frac{53{,}204}{16{,}000} = £3.325/\text{kg}$$

$$\text{Product B} = \frac{217{,}506}{53{,}200} = £4.088/\text{kg}$$

(b)

Production costs:		£
Material P	3,220 kilos at £5.00/kilo =	16,100
Material T	6,440 kilos at £1.60/kilo =	10,304
	9,660 kilos	26,404
Conversion costs		23,796
		50,200

Expected output:	kilos
Materials input	9,660
Normal loss (5%)	(483)
	9,177

$$\text{Cost per unit} = \frac{50{,}200}{9{,}177} = £5.47 \text{ per kilo}$$

Abnormal loss = 9,177 − 9,130 = 47 kilos.

Process account

	£		£
Raw materials	26,404	Finished goods (9,130 × £5.47)	49,943
Conversion costs	23,796	Abnormal loss (47 × £5.47)	257
	50,200		50,200

40 PROCESS ACCOUNT

Key answer tips

Under FIFO, the costs brought forward in opening work in process are wholly attributable to completed units; thus they are excluded from the cost per equivalent unit processed this period (or closing WIP would be absorbing some of them), and added as a lump sum to the cost of completed units.

	Total units	Materials equiv. units		Labour/ overhead equiv. units
Opening stock completed	1,000	0	(50%)	500
Other output (3,800 − 1,000)	2,800	2,800		2,800
	3,800	2,800		3,300

Closing stock	1,300	1,300	(75%)	975
		4,100		4,275

Labour costs:	£
Basic wages: 6 people × 37 hrs × £5.00/hr =	1,110
+ Group bonus: (4,275 - 4,000) × £0.80/unit	220
	1,330

Cost per equivalent unit of production:

Materials: £2,255/4,100 units = £0.55/equivalent unit.

Labour and overhead: (£1,330 + £1,748)/ 4,275 units = £0.72/equivalent unit.

Valuation:		£
Opening stock	(£540 + £355)	895
Current period costs:		
Materials	(2,800 × £0.55)	1,540
Labour and overhead	(3,300 × £0.72)	2,376
Total value of finished output		4,811
Closing stock:		
Materials	(1,300 × £0.55)	715
Labour and overhead	(975 × £0.72)	702
		1,417

Process account

	£		£
Opening stock	895	Finished goods	4,811
Materials	2,255		
Labour	1,330		
Overhead	1,748	Closing stock	1,417
	6,228		6,228

41 TRANSPORT BUSINESS

Key answer tips

The answer to (a) is looking for more than a definition – need to discuss when and where used and any problems experienced.

(a) **Service costing** is a form of operations costing that is used where standardised services are provided, either by an undertaking or by a service cost centre within an undertaking. Service costing is concerned with establishing the costs of the services rendered and with establishing average costs per standardised unit of measurement (unit of service). This unit of measurement is not as easy to establish for service costing as it is for production costing, where product units are easily identified.

(b) (i) A **cost unit** is a quantitative unit of product or service in respect of which costs may be ascertained. The cost unit for a particular company or part of a company will depend on the activities that result in the costs being incurred. For a transport business, the costs will be incurred in providing a transportation service in the form of users and/or lorries. The cost unit chosen will therefore relate to the activities of these vehicles.

Transport costs could be analysed by van or lorry but it is probably more informative to analyse costs as either cost per mile (or kilometre) or cost per ton/mile (or kilogram/kilometre). The latter is most useful where the weight of the goods transported has a significant impact on the costs incurred.

(ii) The question does not state which costs are variable and which are fixed, therefore assumptions have to be made. In the calculations below, it is assumed that the only variable costs are spares and replacement parts, and fuel. (Tutorial note: However, it would be perfectly acceptable if you treat tyre replacement costs as a variable cost item.)

Budgeted capacity = $(3/4 \times 80\% \times 160,000) + (1/4 \times 60\% \times 160,000) = 120,000$ kilometres.

Variable costs based on budgeted capacity	£
Spares, replacement parts: £100 × (120,000/1,000)	12,000
Fuel: £0.40 × (120,000/4)	12,000
	24,000

Annual fixed costs excluding general administration	£
Vehicle depreciation: (£4,000 × 4)	16,000
Basic maintenance: £110 × 4 × (12/6)	880
Vehicle licences: (4 × £140)	560
Vehicle insurance: (4 × £450)	1,800
Tyre replacements: (6 × £90) × (120,000/40,000)	1,620
Drivers (4 × £8,000)	32,000
	52,860

Variable cost per kilometre = £24,000/120,000 = £0.20.

Fixed cost per kilometre = £52,860/120,000 = £0.4405.

Cost of the job (64 kilometres)

	£
Variable cost: 64 × £0.20	12.80
Fixed cost: 64 × £0.4405	28.19
Total cost excluding general administration	40.99
General administration: (+ 25%)	10.25
Full cost	51.24

42 PUBLIC TRANSPORT

Key answer tips

The quickest and clearest way to tackle this part is via a suitably structured profit statement. It needs to show total profit (after all costs - i.e. at the bottom of the statement), but also two contributions as defined, after only some of the costs. Build up the statement so that all three levels can be extracted from the same statement.

The main errors arising on this part, as highlighted in the examiner's comments, were through failing to read/follow the instructions closely enough. There is no excuse for not rounding as required; you may have been thrown a bit by the requirement to show contribution after 'all direct service costs' which will include fixed costs. This is a slightly different view of contribution from the standard 'revenue minus variable costs' - here, we are looking at the contribution of a service operation to the business as a whole, rather than per unit. If the operation were to cease, these fixed costs would not arise. They are 'variable' in this sense.

		Service 1	Service 2	Service 3
		£000	£000	£000
	Revenue	146.2	293.5	271.9
	Variable operating costs	33.6	57.6	47.6
	Contribution	112.6	235.9	224.3
	Service fixed costs	49.7	85.2	70.7
	Contribution less direct service fixed costs	62.9	150.7	153.6
	General fixed costs (see note)	75.0	128.5	113.8
(a)	Net profit/(loss)	(12.1)	22.2	39.8
(b)	Kilometres	56,000	96,000	85,000
	Contribution per kilometre	£2.01	£2.46	£2.64
(c)	Number of vehicles	7	12	10
	Contribution less direct service fixed costs per vehicle (to the nearest £100)	£9,000	£12,600	£15,400

Note: Absorption rate $= \dfrac{312,000}{233,000} = $ £1.339 per kilometre

COSTING METHODS AND TECHNIQUES

ABSORPTION COSTING AND MARGINAL COSTING

43 OATHALL LTD

(a)

	£000	£000
Absorption costing		
Sales (£50 × 100,000)		5,000
Cost of sales:		
Opening stock		–

Production costs		
Variable (£19 × 120,000)	2,280	
Fixed (£3(w) × 120,000)	360	
	2,640	
Closing stock (£22 × 20,000)	(440)	
Under/over absorption	(60)	
		(2,140)
Gross profit		2,860
Selling costs		
Fixed		(150)
Variable (£2 × 100,000)		(200)
Net profit		2,510

Working

Overhead absorption rate = £300,000/100,000 = £3 per unit

(b)

Marginal costing	£000	£000
Sales (£50 × 100,000)		5,000
Cost of sales:		
Opening stock	–	
Production costs		
Variable (£19 × 120,000)	2,280	
	2,280	
Closing stock (£19 × 20,000)	(380)	
Variable selling costs	200	
		(2,100)
Contribution		2,900
Fixed costs		
Production		(300)
Selling		(150)
Net profit		2,450

ACCA marking scheme		
		Marks
(a)	Correct sales figure	½
	Variable production cost figure	½
	Fixed overhead absorption rate	½
	Fixed production cost figure	½
	Calculation of closing stock units	½
	Calculation of closing stock value	½
	Variable and fixed selling costs	1
	Under/over absorption	1
	Including the term gross profit	½
	Layout/presentation	½
(b)	Including variable production costs only	½

	Closing stock evaluation	1
	Including variable selling costs before	½
	contribution	½
	Including the term contribution	1
	Correct fixed costs	½
	Layout/presentation	
Total		10

44 SURAT

(a) **Workings**

Standard cost per unit	£
Direct/variable costs	20
Fixed overhead cost (£4,000/2,000 units)	2
Standard full cost per unit	22

	£
Budgeted fixed costs per month	4,000
Budgeted absorption of overhead (1,800 × £2)	3,600
Budgeted under-absorption	400

(b)

	£000	£000
Sales (1,600 units)		48.0
O/s (150 units × £22)	3.3	
Full cost paid in (1,800 × £22)	39.6	
	42.9	
C/s (350 units × £22)	7.7	
		35.2
		12.8
Budgeted materials		0.4
		12.4
Admin		(3.6)
Selling & distribution		(4.4)
Profit		4.4

Reconciliations	£
Profit under absorption costing	4,400
Add fixed costs in opening stock (150 units × £2)	300
Less fixed costs in closing stock (350 units × £2)	(700)
Profit under marginal costing	4,000

An enterprise might prefer marginal costing since marginal costs include only costs that are relevant for decision-making, i.e. variable costs. Also, the enterprise might not have significant fixed costs, and so marginal costing might be more appropriate.

	ACCA marking scheme	
		Marks
(a)	Calculation of fixed overhead absorption rate	0.5
	Calculation of standard full cost	0.5
	Opening stock units figure	0.5
	Opening stock valuation	0.5
	Calculation of product units	0.5
	Fixed production costs absorbed	0.5
	Closing stock units figure	0.5
	Closing stock valuation	0.5
	Under-absorption calculation	1.0
	Selling costs	0.5
	Presentation	0.5
(b)	Reconciliation statement:	
	Absorption costing profit	0.5
	Fixed costs in opening stocks	0.5
	Fixed costs in closing stocks	0.5
	Marginal costing profit	0.5
	Discussion of why marginal costing could be preferred	2.0
Total		10.0

45 MARGINAL AND ABSORPTION

(a) Total production costs:

		£000
Month 1	= 12,000 units × £23.75 per unit	285.0
Month 2	= 10,500 units × £25 per unit	262.5
Month 3	= 10,000 units × £25.50 per unit	255.0

The variable cost per unit can be estimated using the high-low method.

			£000
Total cost of	12,000 units	=	285
Total cost of	10,000 units	=	255
Variable cost of	2,000 units	=	30

Variable cost per unit = £30,000/2,000 units = £15 per unit.

Fixed costs per period can now be calculated as follows.

			£000
Total production cost of	12,000 units	=	285
Variable cost of	12,000 units	=	180
Fixed production costs		=	105

(b) Total costs in month 4:

	£000
Variable cost of 12,500 units (x £15)	187.5
Fixed production overheads	105.0
Fixed selling and administration overheads	87.0
Total costs	379.5

(c)   Fixed production overhead absorption rate:

= £105,000/12,000 units = £8.75 per unit.

Total production cost per unit = £15 + £8.75 = £23.75.

Absorption costing statement for Month 2	£	£
Sales (10,000 units at £34 per unit)		340,000
Production cost of sales (10,000 × £23.75)		237,500
		102,500
Production overhead absorbed (10,500 × £8.75)	91,875	
Production overhead expenditure incurred	105,000	
Under-absorbed overhead		13,125
		89,375
Selling and administration overhead		87,000
Net profit		2,375

(d)

Marginal costing statement for Month 3	£	£
Sales (11,000 units at £34 per unit)		374,000
Variable cost of sales (11,000 x £15)		165,000
Contribution		209,000
Fixed production overhead	105,000	
Selling and administration overhead	87,000	
Under-absorbed overhead		192,000
Net profit		17,000

(e)   The profit difference in month 2 would be:

500 units at £8.75 per unit = £4,375.

Production volume exceeded sales volume by 500 units in the month, therefore additional fixed overhead will go into the valuation of stock with absorption costing, instead f being charged as a cost of sales. This means that the absorption costing profit would exceed the marginal costing profit by £4,375.

Tutorial note: In month 2, with marginal costing, total contribution would be 10,000 x £19 per unit = £190,000, and deducting total fixed overheads of £192,000 gives a loss of £2,000. This is £4,375 less than the profit of £2,375 that would be reported with absorption costing.

ACCA marking scheme		
		Marks
(a)	Variable cost per unit	2.0
	Fixed cost per month	2.0
(b)	Total variable cost	1.0
	Total fixed cost	1.0
(c)	Fixed production overhead absorption rate	1.0
	Sales	1.0
	Production cost of sales	1.0
	Under-absorbed production overhead	1.5

	Selling and administration overhead	0.5
	Gross profit and net profit	1.0
(d)	Sales	1.0
	Variable cost of sales	1.0
	Contribution	1.0
	Fixed overheads	1.0
(e)	Explanation	2.0
	Figures	2.0
Total		20.0

46   TRADING STATEMENT

(a)   *Workings*

Fixed manufacturing overhead absorption rate = £92,000/20,000 units = £4.60 per unit.

Unit cost and profit	£	£
Unit sales price		14.00
Variable costs	6.40	
Fixed cost	4.60	
Total manufacturing cost		11.00
Manufacturing profit		3.00

Period 2 trading statement

		£000	£000
Sales	(22,000 units × £14)		308.0
Manufacturing cost of sales	(22,000 units × £11)		242.0
			66.0
Overhead absorbed	(21,000 units × £4.60)	96.6	
Overhead incurred		92.0	
Over-absorbed overhead			4.6
Manufacturing profit			70.6

(b)

		£000
Sales	(22,000 units × £14)	308.0
Variable manufacturing costs	(22,000 units × £6.4)	140.8
Contribution		167.2
Fixed manufacturing costs		92.0
Manufacturing profit		75.2

(c)   (i)

		£
Profit in Period 1		35,800
Extra profit on extra sales in Period 2	(22,000 – 15,000) × £3	21,000
Extra overhead absorbed in Period 2	(21,000 – 18,000) × £4.60	13,800
Profit in Period 2		70,600

(ii) The manufacturing profit will differ between absorption costing and marginal costing when there is an increase or decrease in stock levels during the period. In Period 2, there was a reduction in stock levels of 1,000 units. In a marginal costing system, stock contains no fixed costs, whereas in absorption costing, stock includes an amount of fixed costs. When stock levels fall during a period, and absorption costing is used, there will be a release of fixed costs into the cost of sales. In Period 2, this was 1,000 units x £4.60 = £4,600. This explains the difference between marginal costing and absorption costing profit.

	£
Profit in Period 2 using marginal costing	75,200
Fixed overheads in amount of stock reduction	4,600
Profit in Period 2 using absorption costing	70,600

47 PERIODS 1 AND 2

Key answer tips

Always show your workings in this type of question and cross reference them to the final answer. An unusual feature of this question is that selling and administration overheads are absorbed into the unit cost of the product. The treatment of selling and distribution overhead is similar to the treatment of production overhead in an absorption costing system, except that the overhead is absorbed on the basis of sales volume, not production volume.

(a) **Trading and profit and loss account**

	Note	Period 1 £000	Period 2 £000
Sales	(1)	1,275	1,350
Manufacturing cost of sales	(2)	(680)	(720)
Gross profit		595	630
(Under)/over-absorbed manufacturing overhead	(3)	(40)	7
Adjusted gross profit		555	637
Absorbed selling and administration overhead	(4)	(323)	(342)
(Under)/over-absorbed selling/admin overhead	(5)	(15)	-
Net profit		217	295

Notes

(1) Period 1: 85,000 × 15

Period 2: 90,000 × 15

(2) Period 1: 85,000 × 8

Period 2: 90,000 × 8

(3) Period 1: Expenditure £320,000 - Absorbed £280,000 (80,000 × 3.50)

Period 2: Expenditure £315,000 - Absorbed £322,000 (92,000 × 3.50)

(4) Period 1: 85,000 × 3.80

Period 2: 90,000 × 3.80

(5)   Period 1:   Expenditure £270,000 - Absorbed £255,000 (85,000 × 3.00)

   Period 2:   Expenditure £270,000 - Absorbed £270,000 (90,000 × 3.00)

(b)   In a marginal costing system, fixed manufacturing overheads are not included in the valuation of stock. As a result, fixed overhead costs are charged against profit in the period in which they are incurred and profit is not affected, (as in the full absorption method used in (a) above), by production being greater/less than sales.

In Period 1, profit using marginal costing would be greater than that under absorption costing, as production volume is less than the sales volume. The cost of sales is higher with absorption costing and the profit lower, because of the fixed overhead cost in the opening stock that is sold in the period. In Period 2, production volume is higher than sales volume, therefore in an absorption costing system, the production overheads in the cost of sales will be lower than the actual overhead expenditure incurred. Profits using marginal costing will therefore be lower in Period 2.

48   MINOR AND MAJOR

Key answer tips

Draw up a marginal costing answer layout and then insert the figures from separate workings. In your comments in (c), discuss the changes in contribution from each product.

(a)   **Projected profit and loss account for 20X5**
   (Marginal costing)

	Minor	Major	Total
	£000	£000	£000
Sales	7,200	3,800	16,000
Direct costs			
Materials (W1)	1,440	1,260	2,700
Labour (W2)	720	840	1,560
Overheads (W3)	1,440	1,680	3,120
	3,600	3,780	7,380
Contribution	3,600	2,870	6,470
Fixed costs			4,200
Profit			2,270

(b)   **Projected profit and loss account for 20X6**
   (Marginal costing)

	Minor	Major	Major Plus	Total
	£000	£000	£000	£000
Sales	7,200	3,800	5,000	16,000
Direct costs (W4)	3,600	2,160	3,000	8,760
Contribution	3,600	1,640	2,000	7,240
Fixed costs				4,800
Profit				2,440

(c) A profit of £2.27m is forecast for 20X5, rising to £2.44m in 20X6. All products make a positive contribution in each year. Contribution from Minors is the same in each year, whereas from Majors and Major Pluses we forecast a total contribution of £2.87m in 20X5, rising to £3.64m in 20X5. This increase in contribution of £770,000 more than offsets the additional £600,000 of fixed costs and accounts for the forecast increase in net profit.

Workings

(W1) **Direct materials costs, 20X5**

	Units
Number of Minors	120,000
Equivalent units of Majors (70,000 × 1.5)	105,000
	225,000

Total materials costs of £2,700,000 to be allocated in the proportions 120 : 105.

Minors: $£2,700,000 \times \dfrac{120}{225} =$ £1,440,000

Majors: $£2,700,000 \times \dfrac{105}{225} =$ £1,260,000

(W2) **Direct labour costs, 20X5**

	Units
Number of Minors	120,000
Equivalent units of Majors (70,000 × 2)	140,000
	260,000

Minors: $£1,560,000 \times \dfrac{120}{260} =$ £720,000

Majors: $£1,560,000 \times \dfrac{140}{260} =$ £840,000

(W3) **Variable overheads, 20X5**

Total of £3,120,000 allocated in the ratio of labour costs (720 : 840)

Minors: $£3,120,000 \times \dfrac{720}{1,560} =$ £1,440,000

Majors: $£3,120,000 \times \dfrac{840}{1,560} =$ £1,680,000

(W4) **Direct costs, 20X6**

Per unit of Minor: £3,600,000 ÷ 120,000 =   £30

Per unit of Major: £3,780,000 ÷ 70,000 =   £54

Per unit of Major plus:

Materials	£24
Labour	£17
Variable overheads (£17 × $\frac{3,120}{1,560}$)	£34
	£75

49 DUO LTD

Key answer tips

Set out a profit statement for both a marginal and an absorption costing layout and then insert figures from separate workings.

(a) **Profit and loss accounts for period 1 and 2 under marginal costing**

	PERIOD 1		PERIOD 2	
	£	£	£	£
Sales		327,000		246,750
Variable cost of sales:				
Opening stock (W1)	0		13,800	
Variable production cost	168,500		125,500	
	168,500		139,300	
Less: Closing stock (W1)	(13,800)		(22,800)	
Variable cost of sales		154,700		116,500
Contribution		172,300		130,250
Less: Fixed overheads		(110,000)		(82,000)
Profit		62,300		48,250

(b) **Profit and loss accounts for period 1 and 2 based on absorption costing**

	PERIOD 1		PERIOD 2	
	£	£	£	£
Sales		327,000		246,750
Cost of sales:				
Opening stock (W2)	0		22,800	
Full production cost	278,500		207,500	
	278,500		230,300	
Less: Closing stock (W2)	(22,800)		(37,800)	
Cost of sales		255,700		192,500
Profit		71,300		54,250

(c) Stock levels are rising over period one and two thus, total absorption costing, which includes a share of fixed costs in the stock valuation gives a higher reported profit than marginal costing which charges the fixed costs against profit in the period in which they are incurred.

Thus, the reported profit under total absorption costing is £15,000 more over the two periods; as £9,000 of fixed costs are 'carried forward' from period 1 to 2, and a net £6,000 are 'carried forward' from period 2 to 3.

Workings

(W1)			Alpha	Beta	Total
Marginal cost per unit			45	32	
Period 1					£
Closing stock	Units		200	150	
	Value (£)		9,000	4,800	13,800
Period 2					
Closing stock	Units		400	150	
	Value (£)		18,000	4,800	22,800

(W2) **Fully absorbed cost per unit**		Alpha	Beta	Total
		£	£	
Marginal cost per unit		45	32	£
Period 1				
Budgeted labour hours				
= (2,500 × 3) + (1,750 × 2) = 11,000				
Budgeted fixed o'hd expenditure = £110,000				
Fixed o'hd absorption rate per hour = £10				
Fixed overhead cost per unit		30	20	
Full cost per unit		75	52	

Closing stock	Units	200	150	
	Value (£)	15,000	7,800	22,800

Period 2				
Marginal cost per unit		45	32	
Budgeted labour hours				
= (1,900 × 3) + (1,250 × 2) = 8,200				
Budgeted fixed o'hd expenditure = £82,000				
Fixed o'hd absorption rate per hour = £10				
Fixed overhead cost per unit		30	20	
Full cost per unit		75	52	

Closing stock	Units	400	150	
	Value (£)	30,000	7,800	37,800

STANDARD COSTING AND VARIANCE ANALYSIS

50   NEWCASTLE

(a)   ***Workings***

	£	
37,250 kg should cost (× £10)	372,500	
Did cost	345,000	
	_____	
Material price variance	27,500	(F)
	_____	

11,500 units should use (× 3)	34,500	kg of material
Did use	37,250	
	_____	
Usage variance in kg	2,750	kg (A)
	_____	

Standard price per kg = £10
Usage variance in £   £27,500 (A)

	£	
45,350 hours should cost (× £6)	272,100	
Did cost	300,000	
	_____	
Labour Material price variance	27,900	(A)
	_____	

11,500 units should take (× 4)	46,000	hours
Did take	45,350	
	_____	
Labour Efficiency variance in hours	650	hours (F)
	_____	

Standard rate per hour = £6
Efficiency variance in £   £3,900 (A)
The budgeted prime cost per unit is £30 + £24 = £54.

Reconciliation statement

	£	
Budgeted prime cost (12,000 units × £54)	648,000	
Cost volume variance (500 units × £54)	(27,000)	
	_____	
Standard prime cost of units produced (11,500 × £54)	621,000	
Materials price variance	(27,500)	(F)
Materials efficiency variance	27,500	(A)
Labour rate variance	27,900	(A)
Labour efficiency variance	(3,900)	(F)
	_____	
Actual prime cost of units produced (300,000 + 345,000)	645,000	
	_____	

(b)   The adverse labour rate variance shows that the work force was paid at a higher rate per hour than the budget or standard.

The favourable labour efficiency variance shows that the work force worked harder/more quickly than expected, as they made more units than would have been expected in the time that they worked.

Interdependence. Since the work force members were paid more per hour than budget, they might have been motivated to work harder.

ACCA marking scheme		
		Marks
(a)	Calculation of budgeted prime cost	1.0
	Calculation of cost volume variance	1.0
	Calculation of materials price variance	1.0
	Calculation of materials usage variance	1.0
	Calculation of labour rate variance	1.0
	Calculation of labour efficiency variance	1.0
	Calculation of actual prime cost	0.5
	Well-presented reconciliation statement	0.5
(b)	What the rate variance indicates	1.0
	What the efficiency variance indicates	1.0
	Discussion of interdependence	1.0
Total		10.0

51   COMPANY M

Key answer tips

The question asks for a 'format suitable for presentation to management'. It is therefore recommended that the first part of the solution is a summary of the variances and the detailed workings are shown separately.

(a)   **Summary of variances for one accounting period**

(F = Favourable: (A) = Adverse)

	£	
Materials:		
Price	1,885	(A)
Usage	2,610	(A)
Cost	4,495	(A)
Labour:		
Rate:	551	(A)
Efficiency	580	(F)
Cost	29	(F)

Workings

Direct material

	£	
3,770 kgs of material should cost (× £9)	33,930	
Did cost	35,815	
Material price variance	1,885	(A)

	kg	
290 units of output should use (× 12)	3,480	
Did use	3,770	
Material usage variance in kg	290	(A)
Standard price per kilogram	£9	
Material usage variance in £	£2,610	(A)

Direct labour

	£	
2,755 hours should cost (× £4)	11,020	
Did cost	11,571	
Direct labour rate variance	551	(A)

	hours	
290 units of output should take (× 10)	2,900	
Did take	2,755	
Labour efficiency variance in hours	145	(F)
Standard rate per hour	£4	
Direct labour efficiency variance in £	£580	(F)

Assumptions

(1)   Quantity of material purchased = Quantity used.

(2)   Actual hours paid for = Actual hours worked.

(b)   To compile standard costs it is necessary to establish standards, i.e. planned amounts, for each of the following:

Material

Price is established with the assistance of the buying department; it is necessary to take account of quantity discounts and price increases.

Quantity (including an allowance for wastage) should be available from the production department.

Quality/type. This is closely linked to quantity and design of the product and may involve a decision by the production department as to which material is most suitable.

Labour

It is first necessary to identify the tasks that are to be carried out on the product. Then for each tasks the following information is needed:

(i)   level of skill/grade of worker needed

(ii)   time allowed - it may be necessary to use work study to decide on the production method and the associated standard time

(iii)   rate of pay - this will be dependent on the grade of employee and may be subject to a company-wide or national wage agreement.

52   DEPARTMENT 7

Key answer tips

Note that variable overheads vary with standard hours produced and, don't forget to flex the budget.

Tutorial note: Assumption. It is assumed that when the question refers to the variable overhead 'expenditure' variance, it actually intends to refer to the variable overhead total cost variance. The answer has been based on this assumption. If this were not the case, the question would have asked for both the variable overhead expenditure variance and the variable overhead efficiency variance.

(i)

	Std hours
Budgeted production volume	8,000
Actual production volume	8,400
Volume variance in units	400 (F)
Standard fixed overhead cost per standard hour = (£6,750 + £3,250)/8,000	£1.25
Fixed overhead volume variance in £	£500 (F)

(ii)

	£
Budgeted fixed overhead (£6,750 + £3,250)	10,000
Actual fixed overhead (£6,400 + £3,315)	9,715
Fixed overhead expenditure variance	285 (F)

(iii)   The budgeted variable overhead for 8,000 standard hours was £28,000.

The standard variable overhead cost per hour is £28,000/8,000 hours = £3.50

Actual variable overhead expenditure was (£20,140 + £5,960 + £4,480) = £30,580.

Variable overheads	£
8,400 standard hours should cost (× £3.50)	29,400
Actual variable overhead expenditure	30,580
Fixed overhead expenditure variance	1,180 (A)

53   GUNGE

Key answer tips

The question asks for relevant manufacturing cost variances. This should include fixed overheads because there is no indication that they are not manufacturing costs.

(a)   **Direct material**

	£	
37,000 kg of material should cost (× £3)	111,000	
Did cost	120,000	
Material price variance	9,000	(A)

	kg	
9,500 gallons of output should use (× 4)	38,000	
Did use	37,000	
Material usage variance in kg	1,000	(F)
Standard price per kilogram	£3	
Material usage variance in £	£3,000	(F)

Direct labour

	£	
49,000 hours should cost (× £4)	196,000	
Did cost	200,000	
Direct labour rate variance	4,000	(A)

	hours	
9,500 gallons of output should take (× 5)	47,500	
Did take	49,000	
Labour efficiency variance in hours	1,500	(A)
Standard rate per hour	£4	
Direct labour efficiency variance in £	£6,000	(A)

Variable overhead

	£	
49,000 hours should cost (× £5/5 hrs)	49,000	
Did cost	47,000	
Variable overhead expenditure variance	2,000	(F)

Efficiency variance in hours (see above)	1,500	(A)
Standard variable overhead rate per hour	£1	
Variable overhead efficiency variance in £	£1,500	(A)

Fixed overhead

	£	
Budgeted fixed overhead (10,000 × £15)	150,000	
Actual fixed overhead	145,000	
Fixed overhead expenditure variance	5,000	(F)

	units	
Budgeted production volume	10,000	
Actual production volume	9,500	
Volume variance in units	500	(A)
Standard fixed overhead cost per unit	£15	
Fixed overhead volume variance in £	£7,500	(A)

(b) **Sales variances**

	£	
9,500 units should sell for (× £60/unit)	570,000	
Did sell for	588,500	
Sales price	18,500	(F)

	units	
Budgeted sales volume	10,000	
Actual sales volume	9,500	
Sales volume variance in units	500	(A)
Standard profit per unit (£60 - £52)	£8	
Sales margin volume variance in £	£4,000	(A)

Profit reconciliation statement

Period 4

	£	
Budgeted profit	80,000	
Sales margin volume variance	4,000	(A)
Standard profit on actual volume sold	76,000	
Sales margin price variance	18,500	(F)
Cost variances:		
Materials price	9,000	(A)
Materials usage	3,000	(F)
Direct labour rate	4,000	(A)
Direct labour efficiency	6,000	(A)
Variable overhead expenditure	2,000	(F)
Variable overhead efficiency	1,500	(A)
Fixed overhead expenditure	5,000	(F)
Fixed overhead volume	7,500	(A)
Actual profit	76,500	

54 FIXED PRODUCTION OVERHEAD

(a) **Fixed production overhead expenditure variance**

	£	
Budgeted fixed overhead expenditure	2,500,000	
Actual fixed overhead expenditure	2,890,350	
Fixed overhead expenditure variance	**390,350**	**Adverse**

This variance indicates that the company has spent more than originally budgeted.

Fixed production overhead volume variance

Fixed overhead absorption rate/direct labour hour $= \dfrac{£2,500,000}{500,000 \text{ hours}} = £5$.

Budgeted hours/unit = 500,000/62,500 = 8 hours/unit.

Fixed overhead absorption rate/unit = 8 hours × £5/hour = £40 per unit.

(*Tutorial note*: An assumption in this question has to be that fixed overheads are absorbed into product costs at a standard amount per unit - £40 - rather than at a standard amount for each hour worked. Without this assumption, it would not be possible to calculate capacity and efficiency variances in part (b) of the solution. Fixed overheads should therefore be treated in this solution the same way as in a standard costing system.)

	units	
Budgeted volume of production	62,500	
Actual volume of production	70,000	
Fixed overhead volume variance (units)	7,500	Favourable

Fixed overhead rate/unit	£40	
Fixed overhead volume variance (£)	**£300,000**	**Favourable**

This variance indicates that the company has produced more output volume (units) than originally budgeted.

(b) **Fixed production overhead efficiency variance**

	hours	
70,000 units of production should take (× 8 hours)	560,000	
They did take	525,000	
Fixed overhead efficiency variance (hours)	35,000	Favourable

Fixed overhead rate/hour	£5	
Fixed overhead efficiency variance (£)	**£175,000**	**Favourable**

This variance indicates that labour were more efficient than originally budgeted, as they took less time than expected to achieve the production of 70,000 units.

Fixed production overhead capacity variance

	hours	
Budgeted hours of work	500,000	
Actual hours of work	525,000	
Fixed overhead capacity variance (hours)	25,000	Favourable

Fixed overhead rate/hour	£5	
Fixed overhead capacity variance (£)	**£125,000**	**Favourable**

This variance shows that labour worked for more hours than was originally budgeted thus exceeding the budgeted capacity.

(*Note*: The fixed overhead efficiency variance and capacity variance together add up to the fixed overhead volume variance.)

ACCA marking scheme		
(a)	Fixed production overhead expenditure variance £	0.5
	Fixed production overhead expenditure variance adverse	0.5
	Explanation of variance	1.0
	Fixed production overhead volume variance £	0.5
	Fixed production overhead volume variance favourable	0.5
	Calculation of the FOAR/unit	1.0
	Explanation of variance	1.0
(b)	Efficiency variance £	0.5
	Efficiency variance favourable	0.5
	Calculating FOAR/labour hour	1.0
	Explanation of variance	1.0
	Capacity variance £	0.5
	Capacity variance favourable	0.5
	Explanation of variance	1.0
Total		10.0

55   RECONCILIATION STATEMENT

(a)   The question asks for an analysis in as much detail as possible so don't forget to split variances into price and usage/efficiency elements.

Operating statement - Year ended 31 October 20X1

			£
Budgeted profit (W1)			22,312.50

Variances	*Fav*	*Adv*		
	£	£		
Total sales margin variance (W2)	937.50			
Operating variances				
Direct material cost		0		
Direct labour rate (W3)		3,500		
Direct labour efficiency (W4)		4,000		
Vble overhead expenditure (W5)	2,750.00			
Vble overhead efficiency (W6)		1,400		
Fixed overhead expenditure (W7)	2,400.00			
Fixed overhead volume (W8)	500.00			
	———	———		
Total variances	6,587.50	8,900	2,312.50	(A)
	———	———		
Actual profit (W9)			20,000.00	
			———	

Workings

Don't forget to show all workings – give as notes and cross reference to your answer.

(W1)   The selling price per unit is £2.00. Deduct the costs to obtain standard profit per unit:

Costs per unit		£
Material	=	
Labour: 3 minutes at an hourly rate of £10 = 10/60 × 3	=	0.750
Variable overhead: 35% of direct labour cost	=	0.500
Fixed overhead: 40% of direct labour cost	=	0.175
		0.200
		———
		1.625
Selling price		2.000
		———
Standard profit per unit		0.375
		———

Budgeted profit:

59,500 units × £0.375 = £22,312.50.

(W2)   **Total sales margin variance**

	£	£	
Budgeted profit		22,312.50	
Actual sales (62,000 units × £2)	124,000		
Less: Standard cost of actual sales	100,750		
	———		
(62,000 units × £1.625)		23,250.00	
		———	
Total sales margin variance		937.50	(F)
		———	

(W3) **Direct labour rate variance**

	£
3,500 hours should cost (× £10)	35,000
They did cost	38,500
Direct labour rate variance	3,500 (A)

(W4) **Direct labour efficiency variance**

	Hours
62,000 units should take (× 3/60)	3,100
They did take	3,500
Direct labour efficiency variance (hours)	400 (A)
Standard rate per hour	£10
Direct labour efficiency variance (£)	£4,000 (A)

(W5) **Variable overhead expenditure variance**

	£
3,500 hours should cost (× 35% of £10)	12,250
They did cost	9,500
Variable overhead expenditure variance	2,750 (F)

(W6) **Variable overhead efficiency variance**

Efficiency variance in hours (see W4) = 400 hours (A)

Standard variable overhead rate per hour (35% of £10) = £3.50

Variable overhead efficiency variance in £: 400 (A) × £3.50 = £1,400 (A).

(W7) **Fixed overhead expenditure variance**

	£
Budgeted fixed overhead expenditure: £0.20 × 59,500 units	11,900
Actual fixed overhead expenditure	9,500
Fixed overhead expenditure variance	2,400 (F)

(W8) **Fixed overhead volume variance**

	Units
Budgeted production volume	59,500
Actual production volume	62,000
Volume variance (units)	2,500 (F)
Standard fixed overhead rate per unit	£0.20
Fixed overhead volume variance	£500 (F)

(W9) **Actual profit**

	£	£
Sales - 62,000 × £2		124,000
Less:		
Labour	38,500	
Materials - 62,000 × 0.75	46,500	
Variable overheads	9,500	
Fixed overheads	9,500	
		104,000
Profit		20,000

(b) A common sense approach is required here – any sensible answers would gain credit.

Direct labour efficiency variance

(i) Staff which were poorly trained for the job would take longer to produce the goods than the standard.

(ii) Poor staff relationships may have had a negative impact on efficiency.

Direct labour rate variance

(i) A higher wage settlement would mean a higher wage rate.

(ii) Staff members could have been over-skilled for the job and thus earning a higher rate.

(c) *Don't forget here to relate your answer to the case in the question.*

When selecting a method to calculate the overhead absorption rate one should consider the incidence of overheads in the cost centre and reflect this in the choice of rate. A time basis for the absorption of overheads is often used – overheads often increasing in relation to time – a product spending longer in a department incurs more overhead than one spending only a short while. Common examples of this are rates per machine hour and rates per labour hour.

However, which ever method is selected it is essential that data to calculate the standard rate and the actual result for a period are relatively easy to obtain.

SS Ltd only produces one product – thus whichever method is used to obtain an overhead absorption rate the result will be the same.

The method it is currently using to calculate overhead absorption rate is a percentage of direct labour cost. For this method to be used uniform wage rates must apply within a department. It should be noted that with uniform wage rates the result is the same as if the direct labour hour method had been used. SS Ltd has a single wage rate so using a percentage of direct labour cost produced the same results as using the labour hour method.

56   BB LTD

Workings

Standard variable cost per meal = £1.50 + £0.60 = £2.10.

Standard contribution per meal = £5 - £2.10 = £2.90.

(W1)

	£
Budgeted contribution (100,000 meals × £2.90)	290,000
Budgeted fixed costs for the quarter (£500,000/4)	125,000
Budgeted profit	165,000

(W2)

The total sales contribution variance is the sum of the sales price variance and the sales volume (contribution) variance.

	£	
90,000 meals should sell for (× £5)	450,000	
Did sell for (× £4.75)	427,500	
Sales price variance	22,500	(A)

	meals	
Budgeted sales	100,000	
Actual sales	90,000	
Sales volume variance in meals	10,000	(A)

Standard contribution per meal	£2.90	
Sales volume contribution variance	£29,000	(A)

Total sales contribution variance = £22,500 (A) + £29,000 (A)

= £51,500 (A)

Alternative approach: You could also calculate the variance as the difference between budgeted contribution and actual sales revenue minus the standard variable cost of actual sales.

	£	£
Budgeted contribution (10,000 × £160)		290,000
Actual sales	427,500	
Standard variable cost of actual sales	189,000	
(90,000 × £2.10)		
		238,500
Total sales contribution variance		51,500 (A)

(W3)

Food and drink cost	£	
90,000 meals should cost (× £1.50)	135,000	
Did cost	112,500	
Food and drink total cost variance	22,500	(F)

(W4)

	hours	
90,000 meals should take (× 6 minutes)	9,000	
Did take	8,250	
Efficiency variance in hours	750	(F)

Direct labour rate per hour (£0.60 × 60/6 minutes)	£6	
Direct labour efficiency variance in £	£4,500	(F)

(W5)

	£	
8,250 hours of labour should cost (× £6)	49,500	
Did cost	48,675	
Direct labour rate variance	825	(F)

(W6)

	£	
Budgeted fixed overheads for the quarter	125,000	
Actual fixed overheads	120,000	
Fixed overheads expenditure variance	5,000	(F)

Answers (a) to (f)

Profit reconciliation statement
for the quarter ending 31 March 20X2

		£	£	
(W1)	Budgeted profit		165,000	
(W2)	Total sales margin contribution variance		51,500	(A)
			113,500	
(W3)	Food and drink: total cost variance	22,500 (F)		
(W4)	Labour efficiency variance	4,500 (F)		
(W5)	Labour rate variance	825 (F)		
(W6)	Fixed overhead expenditure variance	5,000 (F)		
	Total cost variances		32,825	(F)
	Actual profit		146,325	

(g)   Fixed overhead volume variance, which is the amount of fixed overhead under- or over-absorbed due to actual production volume differing from the budgeted volume.

57   X LTD

(a)   **Direct materials**

	£	
900 units should cost (× £5)	4,500	
Variance	180	(F)
So did cost	4,320	

(b)   **Direct labour**

	£
900 units should cost (× £7.40)	6,660
Variance	980 (A)
So did cost	7,640

(c)   **Variable overhead**

	£
900 units should cost (× £2.30)	2,070
Variance	240 (A)
So did cost	2,310

(d)   **Fixed overhead**

	£
Standard cost of 900 units (× £3.80)	3,420
Total fixed overhead variance	200 (A)
Actual cost	2,610

Tutorial note: The total fixed overhead variance is under-absorbed overhead of £200. Actual overhead costs were therefore £200 more than the overheads absorbed. Overheads are absorbed in standard costing at a standard rate/unit produced, £3.80.

58   VARIANCES

Key answer tips

To calculate a realistic efficiency variance, use the actual attainable hours less the standard hours for actual production.

(a)   **Standard cost per unit**

	£
Material A: 1.2 kg at £11	13.20
Material B: 4.7 kg at £6	28.20
Labour: 1.5 hours at £8	12.00
Overheads: 1.5 at £30	45.00
	98.40

(b)   **Labour rate variance**

	£
215,000 hours should cost (× £8)	1,720,000
They did cost	1,700,000
Labour rate variance	20,000 (F)

Realistic efficiency variance

120,000 units have a standard time of (42 + 37 + 11 minutes per unit)

= 120,000 × 1.5 hours = 180,000 hours.

The budgeted time is 500 × 400 hours = 200,000 hours.

This indicates that the actual hours worked should be converted by a factor of ×
200/180 to convert from ideal labour time to realistic labour time.

Standard rate × (Actual attainable hours − Standard for actual production)

	Hours	
126,000 units should take (× 90/60 hours) × 200/180	210,000	
They did take	215,000	
Labour efficiency variance (hours)	5,000	(A)
Standard rate per hour	£8	
Direct labour efficiency variance (£)	£40,000	(A)

(c) **Material price variance**

Material A

	£	
150,000 kg should cost (× £11)	1,650,000	
They did cost	1,650,000	
Material A price variance	Nil	

Material B

	£	
590,000 kg should cost (× £6)	3,540,000	
They did cost	3,600,000	
Material B price variance	60,000	(A)

Material usage variances

Material A

	Kg	
126,000 units should use (× 1.2 kgs)	151,200	
They did use	150,000	
Material A usage variance (kgs)	1,200	(F)
Standard rate per kilogram	£11	
Material A usage variance (£)	£13,200	(F)
Material A usage variance (kgs)	1,200	(F)

Material B	*Kg*	
126,000 units should use (× 4.7 kgs)	592,200	
They did use	590,000	
Material A usage variance (kgs)	2,200	(F)
Standard rate per kilogram	£6	
Material B usage variance (£)	£13,200	(F)

(d)   The manufacturing environment in which labour variances can provide useful information is one which is relatively stable, i.e. where it is realistic to expect the time taken to make a unit not to change. If it does change, for example if the workforce can be expected to get quicker with practice, then labour variances comparing actual time with a now 'out of date' standard time are of little relevance.

59   LABOUR-INTENSIVE PRODUCT

(a)   *Variable production overhead expenditure variance:*

	£	
9,300 hours should cost (× £3)	27,900	
They did cost	28,900	
Variable overhead expenditure variance	1,000	(A)

(b)   *Variable production overhead efficiency variance:*

	Hours	
5,000 units should take (× 2)	10,000	
They did take	9,300	
Direct labour efficiency variance (hours)	700	(F)
Standard rate per hour	£3	
Variable overhead efficiency variance (£)	£2,100	(F)

(c)   *Fixed production overhead expenditure variance:*

	£	
Budgeted fixed overhead expenditure	120,000	
Actual fixed overhead expenditure	118,000	
Fixed overhead expenditure variance	2,000	(F)

(d)   *Fixed production overhead volume variance*

	Units	
Budgeted production volume (W1)	4,800	
Actual production volume	5,000	
Volume variance (units)	200	(F)
Standard fixed overhead rate per unit (W2)	£25	
Fixed overhead volume variance	£5,000	(F)

Workings

(W1) Budgeted output $= \dfrac{9{,}600\text{hrs}}{2\text{hrs}/\text{unit}} = 4{,}800$ units

(W2) Fixed overhead absorption rate/unit $= \dfrac{\text{Budgeted overheads}}{\text{Budgeted number of units}}$

$= \dfrac{\pounds120{,}000}{4{,}800 \text{ units}} = \pounds25/\text{unit}$

DECISION MAKING

COST BEHAVIOUR, TIME SERIES ANALYSIS

60 LINEAR FUNCTION

(a)

Year	Costs	Cost inflation index	Costs at Year 1 prices
	£		£
1	135,000	/1.000	135,000
2	144,072	/1.035	139,200
3	156,090	/1.075	145,200
4	158,950	/1.100	144,500

High-low method

	Year 1 prices £
Total cost of 75,600 units	145,200
Total cost of 67,200 units	135,000
Variable cost of 8,400 units	10,200

Variable cost per unit = £10,200/8,400 units = £1.214 per unit.

Substituting in Year 1:

	£
Total cost of 67,200 units	135,000
Variable cost of 67,200 units (× £1.214)	81,581
Fixed costs	53,419

Total cost equation at Year 1 prices:

Total cost (£) = 53,419 + 1.214x

where x is the number of units.

(b)   Using the equation in (a) for Years 2 and 4 (at Year 1 prices):

Year	Units	Variable costs £	Fixed costs £	Total costs £
2	71,300	86,558	53,419	139,977
4	75,100	91,171	53,419	144,590

In Year 2, actual costs were below predicted costs by £(139,200 – 139,977) = £777.

This was (£777/£139,977) × 100% = 0.6% below the predicted costs.

In Year 4, actual costs were below predicted costs by £(144,500 – 144,590) = £90.

This was (£90/£144,590) × 100% = 0.1% below the predicted costs.

It should therefore be concluded that the cost equation, adjusted for inflation, is an accurate predictor of costs under existing operating conditions.

(c)

	£
Variable costs at Year 1 prices (77,200 × £1.214)	93,721
Fixed costs at Year 1 prices	53,419
Total costs at Year 1 prices	147,140
Inflation adjustment	1.129
Total costs at Year 5 prices	£166,121

(d)   See chart.

Profit – volume chart: Year 5

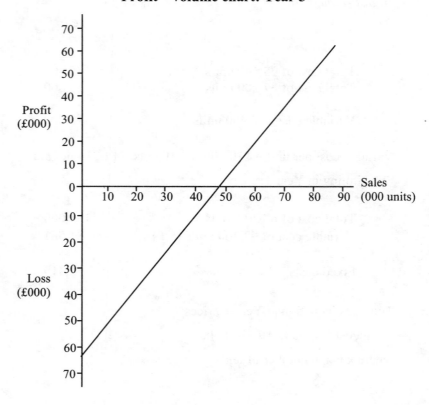

Workings for chart:

Tutorial note: We need two points on the chart, which can then be used to draw the chart, because the graph is a straight line. The points chosen here are the loss at zero sales and the profit at sales of 90,000 units.

Fixed costs at Year 1 prices = £53,419.

Fixed costs at Year 5 prices = £53,419 × 1.129 = £60,310.

This is the loss that would be incurred if sales were zero.

Year 1 selling price = £159,936/67,200 units = £2.38 per unit.

Year 5 sales revenue from 90,000 units 1.15 × £2.38 × 90,000 units = £246,330.

	£	£
Sales revenue		246,330
Variable costs (90,000 × £1.214 × 1.129)	123,355	
Fixed costs (see above)	60,310	
		183,665
Profit at sales of 90,000 units		62,665

61 TOTAL SURVEYS LTD

Key answer tips

First adjust the figures for inflation and then use the high-low method to determine the fixed and variable elements.

(a) Before using the 'high low' method on the data given to estimate the variable element due to change in activity level, the data must be adjusted onto a comparable inflation basis. Thus the 20X5 cost will initially be inflated by 5% to convert it to '20X6 £s':

£6 million × 1.05 = £6.3 million

Change in total (adjusted) cost from 20X5 to 20X6 = £(6.615 - 6.3)m = £315,000

This is attributable to a 20% increase in activity, i.e. the variable cost for 100% activity (20X5 level) = £315,000/0.2 = £1.575 million (in 20X6 £s), giving a variable cost for 20X6 = £1.575m × 1.2 = £1.89 million

Thus the variable cost for 20X7, taking account of a further 25% increase in activity and 4% inflation

= £1.89m × 1.25 × 1.04 = **£2.457 million**

Fixed cost for 20X6 = Total cost - variable cost = £(6.615 - 1.89)m = £4.725 million

Thus the fixed cost for 20X7, taking account of further 4% inflation

= £4.725m × 1.04 = **£4.914 million**

(b) C/S ratio = $\dfrac{\text{Sales - Variable cost}}{\text{Sales}} \times 100\%$

Thus, for 20X7, $\dfrac{\text{Sales - £2.457m}}{\text{Sales}} = 0.8$

=> Sales - £2.457m = 0.8 Sales

=> 0.2 Sales = £2.457m

=> Sales = £2.457m/0.2 = **£12.285 million**

(c) The following comments may be made about the above method of splitting total costs into fixed and variable elements:

- Only two years' worth of data have been used.

- This may lead to an unrepresentative result. More observations need to be used for more reliable estimates. This will obviously present problems if only a limited amount of data is available, e.g. in the early years of a business.

- It has been assumed that activity level and inflation are the only factors influencing cost.

- In practice, there may be many factors influencing cost - e.g. efficiency levels, production process methods, non-activity based cost drivers (set-ups, material orders etc), market resource price changes, learning effects etc - which will be difficult to build into a mathematical analysis.

- Costs and activity level are assumed to be related in a linear fashion.

- Even if activity level is the main influential factor on cost (cost driver) the two may not be linearly related. As activity level increases, costs per unit may change (through overtime, discounts, diminishing returns to a factor etc). These will again present problems in the analysis.

- The results of the analysis have been used to project costs for an activity level and time outside the range of the original data.

Relationships that have existed in the past may be affected by changes proposed for the future - e.g. technological - and by working at an activity level outside past experience. These effects may be quite difficult to quantify and build into the estimates.

Some of these limitations can be overcome to some extent by the use of multiple linear regression, a more complex technique that incorporates more data and variables into the analysis. However, this will still be using data within a particular time span and activity range.

62   COST ANALYSIS

Key answer tips

(a) Take care to answer the question set . It does not say 'write all you know about the different types of cost behaviour'. The main point is to discuss how knowledge of the behaviour helps in cost management; discussion of different types of behaviour (with examples) is required as an *illustration* to the answer.

(b) Remember that the high-low method is so named because it uses data related to the highest and lowest output levels (not necessarily corresponding to the highest and lowest costs).

(a) **Behavioural analysis of costs is important for planning, control and decision-making.**

Different costs may have different behaviour patterns in response to changes in activity, influenced by several factors. At one extreme, certain costs may remain fixed unaffected by changes in activity e.g. capacity costs such as rent and rates. This is unlikely to remain the case, however, for large changes in activity where step increases or decreases in costs are likely to occur. At the other extreme certain costs may be variable with activity e.g. raw materials. However, the change may not be exactly proportional due to relative efficiencies, or economies of scale, at different levels of activity. Other patterns of behaviour may be found.

The fact that various patterns of cost behaviour exist highlights the importance of a behavioural analysis, in order to help to plan and control such costs on an ongoing basis and in order to help to identify incremental costs that may be incurred by decision alternatives.

(b) **High-low method**

		£
High	Total cost of 14,000 units	113,201
Low	Total cost of 11,500 units	102,476
	Variable cost of 2,500 units	10,725

Variable cost per unit = £10,725/2,500 units = £4.29.

Substituting:

	£
Total cost of 14,000 units	113,201
Variable cost of 14,000 units (× £4.29)	60,060
Fixed costs	53,141

Total costs = Fixed costs of £53,141 plus a variable cost of £4.29 per unit.

63 SOUTH

(a)

x units	y £000	xy	x^2
300	3.8	1,140	90,000
400	4.0	1,600	160,000
150	3.0	450	22,500
260	3.5	910	67,600
1,110	14.3	4,100	340,100

$n = 4$

$$b = \frac{4 \times 4,100 - 1,110 \times 14.3}{4 \times 340,100 - (1,110)^2}$$

$$= \frac{527}{128,300} = 0.0041$$

$$a = \frac{14.3}{4} - 0.0041 \times \frac{1,110}{4}$$

$$= 2.437$$

Total cost = 2.437 + 0.0041 × activity (with total cost in £000)

Total cost = 2,437 + 4.1 × activity (with total cost in £)

(b)   Total cost at 200 units = 2,437 + 4.1 × 200 = £3,257

Since the value of 200 units lies within the range of the data (i.e. interpolation) some reliance can be placed upon the value generated. (The degree of reliance can be measured by calculating the correlation coefficient r.)

Total cost at 500 units = 2,437 + 4.1 × 500 = £4,487

Since the value of 500 units lies outside the range of the data (i.e. extrapolation) very little reliance can be placed upon the value generated.

ACCA marking scheme		Marks
(a)	Total for x	0.5
	Total for y	0.5
	xy column	1.0
	x^2 column	1.0
	Calculation of b	1.5
	Calculation of a	1.0
	Stating the total cost equation	0.5
(b)	Calculation of total cost at 200 units	1.0
	Comment on interpolation	1.0
	Calculation of total cost at 500 units	1.0
	Comment on extrapolation	1.0
Total		10.0

64   SAPPHIRE

(a)

x	y	xy	x^2
220	4.5	990	48,400
400	7.0	2,800	160,000
360	5.5	1,980	129,600
380	6.0	2,280	144,400
290	5.0	1,450	84,100
1,650	28.0	9,500	566,500

n = 5

$$b = \frac{(5 \times 9,500) - (1,650 \times 28.0)}{5 \times 566,500 - (1,650)^2}$$

$$= \frac{1,300}{110,000} = 0.0118$$

$$a = \frac{28}{5} - \frac{0.0118(1,650)}{5} = 1.706$$

Total cost = 1.706 + 0.0118 × activity (activity in 000s)

Total cost = 1,706 + 11.8 × activity (with total cost in £)

(b)   (i)   Total cost for 300 units =

1,706 + (11.8 × 300) = £5,246

(ii)   Total cost for 450 units =

1,706 + (11.8 × 450) = £7,016

Note: Since the value of 300 units lies within the range of data, some reliance can be placed upon the value calculated above. However, as 450 units lies outside of the range of data, little reliance can be placed upon the value calculated above.

65   LINEAR RELATIONSHIP

(a)

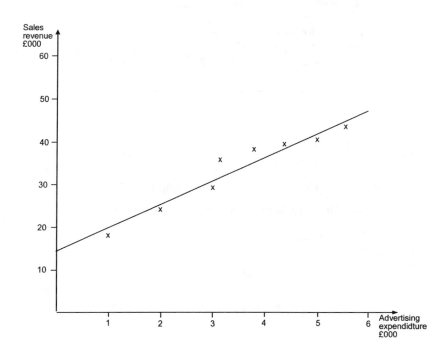

(b)   Regression line: y = a + bx

$$b = \frac{n\Sigma xy\ \Sigma x\ \Sigma y}{n\Sigma x^2\ (\Sigma x)^2}$$

$$a = \frac{\Sigma y}{n} - \frac{b\Sigma x}{n}$$

In this example the advertising expenditure is in the independent variable (×) and the sales revenue the dependent variable (y).

$$b = \frac{(8 \times 1{,}055.875) - (26.35 \times 289.5)}{(8 \times 101.2625) - 26.35^2} = \frac{818.675}{115.7775} = 7.07$$

$$a = \frac{289.5}{8} - 7.07 \times \frac{26.35}{8} = 12.9$$

regression line: y = 12.9 + 7.07x where x and y are in £000.

Line drawn on above graph.

	ACCA marking scheme	
		Marks
(a)	Points plotted correctly	3
	Labeled axes	½
	Presentation	½
	Explanation of axes used	1
(b)	Calculation of b	2
	Calculation of a	1½
	Stating the regression line	½
	Putting the Regression line on the graph from (a)	1
Total		10

CVP ANALYSIS

66 TOOWAMBA

(a) (i)   Total cost for 30,000 units or less = 50,000 + 5Q

Total cost for more than 30,000 units = 100,000 + 5Q

(b)

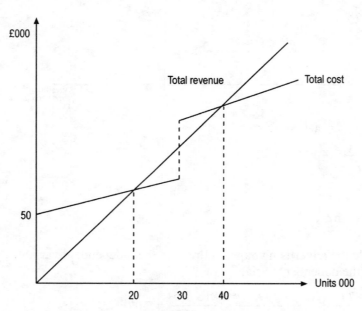

(c)   Implications of having two breakeven points: the product is only profitable between 20,000 and 30,000 units and above 40,000 units, so the production should be set accordingly.

67 TRADING RESULTS

(a) (i)

Price	Volume	Sales	Direct costs	Overheads	Total costs	Profit
£	000 units	£000	£000	£000	£000	£000
2.76	2,110.5	5,825	1,903	3,699	5,602	223
2.53	2,677.5	6,774	2,415	3,881	6,296	478
2.30	3,150	7,245	2,841	4,032	6,873	372
2.07	3,591	7,433	2,850	4,173	7,023	410
1.84	3,937.5	7,245	2,841	4,284	7,125	20

Workings

Sales volume 000s	Direct costs	O'hds production & sales
2,110.5	(67% of 2,841) = 1,903	$4,032 \times (1 - 0.0825) = 3,699$
2,677.5	(85% of 2,841) = 2,415	$4,032 \times (1 - 0.0375) = 3,881$
3,150.0	2,841	$(2,145 + 1,887) = 4,032$
3,591.0	(114% of 0.88) = 2,850	$4,032 \times (1 + 0.035) = 4,173$
3,937.5	(125% of 0.80) = 2,841	$4,032 \times (1 + 0.0625) = 4,284$

(ii)   **Sales and cost functions**

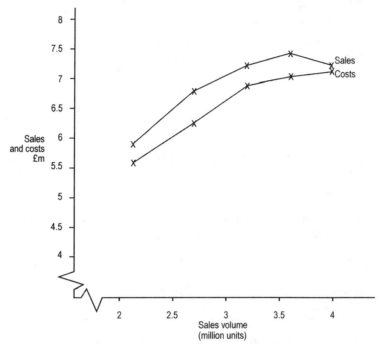

(iii)   The analysis indicates that an increase in selling price of about 10% is justified as profit would be expected to increase to £478,000.

(b)   (i)   Overheads adjusted for inflation:

Period 1 $3,409 \times 1.154$ = 3,934

Period 2 $3,559 \times 1.154/1.052$ = 3,904

Period 3 $3,764 \times 1.154/1.091$ = 3,981

Period 4 $3,913 \times 1.154/1.125$ = 4,014

Period 5   = 4,032

(ii)   High-low method:

$$\text{Variable cost per unit} = \frac{4,032 - 3,904}{3,150 - 2,750}$$

$$= \text{£0.32 per unit}$$

	£000
Cost of 3,150,000 units	4,032
Cost of 2,750,000 units	3,904
Variable cost of 400 units	128
Variable cost/unit	£0.32

At 3,150,000 units:

	£000
Total cost of 3,150,000 units	4,032
Variable cost of 3,150,000 units (× 0.32)	1,008
Fixed costs	———
	3,024

Variable costs = 3,150,000 × 0.32 = £1,008 k

Fixed costs = 4,032,000 − 1,008,000 = £3,024 k

Variable costs are 25% of total costs (1,008/4,032 × 100%) and therefore overheads would be expected to change at a quarter of the rate of any change in sales volume.

68 BREAKEVEN

Key answer tips

To calculate break-even point it is necessary to identify total fixed costs. This can be done using the high/low method. When there is uncertainty regarding the expected level of sales, the best way to approach the question is:

(1) Consider whether previous calculations are relevant. In this case the break-even point, which helps in assessing the riskiness of the two alternatives, has already been calculated.

(2) Calculate the profit expected at each of the activity levels given in the question.

(3) Interpret the break-even and profit/loss figures. In general higher profits are desirable but alternatives which result in losses at low activity levels should be treated with caution.

(a) **Calculation of break-even point when selling via agents**

Assumption

Manufacturing costs vary with sales revenue.

(1) *Calculation of fixed manufacturing costs*

		£
High	Cost when sales = £800,000	410,000
Low	Cost when sales = £600,000	350,000
	Variable cost for sales of £200,000	60,000

Variable manufacturing costs = £60,000/£200,000 = 30% of sales revenue.

Substituting:

	£
Total manufacturing cost when sales = £800,000	410,000
Variable cost when sales = £800,000 (× 30%)	240,000
Fixed manufacturing costs	170,000

Total fixed costs = Fixed manufacturing + fixed administration costs = £170,000 + £160,000 = £330,000

(2)   *Calculation of contribution/sales ratio at 'high' activity level*

	£000	£000
Sales		800
Less: Variable costs:		
Selling 800 × 10%	80	
Manufacturing	240	
		320
Contribution		480

$$\text{Contribution/sales ratio} = \frac{\text{Contribution}}{\text{Sales}} \times 100$$

$$= \frac{480}{800} \times 100$$

$$= 60\%$$

(3)   *Break-even point*

$$\frac{\text{Total fixed costs}}{\text{Contribution sales ratio}} \times 100 = \frac{330}{60\%} \times 100$$

$$= \pounds550,000$$

(b)   **Calculation of break-even point with own sales force**

	£000
Fixed costs, as above	330
Add: Increase in selling costs	60
	390

	£000
Contribution/sales ratio:	
Sales	800
Less: Variable costs	240
Contribution	560

$$\text{Contribution/sales ratio} = \frac{560}{800} \times 100$$

$$= 70\%$$

$$\text{Break-even point} = \frac{\text{Total fixed costs}}{\text{Contribution sales ratio}} \times 100$$

$$= \frac{390}{70\%} \times 100$$

$$= \pounds557,000$$

69   PROFIT VOLUME

Key answer tips

(a)   The question asks for a profit volume chart, so don't do more than one diagram. However you have two periods with different contribution margins, so you will need two lines on the chart. The PV chart can either have sales volume or revenue on the x axis - here you need to use the latter. You only need two points to plot each line - you have one from the question data, and the easiest second point is at sales of zero. Join these two and extend to sales of £1m.

(b)   First work out your target contribution (period 1's profit add back period 2's fixed costs). The C/S ratio gives you the rate at which contribution is generated from sales, so dividing target contribution by C/S will give target sales.

(a)   **Period 1:**

Profit at zero sales	=	(£297.8k)
Profit at £742.7k sales	=	£36.6k
Profit at £1m sales	=	$\left(1m \times \dfrac{334.4}{742.7}\right) - 297.8$
	=	£152.4k

    Period 2:

Profit at zero sales	=	(£312.7k)
Profit at £794.1k sales	=	£72.4k
Profit at £1m sales	=	$\dfrac{\left(1m \times \dfrac{385.1}{794.1}\right)}{} - 312.7$
	=	£172.3k

Profit volume chart

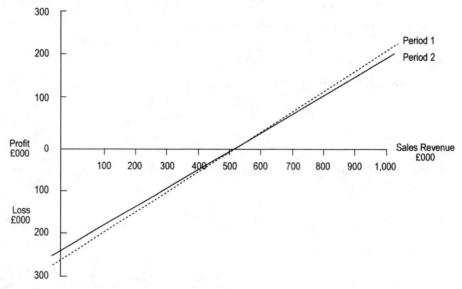

(b)   Sales required to maintain profit $= \dfrac{36.6 + 312.7}{385.1 / 794.1}$

    =   <u>£720k</u>

(c)   (i)   The C/S ratio is the ratio of contribution to sales. It is normally expressed as a percentage, i.e.

$$\frac{\text{Contribution (£)}}{\text{Sales (£)}} \times 100\%$$

        (ii)   The margin of safety is the difference between actual/budgeted sales volume and break-even sales volume (where sales > break-even). It is normally expressed as a percentage of actual/budgeted sales i.e.

$$\frac{\text{Margin of safety}}{\text{Sales (£)}} \times 100\%$$

70   PE LTD

(a)   Each unit of P yields a contribution of £5

Each unit of E yields a contribution of £2

Therefore one sales batch of 4P and 3E yields contribution of:

(4 × £5) + (3 × £2)   = £26

Fixed cost   = £561,600

Therefore breakeven $= \dfrac{£561,600}{£26} = 21,600$ sales batches

This is:

		£
21,600 × 4 = 86,400 of P at £10 =		864,000
Plus 21,600 × 3 = 64,800 of E at £12 =		777,600
Breakeven sales revenue		1,641,600

(b)   Using the same principles each sales batch yields:

(4 × £5) + (4 × £2) = £28

Therefore breakeven $= \dfrac{£561,600}{£28} = 20,057.14$ batches

= 80,228.571 or 80,229 of each product

The sales revenue is; 80,229 × £22 = £1,765,038

(c)   The product mix of 4P to 3E has a lower total sales value requirement to breakeven, but requires more sales of P and less of E to breakeven than the mix of 4P to 4E. The solution depends on the market demand for each product. Whilst product P is more profitable per unit than product E if the market for P cannot support a demand of 86,400 units the second mix is preferable, if this demand for product P does exist then mix (i) is preferable because it is more profitable.

(d)

	Product P	Product E
Contribution/unit	£5	£2
Hours/unit	0.4	0.1
Contribution/hour	£12.50	£20

When there is a shortage of machine hours product E yields the better return per hour than product P. Thus production should concentrate on product E. If all time is spent on product E then (32,000/0.1) 320,000 units can be made which yields a contribution of £640,000 and a net profit of £78,400.

LIMITING FACTORS

71   CUCKFIELD

(a)   Let the number of units of product D made and sold be d.

Let the number of units of product H made and sold be h.

The contribution per unit of D is £8.50 and the contribution per unit of H is £27.

The objective function is therefore to maximise 8.50d + 27h.

This is subject to the following constraints:

$3d + 2h \leq 3,000$ (availability of material A)

$0.5d + 2h \leq 1,000$ (availability of material N)

$1.5d + 1.5h \leq 1,800$ (availability of semi-skilled labour hours)

$d + 1.4h \geq 700$ (minimum skilled labour hours)

$d \geq 0, h \geq 0$ (non-negativity constraints for products D and H)

(b)

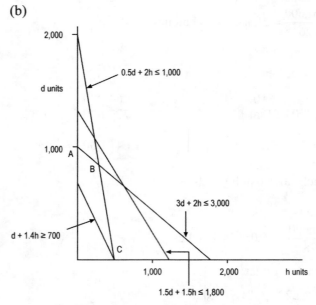

The optimal point will be on either A, B or C.

Tutorial note: Semi-skilled labour hours are not an effective constraint in this problem.

A solution was not required by this question. However, check whether you can solve the problem. Contribution is maximised at point B, where d = 800 and h = 300, so that total contribution is £14,700. Having identified point B as the optimal solution, you can calculate the values for d and h by solving the simultaneous equations 0.5d + 2h = 1,000 and 3d + 2h = 3,000).

ACCA marking scheme		
		Marks
(a)	Constraint equation for Material A	1.0
	Constraint equation for Material N	1.0
	Constraint equation for semi-skilled workers	1.0
	Constraint equation for skilled workers	1.0
(b)	Labelling the axes on the graph	0.5
	Drawing the Material A constraint	1.0
	Drawing the Material N constraint	1.0
	Drawing the semi-skilled workers constraint	1.0
	Drawing the skilled workers constraint	1.0
	Good presentation	0.5
	Stating possible optimal points	1.0
Total		10.0

72   T LIMITED

(a)   Objective is to maximise contribution

Therefore objective function = 24X + 30Y

(b)   Skilled labour (X = 8 hours per unit , Y = 5 hours per unit)

Constraint = $8X + 5Y \leq 1,200$

Semi-skilled labour (X = 5 hours per unit, Y = 5 hours per unit)

Constraint = $5X + 5Y \leq 900$

X max constant demand ≤ 100

Y max constant demand ≤ 150

(c)   See graph

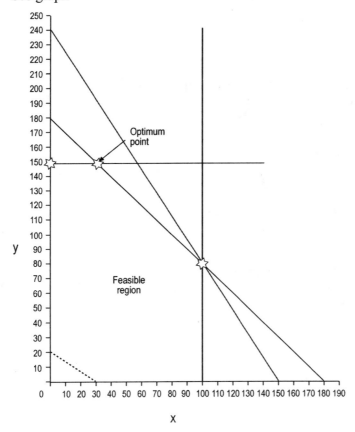

(d)   Optimum point is where the line y = 150 and $5x + 5y \leq 900$ intersect

Substituting Y= 150 into the other formula:

$5X + 5(150) \leq 900$

$5X \leq 150$

$X \leq 30$

Therefore to maximise contribution make 150 Y and 30 X.

73   OPTIMAL PRODUCTION PLAN

(a)   The objective is to maximise profit:

Let a = the number of units of A to be produced

Let b = the number of units of B to be produced

Objective function: Maximise 9a + 23b

Subject to the following constraints:

Non-negativity	$b \geq 0$
Restriction on A	$a \geq 1,000$
Materials	$3a + 4b \leq 30,000$
Labour	$5a + 3b \leq 36,000$

Tutorial note

The constraints and the objective function are shown in the following graph. The objective function line shown here is:

9a + 23b = 103.5.

When a = 0, b = 103.5/23 = 4.5.

When b = 0, a = 103.5/9 = 11.5.

So plot a = 0, b = 4.5 and b = 0, a = 11.5 on the graph and join the points to get an objective function line 9a + 23b = 103.5. This lets us determine the slope of the objective function line.

The figure 103.5 has been chosen because (9 × 23) = 207. However, drawing the line 9a + 23b = 207 would mean joining the points a = 0, b = 9 and b = 0, a = 23, which would not be possible to draw, given the scale of this graph. Therefore 207 has been halved to 103.5, for convenience.(b)

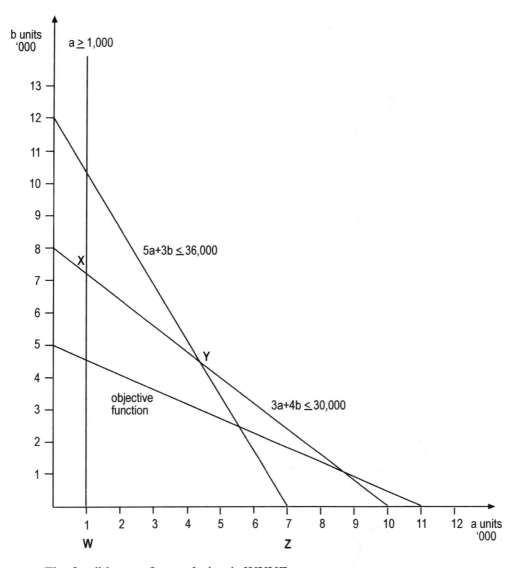

The feasible area for a solution is WXYZ.

The optimal point, where the objective function is maximized, is at point X, the intersect of the a = 1,000 line and the materials constraint line 3a + 4b = 30,000.

At this point, a = 1,000.

Therefore:

(3 x 1,000) + 4b = 30,000

3,000 + 4b = 30,000

4b = 30,000 − 3,000 = 27,000

b = 27,000/4,000

    = 6,750 units

The **optimal production plan** is to make 1,000 units of A and 6,750 units of B.

ACCA marking scheme		
(a)	Defining variables	0.5
	Objective function	0.5
	Non-negativity constraint for b	0.5
	Variable a greater 1,000	1.0
	Material constraint	1.0
	Labour constraint	0.5
(b)	Labelled axes on graph	0.5
	Good presentation	0.5
	Correctly drawn material line	1.0
	Correctly drawn labour line	1.0
	Restriction on a line	0.5
	Plotting the objective function	1.0
	Establishing the optimal point	1.5
Total		10.0

74   PRODUCTION PLANNING

Key answer tips

(i)   Here, you are not required to draw the graph yourself; instead you are given it, and asked to analyse/interpret it. When finding the equations for the constraint lines, don't forget there are two sides to an equation - on the left, the usage of the resource by the products (given in the question) and on the right, the total availability of the resource (deduced from the graph itself)). Ensure that when you define your variables, you state whether they are in unit or '000s units, as this will affect your constraint equations.

(ii)   There are only two constraints, so PQ must be related to the other main element of a linear programming problem - the objective. As well as explaining in general what the line represents, you should use data from the question to illustrate, as asked.

(i)   The feasible region is the area MZYO on the graph:

Equation for line MN:

The constraint is

$0.08A + 0.07B = T$

When A = 0, B = 11,428

When B = 0, A = 10,000

So,

$T = 0.08 \times 10,000 = 800$

or $0.07 \times 11,428 = 800$

So the constraint here is $0.08A + 0.07B = 800$

Equation for line XY:

The constraint is

$0.125A + 0.0625 = V$

When A = 0, B = 16,000

When B = 0, A = 8,000

So,

V = 16,000 ×0.0625 = 1,000

or 8,000 × 0.125 = 1,000

So the constraint here is 0.125A + 0.0625B = 1,000

where:

A = units of Product A

B = units of Product B

These equations simplify to 0.08A + 0.07B = 800

0.125A + 0.0625B = 1,000.

(ii) PQ is a line showing varying combinations of Products A and B all of which produce the same total profit contribution. It is an 'iso-contribution line', used to determine the slope of any total contribution line and is a means of identifying an optimal solution.

For example:

	Product A	Product B
Selling price £/unit	5.00	3.50
Variable cost £/unit	2.80	1.40
Contribution £/unit	2.20	2.10
× Output at points Q and P respectively	× 4,545	× 4,762
= Total contribution (£)	£10,000	£10,000

So the line is 2.20A + 2.10B = 10,000.

RELEVANT COSTS, DECISIONS WITH UNCERTAINTY, PRICING DECISIONS

75 MIKE LIMITED

Relevant cost statement

	Note	£
Material V	1	900
Material I	2	6,500
Material C	3	2,050
Department 1	4	–
Department 2	5	26,000
Overheads	6	–
Minimum contract price		35,450

Notes

1 The historical cost of £10 is not relevant, as it is a sunk cost. The relevant cost is the opportunity cost relating to lost scrap proceeds:

= 300 × £3 = £900.

2   Again, the historical cost is irrelevant, as it is a sunk cost. Since the material is in continuous use in the business, the relevant cost is the current replacement cost of the material

= 1,000 × £6.50 = £6,500.

3   Since there is only 300 kg in stock, 250 kg would need to be purchased at the current replacement cost = 250 × £4 = £1,000. If the current stock of 300 kg is not used for the contract, it would be used to replace material Y in an alternative production process.

Therefore the relevant cost for the stock of 300 kg is = 300 × £7/2 = £1,050, bearing in mind the 2-for-1 substitution.

Total relevant cost for material C = £1,000 + £1,050 = £2,050.

4   Since there is spare capacity in this department, there is no relevant cost.

5   For this department, the two alternatives need to be considered:

Cost of working overtime = 2,000 × £10 ×1.5 = £30,000

Cost of diverting labour = 2,000 × (£10 + £3) = £26,000

It would be cheaper to divert the labour from the other production processes, so the relevant cost for department 2 is £26,000.

6   There will be an increase in overhead expenditure for the relevant costs.

7   The minimum price is the price that just covers the relevant costs of the contract.

ACCA marking scheme	
	Marks
Calculation of relevant cost for material V	0.5
Explanation of historic cost as sunk	0.5
Explanation of relevant cost being opportunity cost relating to lost scrap proceeds	0.5
Calculation of relevant cost for material I	0.5
Explanation of relevant costs being current purchase cost as in continuous use in business	0.5
Calculation of relevant cost for material C	1.0
Explanation of need to buy extra units and relevant cost	0.5
Explanation of the relevant cost of the alternative use for material C	0.5
Calculation of relevant cost of labour in dept 1	0.5
Explanation of there being spare capacity so no relevant cost	0.5
Calculation of relevant cost of labour in dept 2	1.0
Explanation including the need to compare overtime costs with cost of diverting labour	1.0
Calculation of relevant cost of overheads	0.5
Explanation of there being no incremental costs	0.5
Presentation of statement and notes	1.0
Stating minimum price being the total of the relevant costs	0.5
Total	10.0

76   ALBANY

(a)   Marginal cost plus = £30 × 120% = £36

Advantages

–   Simple and easy to calculate

–   Focuses on contribution

–   Can easily adjust the mark-up

Disadvantages

– Selling price might not cover fixed costs

– Ignores price/demand relationship

Total cost plus = £37 × 120% = £44.40

Advantages

– More likely to ensure a profit is made

– Product is not sold below full cost

– Simple and easy to calculate

– Can easily adjust the mark-up

Disadvantages

– Fixed costs need to be allocated to the cost unit which may be ambiguous

– Ignores price/demand relationships

(b) **Any two** of the following pricing strategies should be discussed:

– Price skimming – tends to lead to a high price initially, useful if the product is completely new

– Penetration pricing – go to market with a low price initially to gain market share

– Pricing discrimination – use two different prices in two different markets if there are barriers between the markets e.g. Age, time and location

– Premium pricing – charging a higher price than the competitors as the product can be differentiated

– Costs plus pricing – leads to a price that will cover costs although care needs to be taken with regard to Marginal cost plus to ensure that the plus is large enough to cover fixed costs

– Market price – leads to an acceptable price but one which may vary

– Price to maximise profits although a demand function will need to be established – leads to an optimal price but may not affect the market price.

ACCA marking scheme		Marks
(a)	Calculation of marginal cost plus	1
	Advantage of marginal cost plus	1
	Disadvantage of marginal cost plus	1
	Calculation of fixed cost plus	1
	Advantage of fixed cost plus	1
	Disadvantage of fixed cost plus	1
(b)	Two pricing strategies and impacts required. For each, 1 mark for strategy and 1 mark for impact	4
Total		10

77 NORTHSHIRE HOSPITAL TRUST

Key answer tips

Calculate the total cost per scan, then multiply by 100/90 to reflect the fact that 10% are not successful.

(a) **Cost of satisfactory brain scan on XR1**

Cost per scan

		£
Cost of x-ray plate		40.00
Variable cost	4 hours at (£27,500/1,100) per hour	100.00
Fixed cost	4 hours at (£20,000/1,100) per hour	72.73
Total cost per scan		212.73

10% are blurred, therefore the cost of satisfactory scan is £212.73 $\times \frac{10}{9}$ = £236.37.

(b) In decision making, consider variable costs only, as fixed costs will not be changed by the decision

Variable cost of satisfactory scan on XR1

£140 $\times \frac{10}{9}$ = £155.56.

Variable cost of satisfactory scan on XR50

(W1) 112.60 $\times \frac{100}{94}$ = £119.78

Therefore it is cheaper to use XR50 for the brain scans.

Working

(W1)

	£
Cost of plate	55.00
Variable cost: 1.8 × (£64,000/2,000)	57.60
	112.60

78 JETPRINT LTD

Key answer tips

In part (b) assume that all general overheads are charged to these 100 batches.

(a)

	Producing *10,000 leaflets*	*Producing* *20,000 leaflets*
	£	£
Artwork	65.00	65.00
Machine setting (4 hrs at £22)	88.00	88.00
Paper	125.00	250.00
Ink and consumables	40.00	80.00
Printers' wages (4 hrs at £8/8hrs at £8)	32.00	64.00
	350.00	547.00
General overheads: (£15,000/600 = £25 per hour)	100.00	200.00
Total costs	450.00	747.00
Profit (30/70 × £450: 30/70 × £747)	192.86	320.14

Selling price	642.86	1,067.14
Selling price per thousand leaflets	£64	£53

(b)

	£
Revenue: $(64 \times £64 \times 10) + (36 \times £53 \times 20)$	79,120
Direct costs: $(64 \times £350) + (36 \times £547)$	(42,092)
Overheads	(15,000)
	22,028

Tutorial note: This assumes that only this type of leaflet was produced in the period, and thus all general overheads are charged to it.

(c)   The hours actually worked in the period are:

$(64 \times 4) + (36 \times 8) = 544$ hours.

This compares with the 600 hours that were expected to be worked, i.e. the business is working full capacity. A further 56 hours of work could have been carried out in the period, which presumably would have generated even greater profits. It seems likely that sales are currently the limiting factor, so efforts should be concentrated on sales and marketing so that the currently slack 56 hours can be used in new profitable work.

If it is possible to choose, the slack time should preferably be filled with new 10,000 leaflet jobs, since they offer a higher profit per labour hour:

Profit per labour hour: 10,000 leaflet jobs: $\dfrac{£640 \times 30\%}{4} = £48$

Profit per labour hour: 10,000 leaflet jobs: $\dfrac{£1,060 \times 30\%}{8} = £39.75$

Tutorial note: Strictly this analysis should be done on a contribution basis (Revenue - direct costs), i.e. before general overhead absorption. But this does not change the conclusion.

79   TP LTD

(a)   **£1,650**

Material X is in regular use. The relevant cost of using it for the urgent job would be its replacement cost. This is 150 units × £11 = £1,650.

(b)   **£825**

Material Y is also in regular use. The relevant cost of using it for the urgent job would also be its replacement cost. This is 150 units × £5.50 = £825.

(c)   **£2,025**

The relevant cost of labour is the additional cash that will be spent for the overtime working.

Total hours required for the job = 150 computers × 2 hours each = 300 hours.

Overtime hours required = 30% × 300 hours = 90 hours.

Cost of overtime = 90 hours × (£15 × 150%) per hour = £2,025.

(d) **£2,250**

Variable overheads are not incurred during idle time, therefore the urgent job will give rise to additional variable overhead spending in 300 hours.

Relevant cost = 300 hours × £7.50 per hour = £2,250.

(e) The relevant cost of fixed overhead is zero, because no additional fixed overhead spending will be incurred by the job.

(f) **7,937**

	£
Material cost per computer service	14.40
Labour cost per computer service	30.00
Variable overheads per computer service	15.00
total variable cost per computer service	59.40
Service price	135.00
Contribution per computer service	75.60

Budgeted fixed overheads = 20,000 × £30 = £600,000.

Breakeven output = £600,000/£75.60 = 7,936.5 computer services, i.e. 7,937 services.

(g) **£2,362,500**

Contribution/sales ratio = £75.60/£135 = 0.56 (56%).

	£
Budgeted fixed costs	650,000
Target profit	673,000
Target contribution	1,323,000

Sales revenue required to achieve target profit

= Target contribution/ C/S ratio

= £1,323,000/ 0.56

= £2,362,500

Section 5

MOCK EXAMINATION QUESTIONS

SECTION A – ALL 25 QUESTIONS ARE COMPULSORY AND MUST BE ATTEMPTED. EACH QUESTION WITHIN THIS SECTION IS WORTH 2 MARKS.

1   **Inspection costs for the operations of W in the last six months of 20X3 were as follows.**

Month	Number of units inspected	Total costs of inspection £
July	400	3,510
August	370	3,342
September	510	4,126
October	450	3,790
November	480	3,958
December	350	3,230

On the basis of these figures, the estimated variable cost of inspection per unit was:

A   £5.60

B   £8.09

C   £8.78

D   £9.23

2   **In October BC received three deliveries of a material, as follows.**

1st October   200 kilos at £40 per kilo

8th October   350 kilos at £42 per kilo

19th October   280 kilos at £45 per kilo

There was no opening stock on 1st October.

During October, the following requisitions of the material were made from stores:

6th October   150 kilos

12th October   310 kilos

16th October   70 kilos

24th October   290 kilos

What would be the valuation of the closing stock, using a last in, first out (LIFO) method of stock valuation?

A   £400

B   £420

C   £425

D   £450

3   The following data relates to the stock position of material AA.

Minimum usage	200 units per day
Maximum usage	500 units per day
Maximum re-order lead time	8 days
Minimum re-order lead time	4 days
Re-order level	4,000 units

What is the minimum stock level for material AA?

A   1,900 units

B   2,100 units

C   3,200 units

D   4,000 units

4   **The following budgeted and actual results relate to production activity and overhead costs in WX.**

	Budget	*Actual*
Production overhead costs		
Fixed	£36,000	£39,000
Variable	£9,000	£12,000
Direct labour hours worked	18,000 hours	20,000 hours

An absorption costing system is used and production overhead costs are absorbed into output costs on a direct labour hour basis.

Production overhead during the period was:

A   over-absorbed by £1,000

B   under-absorbed by £1,000

C   under-absorbed by £5,000

D   under-absorbed by £6,000.

5   **A finishing department absorbs production overheads using a direct labour hour basis. Budgeted production overheads for the year just ended were £268,800 for the department, and actual production overhead costs were £245,600.**

If actual labour hours worked were 45,000 and production overheads were over-absorbed by £6,400, what was the overhead absorption rate per labour hour?

A   £5.32

B   £5.60

C   £5.83

D   £6.12

6   **V uses a standard costing system. The data below relates to direct labour.**

Standard direct labour rate	£8 per hour
Standard hours allowed for actual output	6,800 hours
Actual hours worked	6,200 hours

The direct labour rate variance was £744 adverse.

The actual hourly rate of pay was:

A   £7.80

B   £7.89

C   £8.00

D   £8.12

7   **Z manufactures paint in two consecutive processes, and uses process costing methods to record the costs of production. The following information relates to Process 1 for the period just ended.**

Opening work in process	500 litres, 100% complete for material and 60% complete for labour and overhead costs.
	Cost to date: materials £4,500, labour and overhead £1,500
Materials input	18,000 litres
Costs of input materials	£180,000
Labour and overhead costs	£51,600
Output to Process 2	17,000 litres
Closing work in process	1,500 litres, 100% complete for material and 25% complete for labour and overhead costs

If a FIFO basis is used in the process costing system, what is the value of the closing stock?

A   £15,320

B   £16,470

C   £16,500

D   £19,500

8   **In the period just ended RT produced 22,000 units of product X, each with a total cost of £20. The variable cost portion of total cost was 80%, and the remainder was fixed cost.**

During the period, RT sold 19,500 units of product X at a selling price of £25 per unit. There were no opening stocks of product X at the start of the period.

If absorption costing is used to calculate the profit in each period, the profit in the period just ended would be:

A   £10,000 lower than if marginal costing had been used to measure profit

B   £10,000 higher than if marginal costing had been used to measure profit

C   £20,000 higher than if marginal costing had been used to measure profit

D   £40,000 higher than if marginal costing had been used to measure profit

9 A company makes three different products with the same item of direct materials and the same direct labour employees. These products have the following selling prices and unit costs.

	Product N £	Product S £	Product E £
Selling price per unit	30.00	42.00	22.00
Direct materials (£5 per kilogram)	10.00	12.50	7.50
Direct labour (£8 per hour)	8.00	16.00	4.00
Fixed overheads	7.00	8.00	6.00
Total cost per unit	25.00	36.50	17.50
Profit per unit	5.00	5.50	4.50
Sales demand each month	2,000 units	1,600 units	2,200 units

Each month, there is a maximum of 11,500 kilograms of material and 5,800 labour hours available.

If the company wishes to maximise its profit each month, the optimal production plan is:

	Product N units	Product S units	Product E units
A	2,000	1,350	2,200
B	2,000	1,600	2,200
C	2,000	1,600	1,200
D	1,500	1,600	2,200

10 The following information relates to product P.

	£ per unit
Selling price	65
Direct materials cost	22
Direct labour cost	14
Variable production overhead cost	9
Fixed production overhead cost	10

Budgeted output of product P for the year is 12,000 units.

Assuming that there is no stockholding of product P, what number of units must be made and sold to make a profit of £18,000 in the year?

A 4,759 units

B 6,000 units

C 6,900 units

D 13,800 units

11   The standard direct labour cost of Product H is £21 per unit, and each unit is expected to take 3.5 hours to make. The budget was to produce 22,000 units, but in the period, only 21,000 units were actually made. The time required to produce these units was 75,000 hours, which had a labour cost of £431,250.

What was the direct labour efficiency variance in the period?

A   £9,000 Adverse

B   £8,625 Adverse

C   £9,750 Favourable

D   £12,000 Favourable

12   A company budgeted to make 30,000 units of a product P. Each unit was expected to take 4 hours to make and budgeted fixed overhead expenditure was £840,000. Actual production of Product P in the period was 32,000 units, which took 123,000 hours to make. Actual fixed overhead expenditure was £885,600.

What was the fixed overhead capacity variance for the period?

A   £21,000 Favourable

B   £21,600 Favourable

C   £35,000 Favourable

D   £56,000 Favourable

13   The manager of a profit centre needs information about which of the following?

(i)   Revenues of the centre

(ii)   Costs of the centre

(iii)   Assets employed in the centre

A   (i) only

B   (ii) only

C   (i) and (ii) only

D   (i), (ii) and (iii)

14   A company manufactures a product in batches and then holds the items produced in finished goods stock until they are sold. It is capable of replenishing the product at the rate of 100,000 units/year, but annual sales demand is just 40,000 units. The costs of setting up a batch production run are £1,500 and the cost of holding a unit of the product in stock is £25/year.

What is the economic batch quantity for manufacturing this product?

A   2,191 units

B   2,828 units

C   4,472 units

D   10,954 units

15 **What is the deprival value of an asset?**

A   The higher of (1) replacement cost and (2) the lower of net realisable value and economic value in use

B   The higher of (1) replacement cost and (2) the higher of net realisable value and economic value in use

C   The lower of (1) replacement cost and (2) the lower of net realisable value and economic value in use

D   The lower of (1) replacement cost and (2) the higher of net realisable value and economic value in use

16 **Which of the following items would NOT be included in production overhead costs?**

A   Consumable stores (i.e. low-cost items of production materials)

B   Salary of the manager of the raw materials stores

C   Factory rental cost

D   Printing costs of product catalogue

17 **John Jones has worked for the same company for four years, receiving an annual increase in his salary of £500 each year. John is unhappy with his salary increases, because they are insufficient to enable him to maintain his standard of living. He has the following information.**

Year	Annual salary £	Retail Prices Index
1	15,000	280
2	15,500	290
3	16,000	305
4	16,500	315

Using this information and using year 1 as the base year, John has calculated his real annual salary in year 4 (to the nearest £1) to be:

A   £14,118

B   £14,667

C   £15,000

D   £15,750

18 **A company uses regression analysis to establish its selling overhead costs for budgeting purposes. The data used for the analysis is as follows.**

Month	Number of salesmen	Sales overhead costs £000
1	3	35.1
2	6	46.4
3	4	27.0
4	3	33.5
5	5	41.0
	21	183.0

The gradient of the regression line is 4.20.

Using regression analysis, what would be the budgeted sales overhead costs for the month, in £000, if there are 5 salesmen employed?

A   28.87

B   39.96

C   41.00

D   56.76

19   A company that makes and sells a single product has budgeted the following unit costs and profit.

	£
Sales price	8
Variable cost	3
Fixed cost	4
Profit	1

The budgeted profit is £125,000.

What is the margin of safety?

A   20,000 units

B   31,250 units

C   20%

D   25%

20   A company makes two joint products, X and Y, in a common process. Normal loss from this process is 10% of input units and has a scrap value of £1.80unit. Joint process costs are apportioned between the two products on the basis of sales value at the split-off point.

During a particular month, output from the process was 18,000 units of X and 9,000 units of Y. The costs of materials input to the process plus the costs of labour and overheads totalled £102,600. The sales value per unit at split-off point is £4/unit for X and £6/unit for Y.

What was the cost/unit of product X in the month?

A   £3.09

B   £3.26

C   £3.43

D   £3.60

21   TG worked on three jobs in the period just ended, the details of which are as follows.

	Job 1	Job 2	Job 3
	£	£	£
Opening work in progress	3,400	0	25,000
Materials added in the period	15,500	31,900	1,000
Labour costs incurred in the period (£5/hour)	10,000	20,000	5,000

Budgeted and actual overhead expenditure in the period were £94,500. Overhead is absorbed into the cost of jobs on a direct labour hour basis, and actual labour hours worked in the period were as budgeted.

At the end of the period, Job 1 and Job 2 were incomplete.

The value of closing work in progress at the end of the period was:

A   £80,800

B   £111,800

C   £161,800

D   £175,300

---

22   **A factory has two production departments, X and Y, and two service departments C and D. The following information costs relates to the overhead costs in each department.**

	Manufacturing departments		Service departments	
	X	Y	C	D
Overhead costs	£5,000	£7,500	£3,200	£4,600
Proportion of usage of services of C	50%	40%	-	10%
Proportion of usage of services of D	20%	60%	20%	-

Using the reciprocal method of apportioning service department costs, the total overhead costs allocated to department X will be:

A   £5,000

B   £7,520

C   £8,105

D   £12,195

---

23   **A company manufactures four products, for which the unit costs and selling prices are as follows.**

Product	W	X	Y	Z
	£	£	£	£
Variable cost	8	7	12	16
Fixed cost	4	4	6	8
	12	11	18	24
Sales price	16	15	21	23
Profit/(loss)	4	4	3	(1)

The company is aware that it could sub-contract the manufacture of any of these items, and buy them in from external suppliers at a price of £6/unit of W, £8/unit of X, £10/unit of Y and £18/unit of Z. A decision to purchase externally would not have any effect on total fixed costs.

To maximise profitability, which of the four products should the company buy externally?

A   W and Y only

B   W, Y and Z only

C   Z only

D   All four products

24 **A company manufacturing three products had the following budget.**

Product	Budgeted output units	Hours/unit	Total hours
X	8,000	1	8,000
Y	4,000	2	8,000
Z	5,000	4	20,000
			36,000

All three products are manufactured in batches. Production overheads are absorbed into the cost of batches on the basis of labour hours worked (rather than on a rate per unit basis). Budgeted production overheads for the period were £115,200 and actual production overhead expenditure was £108,000.

Actual output for the period was as follows:

Product	Actual output units	Hours
X	9,000	10,000
Y	3,000	7,000
Z	4,000	17,000
		34,000

How much overhead was absorbed into the production costs of Product Z in the period?

A   £48,000

B   £51,000

C   £54,000

D   £54,400

25 **GG manufactures a product that has a selling price of £15 and a variable cost of £6 per unit. Annual fixed costs are £43,875 and annual sales demand is 6,000 units.**

New manufacturing methods are being considered for the product. These would result in a rise of 20% in fixed costs and a reduction in the variable cost per unit to £5. The new manufacturing methods would create a higher-quality product and sales demand would increase to 7,000 units each year at a higher sales price of £20 per unit.

If the changes in manufacturing methods are implemented, and if the selling price is raised to £20, the breakeven level would be:

A   975 units higher

B   1,365 units higher

C   1,950 units lower

D   1,365 units lower

SECTION B – ALL FIVE QUESTIONS ARE COMPULSORY AND MUST BE ATTEMPTED.

1   TRI-D

TRI-D Ltd has three production departments - Extrusion, Machining and Finishing - and a service department known as Production Services which works for the production departments to the ratio of 3:2:1.

The following costs and relevant data, which represent normal activity levels, have been budgeted for the period ending 31 December 20X6:

	Extrusion	Machining	Finishing	Production services	Total
Costs:	£000	£000	£000	£000	£000
Direct wages	58	72	90		220
Direct materials	40	29	15		84
Indirect wages	15	21	8	58	102
Depreciation					84
Rates					22
Power					180
Personnel					60
Insurance					48
Other data:					
Direct labour hours	7,250	9,000	15,000		31,250
Machine hours	15,500	20,000	2,500	2,000	40,000
Floor area (square metres)	800	1,200	1,000	1,400	4,400
Fixed assets	£160,000	£140,000	£30,000	£70,000	£400,000
Employees	40	56	94	50	240

Required:

(a)   Prepare an overhead analysis sheet for TRI-D Ltd for the period ending 31 December 20X6.   **(7 marks)**

(b)   Calculate appropriate overhead absorption rates for the Extrusion, Machining and Finishing Departments.   **(3 marks)**

(Total: 10 marks)

2   TP

TP manufactures paint. The following information relates to April's Process 1 activities at TP.

Material input	1,000 litres, each costing £4.95, which is added at the start of the process
Normal loss	10% of material input
Output to Process 2	880 litres
Labour	£445
Overheads	£267

Both labour and overheads are incurred evenly throughout the process.

Losses are identified when the process is 50% complete. There is no opening or closing work in progress.

Required:

(a)   Calculate the expected equivalent units of output for Process 1.   **(2 marks)**

(b)   Calculate the cost per equivalent unit.   **(2 marks)**

(c)   Prepare the Process 1 account and the abnormal loss account for April.   **(6 marks)**

(Total: 10 marks)

3   HAPPY RETURNS

Happy Returns Ltd operates a haulage business with three vehicles. The following estimated cost and performance data are available:

Petrol	£0.50 per kilometre on average
Repairs	£0.30 per kilometre
Depreciation	£1.00 per kilometre, plus £50 per week per vehicle
Drivers' wages	£300 per week per vehicle
Supervision and general expenses	£550 per week
Loading costs	£6.00 per tonne

During week 26 it is expected that all three vehicles will be used, 280 tonnes will be loaded and a total of 3,950 kilometres travelled (including return journeys when empty) as shown in the following table:

Journey	Tonnes carried (one way)	Kilometres (one way)
1	34	180
2	28	265
3	40	390
4	32	115
5	26	220
6	40	480
7	29	90
8	26	100
9	25	135
	280	1,975

Required:

Calculate the average cost per tonne-kilometre for week 26.   **(10 marks)**

4   FINCH

Finch process and sells one product, product L. The standard cost for one unit of product L is as follows.

	£
Direct material X: 20 kilograms	300
Direct material Y: 5 kilograms	100
Direct labour: 6 hours	42
Fixed production overhead	60
Total standard cost	492

The fixed production overhead in the product cost is based on a monthly production output of 1,000 units of product L, and is absorbed on a direct labour hour basis.

During the month of July 20X3, actual results were as follows.

Units of production	900
	£
Material X: 17,910 kilograms	271,450
Material Y: 4,635 kilograms	97,335
Direct labour: 5,310 hours	39,825
Fixed production overhead	57,000

Required:

(a)   Calculate the material price variance and the material usage variance for both Material X and Material Y.   **(4 marks)**

(b)   Calculate the direct labour rate and efficiency variances.   **(2 marks)**

(c)   Calculate the fixed production overhead expenditure and volume variances.   **(2 marks)**

(d)   Calculate the fixed production overhead efficiency variance and the fixed production overhead capacity variance.   **(2 marks)**

(Total: 10 marks)

5   STRETCH

The managers of Stretch are currently reviewing the profitability of an existing product. In order to help them to reach a decision about future production and sales plans, the accountant has produced some preliminary sales and cost data for next year, as follows.

Anticipated sales	7,000 units at £20 each	£140,000
Direct labour costs	£8 per unit	
Direct material costs	£4 per unit	
Fixed costs	£4 per unit	

Required:

(a)   Calculate the break-even point of sales, in units.   **(1 mark)**

(b)   Calculate the P/V ratio (also called the C/S ratio), and the breakeven sales revenue using the P/V ratio.   **(2 marks)**

(c)   Calculate the margin of safety, both in units and as a percentage amount.   **(2 marks)**

(d)   What would be the effect on the breakeven level of sales if the selling price of the product was reduced to £18 per unit, assuming that the change in sales price has no effect on the costs?   **(2 marks)**

(e)   Determine the number of units of the product that would need to be sold to achieve a profit of £20,000 in the year, assuming that the sales price is held at £20 per unit.   **(3 marks)**

(Total: 10 marks)

Section 6

ANSWERS TO MOCK EXAMINATION QUESTIONS

SECTION A

1 A

Using the high-low method:

		£
High	Total costs of 510 units	4,126
Low	Total costs of 350 units	3,230
	Variable costs of 160 units	896

The variable cost per unit is £896/160 = £5.60.

2 A

Date		Units	Value £	
1 Oct	In	200	8,000	(200 × £40)
6 Oct	Out	(150)	(6,000)	
	Balance	50	2,000	(50 at £40)
8 Oct	In	350	14,700	(350 at £42)
	Balance	400	16,700	
12 Oct	Out	(310)	(13,020)	(310 at £42)
16 Oct	Out	(70)	(2,880)	(40 at £42, 30 at £40)
	Balance	20	800	(20 at £40)
19 Oct	In	280	16,600	(280 at £45)
	Balance	300	17,400	
24 Oct	Out	(290)	17,000	(280 at £45, 10 at £40)
	Balance	10	400	(10 at £40)

Note: You could reach this answer more quickly by identifying that, applying LIFO stock valuation, the 10 units of closing stock are 10 of the units purchased on 1st October.

3 A

The minimum stock level is a warning level, and the stores management should be notified if the actual quantity in stock falls below this level. It is calculated by subtracting from the reorder level the quantity of units that will be consumed if the lead time is average and there is average consumption of the stores item during the lead time.

Minimum level = Reorder level – (Average usage × Average lead time)

It is assumed that the average usage is (200 + 500)/2 = 350 units per day and the average lead time is (8 + 4)/2 = 6 days.

Minimum level = 4,000 – (350 × 6) = 1,900 units.

4 B

Fixed overhead absorption rate = £36,000/18,000 = £2 per direct labour hour.

Variable overhead absorption rate = £9,000/18,000 = £0.50 per direct labour hour.

	£	£
Overheads absorbed:		
Fixed (20,000 × £2)		40,000
Variable (20,000 × £0.50)		10,000
Total overhead absorbed		50,000
Overheads incurred:		
Fixed	39,000	
Variable	12,000	
Total overhead incurred		51,000
Under-absorbed overhead		1,000

5 B

	£
Actual overheads	245,600
Over-absorption of overheads	6,400
Overheads absorbed	252,000

Absorption rate = £252,000/45,000 hours = £5.60 per direct labour hour.

6 D

	£
6,200 hours should cost (× £8)	49,600
Labour rate variance	744 (A)
6,200 hours did cost	50,344

Actual rate per hour = £50,344/6,200 hours = £8.12 per hour.

7   C

	Total units	Equivalent units Materials	Labour /overhead
Opening WIP completed	500	0	200
Other finished output	16,500	16,500	16,500
	17,000	16,500	16,700
Closing work in process	1,500	1,500	500
Total	18,500	18,000	17,200
Costs		£180,000	£51,600
Cost per equivalent unit		£10	£3

Value of closing work in progress = $(1,500 \times £10) + (500 \times £3) = $ **£16,500**.

8   B

Closing stock is $(22,000 - 19,500) = 2,500$ units.

There was no opening stock.

With absorption costing, closing stock will include a fixed overhead cost element of 20% of £20 = £4 per unit.

The fixed costs in closing stock are therefore 2,500 units × £4 = £10,000 in total.

In marginal costing, all fixed costs are charged against profits of the period in which they arise. With absorption costing, the fixed overhead in closing stock is not charged against profits, but is carried forward in the closing stock value.

The absorption costing profit will therefore be £10,000 higher than profit calculated by the marginal costing method.

9   A

To meet maximum sales demand, the materials and labour requirements are as follows.

		Materials kilos		Labour hours
2,000 units of N	(× 2)	4,000	(× 1)	2,000
1,600 units of S	(× 2.5)	4,000	(× 2)	3,200
2,200 units of E	(× 1.5)	3,300	(× 0.5)	1,100
		11,300		6,300
Available		11,500		5,800
Surplus/(shortfall)		200		(500)

Labour hours are a limiting factor.

Product	Contribution per unit	Hours per unit	Contribution per hour	Priority
	£		£	
N	12.00	1.00	12.00	2nd
S	13.50	2.00	6.75	3rd
E	10.50	0.50	21.00	1st

The profit-maximising output is now calculated as follows.

Product	Units	Hours
E	**2,200**	1,100
N	**2,000**	2,000
		3,100
S (balance)	**1,350**	2,700
		5,800

10   C

Contribution per unit = £(65 – 22 – 14 – 9) = £20.

	£
Budgeted fixed costs (12,000 × £10)	120,000
Required profit	18,000
Required contribution	138,000

Volume of sales required to achieve target contribution and profit = £138,000/£20 per unit = 6,900 units.

11   A

	hours	
21,000 hours should take (× 3.5 hours)	73,500	
They did take	75,000	
Efficiency variance in hours	1,500	Adverse

Standard labour rate/hour (£21/3.5 hours)	£6
Direct labour efficiency variance in £	**£9,000 Adverse**

12   A

Budgeted hours of work = 30,000 units × 4 hours = 120,000 hours.

Fixed overhead absorption rate/hour = £840,000/120,000 hours = £7/hour.

	hours	
Budgeted hours of work	120,000	
Actual hours of work	123,000	
Capacity variance in hours	3,000	Favourable

Standard fixed overhead rate/hour	£7
Fixed overhead capacity variance in £	**£21,000 Favourable**

13   C

The manager of a profit centre needs to know about the profits of the centre, i.e. revenues and costs. (Revenues only are appropriate for a revenue centre; costs only for a cost centre; and revenues, costs and assets employed for an investment centre.)

14   B

$$\textbf{Economic batch quantity} = \sqrt{\frac{2C_0D}{C_h\left(1-\dfrac{D}{R}\right)}}$$

$$= \sqrt{\frac{2(1,500)(40,000)}{25\left(1-\dfrac{40,000}{100,000}\right)}}$$

$$= \sqrt{\frac{120\text{million}}{15}}$$

$$= \sqrt{8,000,000}$$

$$= 2,828 \text{ units.}$$

15   D

This question might seem complicated.

The deprival value of short-term assets, such as materials, is their relevant cost. The relevant cost of materials is their replacement cost, unless they are not worth replacing. If they are worth replacing, their economic value in use must exceed their replacement cost. Relevant cost/deprival value is therefore usually the lower of replacement cost and economic value in use.

If materials in stock are not worth replacing, their relevant cost is the higher of their net realisable value from disposal (disposal value) and the profit that would be obtained by making the best economic use of them (their economic value in use).

Deprival value is therefore the lower of (1) replacement cost and (2) the higher of disposal value and economic value in use.

16   D

Consumable stores are generally treated as overhead costs because they are low-value items, and it is therefore not worth treating them as direct production costs. The stores manager is a production overhead rather than an administration overhead. The printing costs of a catalogue are marketing costs, and so would be treated as selling and distribution (or marketing) overheads.

17   B

His year 4 salary in 'real' terms (year 1 terms) is £16,500 × 280/315 = £14,667.

18   B

$$a = \frac{\sum y}{n} - \frac{b\sum x}{n}$$

$$a = \frac{183.0}{5} - \frac{4.2(21)}{5} = [36.6 - 17.64] = 18.96.$$

If there are 5 salesmen in the month, expected costs will be, in £000:

$18.96 + (4.2 \times 5) = \textbf{39.96}$.

19   C

Budgeted profit= £125,000

Budgeted profit/unit = £1

Therefore budgeted sales = 125,000 units.

Budgeted fixed costs = 125,000 units × £4 = **£500,000**.

Contribution/unit = £8 - £3 = £5.

Breakeven point = £500,000/£5 = 100,000 units.

Margin of safety = 125,000 − 100,000 = 25,000 units.

Margin of safety is normally measured as a percentage of the budgeted sales, which in this case is 25,000/125,000 = 0.20 or 20%.

20   A

	units
Output 'good' units from process (18,000 + 9,000)	27,000
Normal loss (× 10/90 of output = 10% of input)	3,000
	30,000

	£
Total cost of process	102,600
Less: scrap value of normal loss (3,000 × £1.80)	5,400
Costs of good output	97,200

	£
Sales value of output at the split-off point =	
Product X (18,000 × £4)	72,000
Product Y (9,000 × £6)	54,000
Costs of good output	126,000

Costs apportioned to X = £97,200 × 72,000/126,000 = £55,543.

Cost per unit of X = £55,543/18,000 units = **£3.09**.

21   C

Budgeted labour hours = £(10,000 + 20,000 + 5,000)/£5 per hour = 7,000

Overhead recovery rate = £94,500/7,000 hours = £13.50 per labour hour.

		Job 1		Job 2
		£		£
Opening WIP		3,400		0
Material costs		15,500		31,900
Labour costs	(2,000 hours)	10,000	(4,000 hours)	20,000
Overheads		27,000		54,000
		55,900		105,900

Total closing WIP = £55,900 + £105,900 = £161,800.

22   C

Let the overhead apportioned from service department C be £C.

Let the overhead apportioned from service department D be £D.

$$C = 3,200 + 0.20D \quad .....(1)$$

$$D = 4,600 + 0.10 \text{ C} \quad ....(2)$$

Substitute (1) in (2)

$$D = 4,600 + 0.10(3,200 + 0.20D)$$

$$D = 4,600 + 320 + 0.02D$$

$$0.98D = 4,920$$

$$D = 5,020.$$

Substitute in (1)

$$C = 3,200 + 0.20 (5,020)$$

$$C = 4,204.$$

Total overhead for Department X = 5,000 + 0.50C + 0.20D

$$= 5,000 + 0.50(4,204) + 0.20 (5,020)$$

$$= 5,000 + 2,102 + 1,004$$

$$= 8,106.$$

Allowing for a rounding difference, this is answer C.

Note: You could have reached the same answer by the repeated distribution method.

23   A

Tutorial note: This question tests your understanding of the 'make or buy' decision. Compare the cost of buying with the costs that would be saved by buying externally – i.e. the marginal cost of manufacturing internally (given that fixed cost expenditure would not be affected by the decision.)

	W	X	Y	Z
	£	£	£	£
P cost of manufacture	8	7	12	16
al purchase cost	6	8	10	18
ving/(net cost) with external purchase	2	(1)	2	(2)

Costs would be reduced by purchasing products W and Y externally but it would be more expensive to buy X and Z externally.

24 D

Production overhead is absorbed into the cost of output on the basis of labour hours worked, not on a unit basis. The overhead absorption rate is:

Budgeted overheads/budgeted labour hours = £115,200/36,000 hours

= £3.20 /hour.

Overhead absorbed into the cost of Product Z units manufactured was therefore:

17,000 hours × £3.20 = **£54,400**.

25 D

Original contribution per unit = £15 - £6 = £9.

Original breakeven point = £43,875/£9 = 4,875 units.

New contribution per unit = £20 - £5 = £15.

New fixed costs = £43,875 × 120% = £52,650.

New breakeven point = £52,650/£15 per unit = 3,510 units.

The new breakeven point is 1,365 units lower than the original breakeven point.

SECTION B

1 TRI-D

Key answer tips

You need to choose an appropriate allocation method for each type of overhead and produce a table which allows you to calculate total overheads for each department.

(a)

Item	Basis	Total	Extrusion	M/chining	Finish'g	Prod services
		£000	£000	£000	£000	£000
Indirect wages	Allocated	102	15.00	21.00	8.00	58.00
Dep'n	Fxd assets	84	33.60	29.40	6.30	14.70
Rates	Floor area	22	4.00	6.00	5.00	7.00
Power	M/c hours	180	69.75	90.00	11.25	9.00
Personnel	Employees	60	10.00	14.00	23.50	12.50
Insurance	Fxd assets	48	19.20	16.80	3.60	8.40
		496	151.55	177.20	57.65	109.60

Reapportion	Prod serv (3:2:1)	-	54.80	36.53	18.27	(109.60)
		496	206.35	213.73	75.92	Nil

Tutorial note: There are alternative acceptable bases for apportionment. For example, the insurance premium cost may be apportioned on the basis of floor area - the most 'fair' basis will depend upon the nature of the insurance (contents, buildings etc).

(b)   Absorption rates $= \dfrac{\text{Apportioned overheads}}{\text{Relevant measure of activity}}$

It is assumed that the machinery-based Extrusion and Machining departmental overheads will be absorbed on the basis of machine hours, whilst Finishing, being labour-intensive, will have its overheads absorbed on the basis of direct labour hours.

	Extrusion	*Machining*	*Finishing*
Apportioned overheads	£206,350	£213,730	£75,920
Direct labour hours			15,000
Machine hours	15,500	20,000	
Absorption rate	£13.31/hr	£10.69/hr	£5.06/hr

Tutorial note: Your answer could argue in favour of a different absorptionbasis for each department, but your answer must state the basis you have selected and why, to pick up marks.

2   TP

(a)

	Total	*Equivalent units*	
	units	*Materials*	*Labour and overhead*
Output units	880	880	880
Normal loss	100	0	0
Abnormal loss	20	20	10
	1,000	900	890

(b)

	Materials	*Labour and overhead*
Cost (1,000 × £4.95)	£4,950	
(£445 + £267)		£712
Cost per equivalent unit	£5.50	£0.80

(c)

Process 1 account

	units	£		units	£
Materials	1,000	4,950	Process 2	880	5,544
Labour		445	Normal loss	100	-
Overhead		267	Abnormal loss	20	118
		5,662			5,662

Workings

Output to Process 2 = 880 units × (£5.50 + £0.80) per unit = £5,544.

Abnormal loss = 20 equivalent units × £5.50 + 10 equivalent units × £0.80

= £110 + £8 = £118.

Abnormal loss account

	£		£
Process 1	118	Profit and loss account	118

3 **HAPPY RETURNS**

Key answer tips

Calculate the cost per tonne kilometre over the outward journeys only, as this is the chargeable element of the journey.

Total costs, week 26

	£/km		£
Petrol	0.50		
Repairs	0.30		
Depreciation	1.00		
(Two-way journeys: 1,975 × 2 = 3,950)	1.80	× 3,950	7,110

	£/week		
Depreciation (£50 × 3)	150		
Wages (£300 × 3)	900		
Supervision and general expenses	550		
			1,600
Loading costs		(£6 × 280)	1,680
			10,390

Tonne-km week 26

Journey	Tonnes	One-way km	Tonne-kms
1	34	180	6,120
2	28	265	7,420
3	40	390	15,600
4	32	115	3,680
5	26	220	5,720
6	40	480	19,200
7	29	90	2,610
8	26	100	2,600
9	25	135	3,375
			66,325

Average cost per tonne-kilometre = £10,390/66,325 = **0.157**

Tutorial note: As the vehicles make their return journeys empty, it is assumed that the cost should only be averaged over the outward, freight-carrying journey.

4 FINCH

(a)   Standard cost per kilogram of Material X = £300/20 = £15.

Standard cost per kilogram of Material Y = £100/5 = £20.

		£	
17,910 kilograms of X should cost (× £15)		268,650	
Did cost		271,450	
Material X price variance		2,800	(A)

		£	
4,635 kilograms of Y should cost (× £20)		92,700	
Did cost		97,335	
Material Y price variance		4,635	(A)

			Material X kg		Material Y kg
900 units of production:					
Should use	(× 20)		18,000	(× 5)	4,500
Did use			17,910		4,635
Material usage variance			90 (F)		135 (A)
Standard price per kg			£15		£20
Material usage variance in £			£1,350 (F)		£2,700 (A)

(b)   Standard rate per labour hour = £42/6 hours per unit = £7.

		£	
5,310 hours of labour should cost (× £7)		37,170	
Did cost		39,825	
Direct labour rate variance		2,655	(A)

		Hours	
900 units of production:			
Should take	(× 6)	5,400	
Did take		5,310	
Labour efficiency variance		90	(F)
Standard rate per hour		£7	
Direct labour efficiency variance in £		£630	(F)

(c)

	£	
Budgeted fixed production overhead (£60 × 1,000)	60,000	
Actual fixed production overhead	57,000	
Fixed production overhead expenditure variance	3,000	(F)

	Units
Budgeted production volume	1,000
Actual production volume	900
Fixed production overhead volume variance	100 (A)
Fixed production overhead cost per unit	£60
Fixed production overhead volume variance in £	£6,000 (A)

(d) Standard fixed production overhead rate per hour = £60/6 hours = £10.

Efficiency variance in hours (same as labour efficiency variance) = 90 hours (F).

Fixed production overhead efficiency variance in £ = 90(F) × £10 = £900 (F)

	Hours
Budgeted capacity in hours (1,000 units × 6)	6,000
Actual hours worked	5,310
Fixed production overhead capacity variance	690 (A)
Fixed production overhead cost per hour	£10
Fixed production overhead capacity variance in £	£6,900 (A)

5 STRETCH

It is assumed that budgeted production and sales volumes are the same quantity.

Contribution per unit = £(20 − 8 − 4) = £8

Budgeted sales in units = £140,000/£20 per unit = 7,000 units.

Budgeted fixed costs = 7,000 units × £4 per unit = £28,000.

(a) Breakeven point is where total contribution = total fixed costs.

= £28,000/£8 per unit = 3,500 units of sales.

(b) The profit/volume ratio (contribution/sales ratio) = £8/£20 = 0.40 or 40%.

The breakeven point can be calculated in terms of sales revenue as:

Required contribution divided by the C/S ratio

= £28,000/0.40

= £70,000.

(c) The margin of safety = Budgeted sales − Breakeven sales

= 7,000 units − 3,500 units = 3,500 units.

This is 50% of the budgeted sales volume.

(d) If the selling price is reduced from £20 to £18, the contribution per unit will fall from £8 to £6.

The breakeven point would rise to £28,000/£6 per unit = 4,667 units.

(e) To achieve a total profit of £20,000, the total contribution must be (£28,000 + £20,000) = £48,000.

If the contribution per unit is £8, the sales volume required would be £48,000/£8 per unit = 6,000 units.

Section 7

DECEMBER 2003 EXAMINATION QUESTIONS

SYLLABUS NOTE

The syllabus for paper 1.2 has been reduced from 2004, starting with the June sitting for the written examination (and earlier in the year for the computer-based examination). Consequently, some of the questions in the December 2003 paper are no longer relevant to the paper 1.2 syllabus, and are examinable instead in paper 2.4. All these questions that were in the December 2003 paper but which are not relevant to the current syllabus have been removed.

Nine of the Section A questions are no longer relevant to the paper 1.2 syllabus. The remaining 16 Section A questions and all the Section B questions ARE still relevant. The remaining 16 Section A questions have been re-numbered.

SECTION A – ALL the questions in this section are compulsory and MUST be attempted. Each question within this section is worth 2 marks. (Only 16 questions included, therefore 32 marks in total.)

1   **A cost is described as staying the same over a certain activity range and then increasing but remaining stable over a revised activity range in the short term.**

What type of cost is this?

A   A fixed cost

B   A variable cost

C   A semi-variable cost

D   A stepped fixed cost.

2   **A company which uses marginal costing has a profit of £37,500 for a period. Opening stock was 100 units and closing stock was 350 units.**

The fixed production overhead absorption rate is £4 per unit.

What is the profit under absorption costing?

A   £35,700

B   £36,500

C   £38,500

D   £39,300

3   A company values stocks using the weighted average value after each purchase. The following receipts and issues have been made with regards to materials for the last month:

Date	Receipts			Issues
	Units	£/unit	Valuation	Units
Brought forward	100	£5	£500	
4th	150	£5.50	£825	
16th				100
20th	100	£6	£600	
21st				75

What is the value of the closing stock using this weighted average method?

A   £1,012.50

B   £976.50

C   £962.50

D   £925.00

4   The following could relate to optical mark readers:

(i)   Specialist pens are always required for use.

(ii)   Data entry is quick.

(iii)   Computers carry out most of the work.

Which of the above would be considered to be advantages of using optical mark readers?

A   (i) and (ii) only

B   (i) and (iii) only

C   (ii) and (iii) only

D   (i), (ii) and (iii)

5   Which of the following would be best described as a short-term tactical plan?

A   Reviewing cost variances and investigate as appropriate

B   Comparing actual market share to budget

C   Lowering the selling price by 15%

D   Monitoring actual sales to budget

6   A company incurs the following costs at various activity levels:

Total cost £	Activity level Units
250,000	5,000
312,500	7,500
400,000	10,000

Using the high-low method what is the variable cost per unit?

A   £25

B   £30

C   £35

D   £40

7 **A company uses process costing to establish the cost per unit of its output.**

The following information was available for the last month:

Input units   10,000

Output units   9,850

Opening stock   300 units, 100% complete for materials and 70% complete for conversion costs

Closing stock   450 units, 100% complete for materials and 30% complete for conversion costs

The company uses the weighted average method of valuing stock.

What were the equivalent units for conversion costs?

A   9,505 units

B   9,715 units

C   9,775 units

D   9,985 units

8 **The following graph has been established for a given set of constraints:**

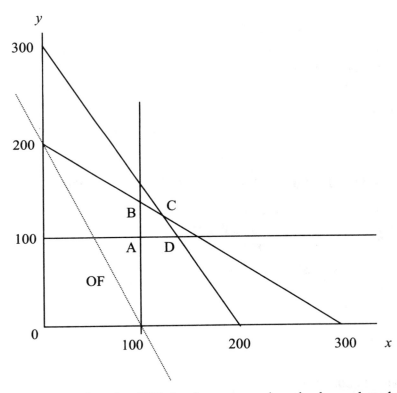

The objective function (OF) for the company has also been plotted on the graph and the feasible region is bounded by the area ABCD.

At which point on the graph will profits be maximised?

A

B

C

D

9   A company has just secured a new contract which requires 500 hours of labour.

There are 400 hours of spare labour capacity. The remaining hours could be worked as overtime at time and a half or labour could be diverted from the production of product X. Product X currently earns a contribution of £4 in two labour hours and direct labour is currently paid at a rate of £12 per normal hour.

What is the relevant cost of labour for the contract?

A   £200

B   £1,200

C   £1,400

D   £1,800

10   A company uses variance analysis to control costs and revenues.

Information concerning sales is as follows:

Budgeted selling price	£15 per unit
Budgeted sales units	10,000 units
Budgeted profit per unit	£5 per unit
Actual sales revenue	£151,500
Actual units sold	9,800 units

What is the sales volume profit variance?

A   £500 favourable

B   £1,000 favourable

C   £1,000 adverse

D   £3,000 adverse

11   A company has the following budgeted information for the coming month:

Budgeted sales revenue	£500,000
Budgeted contribution	£200,000
Budgeted profit	£50,000

What is the budgeted break-even sales revenue?

A   £125,000

B   £350,000

C   £375,000

D   £450,000

12   Which of the following is correct?

A   When considering limiting factors the products should always be ranked according to contribution per unit sold

B   If there is only one scarce resource linear programming should be used

C   In linear programming the point furthest from the origin will always be the point of profit maximisation

D   The slope of the objective function depends on the contributions of the products

13 A company has over absorbed fixed production overheads for the period by £6,000. The fixed production overhead absorption rate was £8 per unit and is based on the normal level of activity of 5,000 units. Actual production was 4,500 units.

What was the actual fixed production overheads incurred for the period?

A   £30,000

B   £36,000

C   £40,000

D   £42,000

14 A company uses process costing to value its output. The following was recorded for the period:

Input materials	2,000 units at £4.50 per unit
Conversion costs	£13,340
Normal loss	5% of input valued at £3 per unit
Actual loss	150 units

There were no opening or closing stocks.

What was the valuation of one unit of output to one decimal place?

A   £11.8

B   £11.6

C   £11.2

D   £11.0

15 Which of the following are correct with regard to regression analysis?

(i)   In regression analysis the n stands for the number of pairs of data.

(ii) Σx^2 is not the same calculation as $(\Sigma x)^2$

(iii) Σxy is calculated by multiplying the total value of x and the total value of y

A   (i) and (ii) only

B   (i) and (iii) only

C   (ii) and (iii) only

D   (i), (ii) and (iii)

16 The following information relates to labour costs for the past month:

Budget		
	Labour rate	£10 per hour
	Production time	15,000 hours
	Time per unit	3 hours
	Production units	5,000 units

Actual		
	Wages paid	£176,000
	Production	5,500 units
	Total hours worked	14,000 hours

There was no idle time.

What were the labour rate and efficiency variances?

	Rate variance	Efficiency variance
A	£26,000 adverse	£25,000 favourable
B	£26,000 adverse	£10,000 favourable
C	£36,000 adverse	£2,500 favourable
D	£36,000 adverse	£25,000 favourable

(32 marks)

Section B – ALL FIVE questions are compulsory and MUST be attempted

1   RECIPROCAL

A business operates with two production centres and three service centres. Costs have been allocated and apportioned to these centres as follows:

Production Centres		Service Centres		
1	2	A	B	C
£2,000	£3,500	£300	£500	£700

Information regarding how the service centres work for each other and for the production centres is given as:

	Work done for:				
	Production Centres		Service Centres		
	1	2	A	B	C
By A	45%	45%	-	10%	-
By B	50%	20%	20%	-	10%
By C	6%	40%	-	-	-

Information concerning production requirements in the two production centres is as follows:

	Centre 1	Centre 2
Units produced	1,500 units	2,000 units
Machine hours	3,000 hours	4,500 hours
Labour hours	2,000 hours	6,000 hours

Required:

(a)   Using the reciprocal method calculate the total overheads in production centres 1 and 2 after reapportionment of the service centre costs.   **(7 marks)**

(b)   Using the most appropriate basis establish the overhead absorption rate for production centre 1. Briefly explain the reason for your chosen absorption basis.   **(3 marks)**

(Total: 10 marks)

2   SKETCH A CHART

Break-even charts and profit-volume charts are commonly associated with cost-volume-profit analysis (break-even analysis).

Required:

(a)   (i)   Sketch a break-even chart and indicate where the break-even point would be for a single product firm.

Clearly label the axes and indicate the following lines:

–   total revenue

–   variable cost

–   fixed costs, and

–   total cost.

(ii)   How would contribution be established from your chart in (a)(i)?   **(6 marks)**

(b)   (i)   Sketch a profit-volume chart and indicate where the break-even point would be for a single product firm.

Clearly label the axes and indicate the profit line and fixed costs.

(ii)   How would contribution be established from your chart in (b)(i)?
[*Note:* no specific numbers are required.]   **(4 marks)**

(Total: 10 marks)

3   FLEXED BUDGET VARIANCES

A company has obtained the following information regarding costs and revenue for the past financial year:

Original budget:
Sales	10,000 units
Production	12,000 units

Standard cost per unit:

	£
Direct materials	5
Direct labour	9
Fixed production overheads	8
	——
	22
	——
Selling price	30

Actual results:
Sales	9,750 units
Revenue	£325,000
Production	11,000 units
Material cost	£65,000
Labour cost	£100,000
Fixed production overheads	£95,000

There were no opening stocks.

Required:

(a)   Produce a flexed budget statement showing the flexed budget and actual results. Calculate the variances between the actual and flexed figures for the following:

  –   sales

  –   materials

  –   labour, and

  –   fixed production overhead.   **(7 marks)**

(b)   Explain briefly how the sales and materials variances calculated in (a) may have arisen.   **(3 marks)**

(Total: 10 marks)

4   EOQ METHOD

A business currently orders 1,000 units of product X at a time. It has decided that it may be better to use the Economic Order Quantity method to establish an optimal reorder quantity.

Information regarding stocks is given below:

Purchase price	£15/unit
Fixed cost per order	£200
Holding cost	8% of the purchase price per annum
Annual demand	12,000 units

Current annual total stock costs are £183,000, being the total of the purchasing, ordering and holding costs of product X.

Required:

(a)   Calculate the Economic Order Quantity.   **(2 marks)**

(b) Using your answer to (a) above calculate the revised annual total stock costs for product X and so establish the difference compared to the current ordering policy.

(4 marks)

(c) List ways in which discounts might affect this Economic Order Quantity calculation and subsequent stock costs. **(4 marks)**

(Total: 10 marks)

5 MARGINAL COSTS AND REVENUES

A company manufactures a single product, product Y. It has documented levels of demand at certain selling prices for this product as follows:

Demand	Selling price per unit	Cost per unit
Units	£	£
1,100	48	22
1,200	46	21
1,300	45	20
1,400	42	19

Required:

Using a tabular approach calculate the marginal revenues and marginal costs for product Y at the different levels of demand, and so determine the selling price at which the company profits are maximised. **(10 marks)**

Section 8

ANSWERS TO DECEMBER 2003 EXAMINATION QUESTIONS

SECTION A

1   D

Many items of fixed costs are stepped in nature, rising to a new higher fixed amount when the volume of activity rises above a level that triggers an increase in cost.

2   C

	£
Marginal costing profit	37,500
Add: fixed costs in closing stock (350 units × £4)	1,400
Less: fixed costs in opening stock (100 units × £4)	(400)
Absorption costing profit	38,500

3   B

	Receipts and issues	
Units	*Price per unit*	*Cost*
	£	£
100	5.00	500.0
150	5.50	825.0
250	5.30	1,325.0
(100)	5.30	(530.0)
150		795.0
100	6.00	600.0
250	5.58	1,395.0
(75)	5.58	(418.5)
175	5.58	**976.5**

4   C

An unusual question, presumably related to the IT aspect of the syllabus. Optical mark readers avoid the need for keying in data manually, so statements (ii) and (iii) are correct. Statement (i) is clearly wrong: how can requiring a specialist pen be regarded as an advantage?

5   C

Lowering a selling price, presumably to increase sales volume, is a short-term decision/plan. The measures in A, B and D are not planning decisions at all: they are all monitoring/control activities.

6   B

	£
Total cost of 10,000 units	400,000
Total cost of 5,000 units	250,000
Variable cost of 5,000 units	150,000

Therefore the variable cost is £150,000/5,000 units = £30 per unit.

7   D

	Total units		Conversion costs *equivalent units*
Output	9,850		9,850
Closing stock	450	(× 30%)	135
Total			9,985

8   D

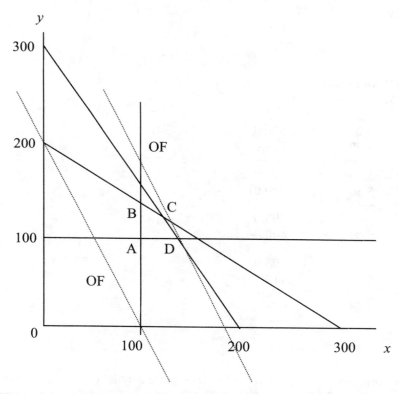

You might notice that the slope of the contribution line in the diagram in the question is steeper than the slope of the constraint line joining points C and D. It therefore follows that the outermost point in the feasible area, that will give the optimal solution to the linear programming problem is point D rather than point C.

9   C

The relevant cost of labour is the lower cost of (1) the cost of working overtime and (2) the cost of diverting labour from other work.

Incremental cost of working overtime

	£
Incremental cost of using 400 hours spare capacity	0
Incremental cost of overtime: 100 hours × £12 × 150%	1,800
	1,800

Incremental cost of diverting labour from other work

	£
Labour cost: 100 hours × £12	1,200
Contribution forgone: 100 hours × £2	200
	1,400

It would be cheaper to divert labour from other work, and the relevant cost is £1,400.

10   C

	units
Budgeted sales units	10,000
Actual sales units	9,800
Sales volume variance (units)	200 (A)
Standard profit/unit	£5
Sales volume profit variance (£)	£1,000 (A)

11   C

$$\text{Breakeven point} = \frac{\text{fixed costs}}{\text{C/S ratio}}$$

	£
Budgeted contribution	200,000
Budgeted profit	50,000
Therefore budgeted fixed costs	150,000

Contribution/sales ratio = £200,000/£500,000 = 0.40.

$$\text{Breakeven point} = \frac{£150,000}{0.40} = £375,000$$

12   D

Statement D is correct.. Statement A is incorrect: products should be ranked according to the contribution they earn for each unit of limiting factor. Statement B is incorrect: linear programming is not required when there is only one limiting factor – products can simply be ranked according to the contribution they earn per unit of limiting factor. Statement C is incorrect, because the point furthest from the origin might not be in the feasible area for a practicable solution.

13   A

	£
Absorbed fixed overheads (4,500 × £8)	36,000
Over-absorbed fixed overhead	6,000
Therefore actual fixed overheads	30,000

14   B

	Total units	Equivalent units
Normal loss	100	0
Abnormal loss	150	150
	250	150
Output (2,000 – 250)	1,750	1,750
	2,000	1,900

Costs	£
Input materials (2,000 × £4.50)	9,000
Scrap value of normal loss (100 × £3)	300
	8,700
Conversion costs	13,340
	22,040

Cost per unit = £22,040/1,900 equivalent units = £11.60.

15   A

This question is a simple test of your understanding of the meaning of the elements in a regression analysis formula. Statements (i) and (ii) are correct, but statement (iii) is wrong. The total value of x multiplied by the total value of y would be written as $\Sigma x \ \Sigma y$, not as Σxy.

16   D

	£
14,000 hours should cost (× £10)	140,000
They did cost	176,000
Labour rate variance	36,000 (A)

	hours
5,500 units should take (× 3 hours)	16,500
They did take	14,000
Labour efficiency variance in hours	2,500 (F)
	£10
Labour efficiency variance in £	£25,000 (F)

SECTION B

1   RECIPROCAL

(a)

	Production Centre		Service Centre		
	1	2	A	B	C
	£	£	£	£	£
Allocated/apportioned costs	2,000	3,500	300	500	700
Apportion B	250	100	100	(500)	50
	2,250	3,600	400	0	750
Apportion C	450	300	-	-	(750)
	2,700	3,900	400	0	0
Apportion A	180	180	(400)	40	0
	2,880	4,080	0	40	0
Apportion B	20	8	8	(40)	4
Apportion C	2	2	-	-	(4)
Apportion A	4	4	(8)	-	-
Production centre overheads	2,906	4,094			

The total amount for overheads in production centre 1 is £2,906 and in production centre 2 is £4,094.

Tutorial note: If you apportion the service department costs in a different order, the end solution should still be the same.

(b) Overhead absorption rate for production centre 2. Since budgeted machine hours are more than budgeted labour hours, it would appear that this department is machine-intensive and a machine hour absorption rate would therefore be more appropriate.

Budgeted overhead expenditure = £2,906

Budgeted machine hours = 3,000

Absorption rate = £0.969 per machine hour (£2,906/3,000).

ACCA marking scheme		Marks
(a)	Reapportionment: 1 mark for each correct line using correct %s: maximum marks. Note: any method with sound bases for allocation should be accepted and given full credit.	6.0
	Conclusion	1.0
		7.0
(b)	Reason for using basis	1.0
	Using correct overhead figure from (a)	0.5
	Using machine hours as a basis	0.5
	Using the correct machine hours figure	0.5
	Correct calculation	0.5
		3.0
Total		10.0

2 SKETCH A CHART

(a) (i)

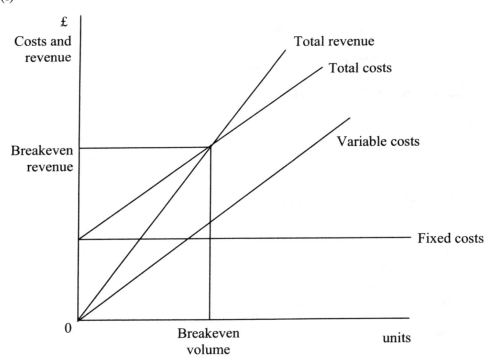

(ii) Contribution would be established by taking the difference between the total revenue line and the Variable costs line.

(b)　(i)

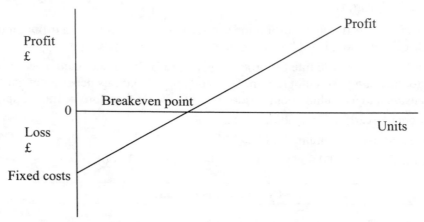

(ii)　Contribution would be established by taking the difference between profit and fixed costs.

ACCA marking scheme			
			Marks
(a) (i)		Correctly labelled axes	1.0
		Total revenue line	0.5
		Variable cost line	0.5
		Fixed cost line	0.5
		Total cost line	0.5
		Break-even point	1.0
	(ii)	Total revenue – variable costs	2.0
			6.0
(b) (i)		Correctly labelled axes	0.5
		Profit line	0.5
		Fixed costs	0.5
		Break-even point	0.5
	(ii)	Profit – fixed costs	2.0
			4.0
Total			10.0

3　FLEXED BUDGET VARIANCES

(a)

	Flexed budget units		Actual results units	Variance
Sales	9,750		9,750	
Production	11,000		11,000	
	£		£	£
Sales (price)	292,500	(= £30 × 9,750)	325,000	32,500 (F)
Cost of sales:				
Opening stock	0		0	
Production costs				
Materials	55,000	(= £5 × 11,000)	65,000	10,000 (A)
Labour	99,000	(= £9 × 11,000)	100,000	1,000 (A)
Fixed production overhead	96,000	(see note)	95,000	1,000 (F)
	250,000		260,000	
Closing stock	(27,500)	(= £22 × 1,250)	(27,500)	
	222,500		232,500	
Profit	**70,000**		**92,500**	22,500 (A)

Note:

In the flexed budget, the fixed overhead absorbed would be £88,000 (= 11,000 units × £8). However, the budgeted fixed overhead expenditure is the same as in the master budget, £96,000, and in the flexed budget there is budgeted under-absorbed overhead of £8,000. This is because the original fixed overhead budget was 12,000 units × £8 = £96,000. The flexed budget should show the budgeted fixed overhead expenditure. Showing it as absorbed overhead of £88,000 and under-absorbed overhead of £8,000 would be a perfectly acceptable solution.

(b) The sales price variance has arisen because the actual average sales price per unit is higher than the budgeted unit sales price.

The material variance may have arisen either because (i) the quantity of materials used in production was more than expected for making 11,000 units, or (ii) the price paid for materials was higher than expected. The total material variance could also be a combination of 'usage' and 'price' variances.

ACCA marking scheme		
		Marks
(a)	Flexed budget	
	Sales units	0.5
	Production units	0.5
	Sales revenue	0.5
	Material cost	0.5
	Labour cost	0.5
	Fixed cost	0.5
	Closing stock	1.0
	Actual figures – all of them	1.0
	Variances	
	Sales revenue	0.5
	Material cost	0.5
	Labour cost	0.5
	Fixed cost	0.5
		7.0
(b)	Sales price	1.0
	Mentioning materials price	1.0
	Mentioning materials usage	1.0
		3.0
Total		10.0

4   EOQ METHOD

(a) Economic order quantity $= \sqrt{\dfrac{2C_0 D}{C_h}}$

$EOQ = \; = \sqrt{\dfrac{2 \times 200 \times 12{,}000}{£1.20}}$

= 2,000 units.

(b)

		£
Revised stock costs:		
Purchase costs	(12,000 × £15)	180,000
Order costs	(£200 × 12,000/2,000 orders)	1,200
Holding costs	(8% × £15) × (2,000/2 units)	1,200
		182,400
Current stock costs		183,000
Saving by purchasing EOQ		600

(c)   Discounts are likely to increase the EOQ, because the holding cost (8% of purchase cost) will be reduced.

Since the purchase price is lower, the total purchase cost will be reduced.

Total order costs will be lower. (As the order cost uses the EOQ to divide the total demand, this cost will be reduced as the EOQ has increased.)

The holding cost will change as it uses both the increased EOQ and a reduced purchase price.

ACCA marking scheme		
		Marks
(a)	Correctly putting in the order cost	0.5
	Correctly putting in the annual demand	0.5
	Correctly putting in the holding cost	0.5
	Calculation	0.5
		2.0
(b)	Purchase cost	1.0
	Order cost	1.0
	Holding cost	1.0
	Saving	1.0
		4.0
(c)	Effect on EOQ	1.0
	Effect on purchase costs	1.0
	Effect on order costs	1.0
	Effect on holding costs	1.0
		4.0
Total		10.0

5   MARGINAL COSTS AND REVENUES

Demand	Sales price/unit	Total revenue (note 1)	Marginal revenue	Cost/unit	Total cost (note 2)	Marginal cost
units	£	£	£	£	£	£
1,100	48	52,800		22	24,200	
1,200	46	55,200	2,400	21	25,200	1,000
1,300	45	58,500	3,300	20	26,000	800
1,400	42	58,800	300	19	26,600	600

Notes:

1   Total revenue = demand in units × sales price per unit.

2   Total cost = demand in units × cost per unit

Solution

Profits are maximised at 1,300 units. Below this level, marginal revenue exceeds marginal cost for additional units produced and sold. Above 1,300 units, the marginal cost of producing more units is higher than the marginal revenue obtained from selling a larger volume. Profits are therefore maximised at a selling price of £45.

ACCA marking scheme	
	Marks
Calculation of total revenue (0.5 per correct entry)	2.0
Calculation of marginal revenue (0.5 per correct entry)	2.0
Calculation of total cost (0.5 per correct entry)	2.0
Calculation of marginal revenue (0.5 per correct entry)	2.0
Profit maximising point	2.0
Total	10.0